Feminism
and
Recent Fiction in English

Feminism and Recent Fiction in English

Edited by

SUSHILA SINGH

PRESTIGE

Published by
Prestige Books International
New Delhi 110060
prestigebooks@gmail.com

ISBN: 978-93-82186-11-3

Rs. 600

Printed in India

Contents

Preface

> Men have had every advantage of us in telling their own story. Education has been theirs in so much higher a degree; the pen has been in their hands.
>
> Jane Austen, *Persuasion*

Feminist literary criticism offers new readings of literature, re-evaluating literary expressions by both women and men, documenting the impact of sexist assumptions on writers, challenging literary judgements that deny the female voice an equal role with the male. Human experience, for centuries, has been synonymous with the masculine experience with the result that the collective image of humanity has been one-sided and incomplete. Woman has not been defined as a subject in her own right but merely as an entity that concerns man either in his real life or in his fantasy life. There has existed, all the same, a distinctively female literary tradition grown out of the anxieties of a woman's life. Women writers have been drawn more to fiction writing than to the other genres of poetry and drama. The very reality of woman's life situation, its "interrupted" nature, perhaps, is the reason for a close affinity between women and fiction writing.

Systematic subject-deprivation of woman has been a fact as much in life as in literature. Feminist consciousness seeks to analyze and understand the material conditions through which gender has been constructed within specific languages and bodies of literature. The strong wave of feminism in the 1960s and 1970s helped theorize a woman's discourse. Since fiction as a literary genre has religiously kept close to the path of realism, recent fiction responds emphatically to this new awakening.

A feministically read text can lead to a better understanding of the woman condition, thereby subverting the male strategies of oppression. Thus, the very basis of feminism is reformist. As the historian Linda Gordon says, feminism is "an analysis of women's subordination for the purpose of figuring out how to change it." At the same time, while dealing with feminism as an ideology and also as a critical tool, it is essential to take note of the fact that it assumes different configurations in accordance with racial, class and cultural variations. As a literary discourse, it is part of the modernist search for new modes of conceptuality to change the existing pattern of gender relationships. Feminism, thus, offers a fresh perspective for critical analysis linking the study of literature with real life contexts.

The feminist goal of equality with men has undergone a significant change in recent years. The woman-centred perspective now locates specific virtues in the female experience. This concept of the valorization of difference isolates and defines those aspects of woman's experience which prove to be the potential source of their strength with a promise of better future for humanity. This is a kind of "subaltern consciousness" that articulates the hidden and suppressed voice, thereby generating power in the victims out of their own victimization. As Gayatri Spivak rightly says, "the agency of change is located in the insurgent or the subaltern."

This book owes its genesis to a seminar on the subject held in November 1989 at the Women's College of the Banaras Hindu University during its Diamond Jubilee Year. Out of twenty-one papers presented, eighteen find place in this volume. The other five are invited articles. These essays discuss recent Indian-English, British, American (including

Black American), and Canadian fiction under the feminist perspective. Broadly, the essays fall into two categories—conceptual and analytical. Significantly, a good number of these focus attention on Indian-English texts. There is indeed a genuine need for an intensive study in this area from the feminist point of view. How with a change in the cultural, racial and class context the woman situation also changes is evident from the study of the British, American and Canadian texts represented here.

This publication aims to review the key issues related to the discipline of feminism and its application in the reading of recent fiction in English. The book is addressed not only to the students of literature but to all humanists with a commitment to a just social order.

Many people have helped in the making of this book. First of all I wish to express heartfelt thanks to all fellow contributors whose instantaneous and warm co-operation made this anthology of critical essays possible.

My revered teacher, Professor T.N. Singh, has been a constant source of inspiration and guidance for which I am profoundly indebted to him. I owe deep gratitude to Professor R.P. Rastogi, Vice-Chancellor, Banaras Hindu University, for encouragement and generous support. To Professor Annapurna Shukla and to Professor Usha Kiran Mehra, I remain grateful; without their support the volume could never have come into existence.

My chief debts are to: Professors Chaman Nahal, Meenakshi Mukherjee, O.P. Mathur, T.R. Sharma, Ramesh K.Srivastava, R.S. Pathak and R.R. Mehrotra for helping in more ways than one. Also my special thanks are due to Dr. R.K. Dhawan for his interest in the book, and to my husband, Professor K. P. Singh for his unfailing help as ever.

I am thankful to the University Grants Commission for sponsoring the seminar and the Banaras Hindu University for subsidizing the publication. The Prestige Books have taken pains in producing the book elegantly; my sincere appreciation for a fine job done.

Banaras Hindu University SUSHILA SINGH

Feminism and Fiction: Some Reflections

T.N. SINGH

Feminism as a precisely defined concept relating to sociological and literary studies is a phenomenon of recent development. The discussion of feminism in literary context, particularly in the context of recent fiction in English should prove an endeavour of a highly innovative nature representing a significant departure from the traditional mode of critical evaluation. I believe, we should consider feminism as a fictional strategy forged by writers in accordance with the pressures and challenges to which they have been subject, for projecting a feminist view of life and its problems. Criticism so far has been unable to take note of this strategy because of the age-old dominance of the male view in the world of letters. Naturally, therefore, we have not been able to see things as these feminist writers would want us to see them. As a critical tool, feminism should aim at providing us an altogether new awareness of the woman's role in the modern complex world.

About two hundred years back, Jane Austen as a writer had a sensitive awareness of the constraints and handicaps of her sex. This may be said of other women writers of the nineteenth century as well. Social decorum and prudish notions of morality proved in their case tyrannically inhibiting factors. Men could very well ignore them. But for a woman, a defiant attitude towards these rigid norms could not but have disastrous consequences for her literary career. A woman writer had to restrict herself only to certain permissible areas of life. Many other domains of human experience that were no less vital remained forbidden to her. Her creative talent, thus, never found a full-throated expression.

Social environment has changed since then. Women writers in the contemporary world enjoy a greater measure of freedom, No area of life remains the exclusive male preserve now. We find women exploring the hitherto prohibited regions of experience with an unusual sense of candour and boldness.

The moot question, however, is whether the new endeavour by modern women writers has succeeded in demolishing the traditional image of woman as a mere sex-object. Feminist writing will have justified itself only by bringing about a radical transformation in public attitude towards man-woman relationship. It must make people realize that love-making and domesticity are by no means the sole concern of women. They have as much to do with the rough and tumble of life as men. Feminism as such has to attempt a new definition of woman's role in the wider social frame.

It is worth noting that almost the whole gamut of feminine writing is marked by a tinge of sadness. Even where the atmosphere is gayfully comic, one has the feel of a grave note. This may be due, perhaps, to a disturbing awareness of the precarious nature of woman's position in society. Even today an average woman feels uncertain about her identity as a social being. Conditions of life have no doubt improved a tremendous deal since the days of Jane Austen. Women today have a greater share in social responsibilities. They have also an infinite number of avenues open before them. We have examples of women outshining men in many spheres. Notwithstanding all this, the general notion about woman as a shadow-figure to a male caretaker, be he a father, a husband or a son, continues to persist. The situation calls for a concerted effort to demolish such notions and to affirm the dignity of woman in the family as well as in the wider social life.

The problem, therefore, with which we are concerned, is not purely literary. It has many other implications—social, political, psychological and economic. Recent fiction, of course, will be the theme of our deliberations. But, I hope, we will discuss it in the context of the contemporary social reality. We have to guard against the theme of feminism becoming a matter of pompous academic exercise. We shall be happy if this seminar assumes the form of a vigorous movement—a movement which does not stop till our collective thinking has undergone a complete change vis-a-vis the role of women in the more serious affairs of life. To achieve this task, we should discuss problems with an open mind, subjecting to a close scrutiny all such theories that are anti-feminist. Our aim should be to give a radically new orientation to the traditional mode of thought and life.

Feminism in English Fiction: Forms and Variations

CHAMAN NAHAL

While discussing feminism, one is confronted with parallel or comparative models from different cultures. There are so many of them: the English feminism, the Canadian feminism, the African feminism, the Australian feminism, the New Zealand feminism. One has to listen to Patricia Grace to realize how effective New Zealand feminism is. Outside the orbit of literature written in English, there is French feminism which is very-very pronounced. Of Marxist feminism, I have personal experience at least of two countries—Soviet Russia and North Korea. So, which model one should follow for the sake of comparisons. The problem is the problem of definition. What is the definition of feminism that we have in mind while dealing with feminism and recent fiction in English.

So far the legal terminology is concerned, the term "man" includes the term "woman." What exactly do we mean by feminism? Does it merely mean female-ism or femaleness, the qualities which all women possess, not only human females but may be the other females in the non-human world. Though we cannot listen to them, perhaps they also feel the same constraints, same pressure of motherhood and child-bearing. Or, feminism means a sense of personal courage. If that is so, is this so very new that we are talking about it today? There are numerous fine examples of women having personal courage. We have Rosalind in Shakespeare's *As You Like It*, who puts on man's clothes and goes about looking for her lover. What about Sita herself? Though Sita is normally cited as an example of anti-feminism, of submission, Sita must have been very courageous to have resisted a man like Ravana for one full year. After all she was totally at his disposal and he could have outraged her whenever he wanted. Sita was able to resist him; she must have been very courageous.

Or, feminism is a kind of social revolt against convention, like living outside marriage. Even then we have had examples earlier. Within literature, we have the example of Elizabeth Barrett Browning and of George Eliot who in the nineteenth century lived outside of marriage. So what do we mean by feminism? I have a definition to offer, but first I propose to problematize the issue.

Even unmarried girls feel the constraints of parents, of ethnic communities to which they belong, the social groups in which they live, of the schools they go to. I have known of girls going to English convents. Because they write with the left hand, and the left hand was the hand of devil, the nuns used to punish them. In one case I know of a girl who developed a stammer because of the punishment she received at the hands of the nuns.

Therefore, while talking of feminist tensions, probably we are talking of the tensions of life. The feminist tensions are the tensions of living whether one is a man or a woman. I would say, even a man would feel the same tensions living together in marriage. Marriage is an impossible situation institutionally for two people to live together. Several minor/major decisions—which paper to read, whether to have tea or coffee, to go out or stay home, to have a child or not—cut into the fabric of every marriage. So what do we mean by feminism? So far, feminism has not been defined in precise terms. What has been offered is a prescription of feminism.

For instance, if we take into account Simone de Beauvoir's *The Second Sex* or some of the other French writers, they are very much concerned about the physical suppression of women. Therefore, according to the French models of feminism, it would imply the greater sexual expression. If we take into account the British models, all feminists slowly become respectable, or reclaimed into the male world order. If we consider American models, they are more outspoken.

By way of coming to a definition of feminism,, I mention Carson McCullers's *The Ballad of the Sad Café*. This is the American assertion of self expression. Typically American, the story is of a young woman in a small village. There is the main street and along comes the peddler. The young woman is very tall, she married a man at one time; she fell out with him. He has gone away, has been in a prison, and she has not seen him for a long time. She is alone; the father is dead. One day a strange hunchback comes into the town and slowly works into her consciousness by telling her that he is an old relation of hers. The two of them start a cafe which thrives and flourishes. In the course of time, the one-time husband, who has been released from the jail, comes back. The point of interest lies here. They have to decide now who is going to stay in the village. It is clear that the young woman will have to fight physically. A match means a physical match. The day of the fight comes, and this woman is actually about to beat the man and then the hunchback jumps on her back and she is floored, downed in defeat. The man wins. The woman loses by default. But there is this strong expression of self-assertion.

In the North Korean Marxist variety, there is a strong sense of feminine loyalty to the party as exhibited by the guide—a woman of twenty-one who looked after me during my stay in that country.

Therefore, there is the problem of definition. Some one might say why have a definition; having a definition is too schematic. But that is the whole business of literature. I think literature is not a teachable subject. Either one likes a writer or does not like a writer. If you do not like Lawrence, what can I do? You do not like him, I like him very much. But to teach a writer we have to have definitions, labels—just to understand, just to problematize the subject.

Before coming to my definition of feminism, I want to mention how women writers have explored the problem—Virginia Woolf in *A Room of One's Own*, Simone de Beauvoir I have already mentioned. There is Kate Millett's *Sexual Politics* and other books. And, then we have the male reply.

Now the question is whether feminism is some kind of chauvinistic aggressive way of living, like dressing up like a man. In 1968, women dressed up like men to assert themselves. Now there is a reverse trend in America amongst men. They also want to hit back. If a woman can dress up like man, why cannot a man dress up like a woman. If there are feminist texts, there are also masculine texts. There is a very fine book by Norman Mailer called *The Prisoner of Sex* which is his reply to this kind of chauvinistic expression of feminism.

I define feminism as a mode of existence in which the woman is free of the dependence syndrome. There is a dependence syndrome: whether it is the husband or the father or the community or whether it is a religious group, ethnic group. When women free themselves of the dependence syndrome and lead a normal life, my idea of feminism materializes.

I come to the second point: where do we go from there after securing freedom? We read good number of feminine texts partly to have vicarious pleasure, partly to see how women feel, because women have somehow claimed that what they feel, they alone can feel. Katherine Anne Porter, in a review of *Lady Chatterley's Lover* argued that how can Lawrence write about the sexual feelings of a woman. He is only a man. If we follow this argument, then one has to be a hermaphrodite to write a novel.

Let us have a look at what women writers are doing. For instance, Doris Lessing's *The Golden Notebook* (1962) is a very complicated and difficult book to read. There are so many diaries, different forms of diaries, then there are different journal entries. The story is about Anna Wulf and Molly. After about five hundred pages, struggling against men, both of them become respectable females in Labour movement, The point is after having broken down the models of living, what do they achieve. Do the feminist writers have a replacement model? My contention is they do not have a replacement model. The women writers have broken down the orthodox model. But where do they go from there? Anna and Molly, where do they go? Ultimately they are absorbed into the male world of the Labour party.

Another example I give from the American writer Marilyn French's *The Women's Room* (1977). Again, the story is of a woman who goes through a bad marriage in the 50s. I do not know why always marriage should be selected to hit at. The woman frees herself from that marriage but after the second half the novel collapses. There is practically nothing in the novel and in the end her daughter is raped which further adds to her sense of aggravation. But where is the replacement model?

Another example we have from an African novel, Chinua Achebe's *Arrow of God* (1964). There is the High Priest Ezeulu. He lives by rhythms of seasons, the people of his tribe Ulu. In the end he refuses to make the ceremonial announcement of the feast of the New Yams, without which the harvest cannot be gathered. Suffering and hunger follow. There is nothing to eat. The clan turn to the Christian Priest who saves them from starvation and ruin. So here we have a replacement model.

I would like to examine whether we have a replacement model in feminine fiction. It is very difficult to construct a replacement model. One cannot escape the myths—the conditioning myths with which one has grown up. Unless we construct new myths, we cannot construct replacement model. We all revere Sita and Savitri; they did something out of loyalty, out of dedication. We may not like it today, but can we disown them? We cannot escape the myths. So, the replacement models are to be constructed in the context of the myths we already have.

Now I examine how well feminism has been presented and how replacement models are possible within the Indian context in my survey of Indian writing in English. I am sorry to say our older writers whom we may call the first generation of Indian English Writing—R.K. Narayan, Raja Rao, Mulk Raj Anand—missed out on great opportunity. They had freedom struggle and so many women in it to write about. They have bypassed our freedom movement which is a matter of surprise to some of us. Even fifty years after the Second World War, the British and American writers are writing about it. In the freedom movement from 1915 to 1947, we had the most riot period in the Indian history when Indian women played such a glorious role: Vijaya Lakshmi Pandit, Sarojini Naidu. For instance, when Gandhiji was arrested in the Salt Satyagraha which he was leading, it was Sarojini Naidu who led the Satyagrahis. So the historic role played by Indian women in their own capacity definitely provides an alternative replacement model. This rich resource has been completely left out.

The only man writer I can think of in addition to myself who talked of women's role is Bhabani Bhattacharya. His *So Many Hungers* is a good feminist novel if read that way. His character, Kajoli, shows great courage in the face of all odds, and is really not dependent on anyone, neither on her grandfather, nor on her husband. She is dependent in the way we are connected to people. And then she goes to Calcutta where she is sold into prostitution and she saves herself by selling newspapers. In this respect, it is a great novel.

Let us consider what are the bases on which the replacement models can be constructed. There has to be some basis for new myths. One such basis can be of protest. The best example is Nayantara Sahgal. All her novels talk about women who are oppressed by marriage, by political circumstances, by accidents of history. They try to break out of that shell: *A Time to Be Happy, This Time of Morning, The Day in Shadow, A Situation in New Delhi, Rich Like Us*. One could go on. Particularly, *The Day in Shadow* is a very good feminist novel. Within the limitation that I have imposed upon, women try to establish a model.

Then, one can establish an order through defiance. One is driven to a situation where there is no way but to hit back. I would refer those women writers who have tried to hit back. They are brave women because it is very difficult to hit back, and the constraints are so many in Indian living. I am not talking about the physical fight in American sense, I am talking about hitting back with whatever force one has.

One such writer is Raji Narasimhan whose novel *Forever Free* (1979) is a very good example of establishing a different model of living through defiance. The principal character, the woman called Shree, undergoes discord in marriage. Her husband has strange ways of looking at things for which she is not responsible at all. For example, one of her husband's beliefs is if the second toe is larger than the main toe, then the woman is surely an adulteress. She is condemned rightaway without even being given any chance to be tried. What does a woman do in such a situation? There is no choice but to hit back. That is what the girl does in the novel.

Another novel here I mention is a novel by Uma Vasudev. Her novel *The Song for Anasuya* (1978) is of this kind, of paying back the men in their own terms. Some of the men writers have done that like Dreiser in *Sister Carrie*. Sister Carrie tries the ladder of success the way men do. She first picks up Charles Drouet, then George Hurstwood; then discards them both to rise. This is the way of the world. In Uma Vasudev's novel, Anasuya is a woman who uses men and discards them. And, why not? If a man can do this, why can't a woman do this?

The illustrations I am giving are from the novels and not from rhetorical books written on the subject. My concern is with the models as they appear in fiction. Uma Vasudev's novel is a good illustration of a woman who uses men as she wants to and is happy with herself. After all, this is what matters. The whole aim of living is to develop our personality to its optimum potentiality. How to optimize the business of living? The very concept of feminism as articulated by the novelists we are discussing is concerned with this very theme.

Yet another model that I take up now is dearer to my heart and closer to the Indian sensibility. Here a replacement model can be established through conformity. Conforming to the myths, one can still bring about a change. A fine example is Rama Mehta's novel *Inside the Haveli* (1977). A girl from Bombay, Geeta, is married into a Rajasthani family and the door is locked upon her. Haveli is a common metaphor in Indian fiction. Same metaphor we have in Attia Hosain's novel *Sunlight on a Broken Column* (1961). So in Rama Mehta's novel, the door is locked upon Geeta. What does she do? Does she walk out? Does she break the door and go out, or does she slowly change everyone in the Haveli. She does that to a large extent through patience, through understanding. She changes her father-in-law. She changes her husband whom initially she could not see during the day time. She would see him only in the dark. She changes all that.

Another writer is Kamala Markandaya whose novels are complete without the dependence syndrome. I do not know why she does that. Her novel *Nectar in a Sieve* (1954) is a fine illustration of change through conformity. Rukmani in that novel accepts everything. She accepts Nathan's adultery, Ira's prostitution, she accepts all misfortunes. However, it is difficult to understand why in the novels of Kamala Markandaya, there has to be a white man to aid her. This dependence is difficult to explain.

Therefore, what I am trying to suggest is that while discussing feminism and recent fiction, first of all we should examine the definition of feminism; and then we should try and see if we can construct a replacement model. Do not tell us where the woman has left. Ibsen has done a lot of damage to us in *A Doll's House*. Nora walks out but walks out to where? Let us pick up the story from where Nora walks out. Lastly, there should be an autonomous feminine critical theory. I don't think it exists. I am aware of the work of Elaine Showalter but it does not go beyond finding parallels with other forms of criticism. They have not developed an independent literary theory through which they examine the works written by women writers.

Recent Trends in Feminist Thought: *A Tour de Horizon*

SUSHILA SINGH

> We cannot rely on existing ideologies as they are products of a male supremacist culture.
>
> Redstockings's Manifesto
> NY 1969

> The situation of woman is that she—a free and autonomous being like all creatures—nevertheless finds herself living in a world where men compel her to assume the status of the Other.
>
> Simone de Beauvoir

Legal, economic and social restrictions on the basic rights of women have existed throughout history and in all civilizations. Through the long line of women writers, who protested against the inequities from Christine de Pisan to Mary Wollstonecraft and through Simone de Beauvoir to present-day feminist thinkers, an outlook, a "theory," a feminist thought system evolves. The feminist consciousness is the consciousness of victimization. As a philosophy of life, it seeks to discover and change the more subtle and deep-seated causes of women's oppression. It is a concept of "raising of the consciousness" of an entire culture. The present paper is an attempt to discuss different strands of feminism analyzing it into all its complexities. It has assumed different configurations in relation to post-modernist approaches. Seen only as an agnostic struggle against all forms of patriarchal and sexist oppression, theoretically it becomes an impossibility. As soon as the oppressional conditions are removed, it ceases to exist. The very concept of equality has undergone tremendous change in the light of new French feminist theories of *différence*. Through the process of *gynesis*, a female discourse has been evolved by deliberate valorization of repressed femininity. The French post-modernist theory of Lacan, Derrida and Deleuze has been used in the process of *gynesis*. Because "post-feminism" has the danger of delimitation and exclusion, materialist feminist theory is offered. Now all the different strands can be divided into two relational and individualist theories. Currently relational feminism is being widely accepted as it avoids all the negativisms associated with extremities of the individualist theories. The present-day feminism thought encompasses a moral vision and emerges as a holistic, anti-militaristic and life-affirming philosophy.

Toril Moi has used the term "post-feminism" to cover the different configurations of feminism and post-modernism present today. Present-day feminist theorists believe that, strictly speaking, feminism is an impossible position. The agnostic definition of feminism sees it as the struggle against all forms of patriarchal and sexist oppression. Such an oppositional definition posits feminism as the necessary *resistance* to patriarchal power. Logically, then, the aim of feminism as an emancipatory theory becomes to abolish itself along with its opponent. "In a non-sexist, non-patriarchal society, feminism will no longer exist."[1] As such, feminism is an impossible undertaking. Feminism is committed to the struggle for equality for women, an effort to make women become *like* men. But the struggle for equal rights historically and politically emphasizes the *value* of women *as they are*. The very argument rests precisely on the fact that women are *already* as valuable as men. But in the situation of women's lack of equal rights, this value must be located as *différence*, not as equality. Women are of equal human value in their own way.

When feminism asserts the value of women as women, then it truly and efficiently counters the systematic devaluation of women under patriarchy. Equality and difference thus are not antithetical. But a discourse of female difference, articulated in isolation, runs the risk of echoing the very patriarchal prejudices against which the champions of equality are struggling.

Accepting the constraining logic of sameness and difference, Julia Kristeva suggests a third space for feminism to operate—the space which deconstructs all identity, all binary oppositions. But again in deconstructing patriarchal metaphysics, the risk of deconstructing the very logic that sustains the two forms of feminism of sameness and difference cannot be avoided. And therefore the three "spaces" of feminism are logically and often strategically incompatible. As such, Toril Moi suggests at once to live out the contradictions of all three feminisms and agnostically take sides to demolish patriarchy. But that does not mean that the individual is entirely free to choose his/her political position. As Freud and Lacan rightly believe, what we say is never quite what we think we say. Derrida has also shown that every discourse engenders its own blind spots and contradictions. And Marx clearly outlined that our specific material position in society and history crucially limits the range of ideological and political options available to us. That means that the choice places itself within the constraints, the limits of analytical self-reflection.

The post-modern feminists are wary of labels or definitions of any kind. And therefore the word "feminism" particularly troubles Alice Jardine:

> Who and what, then do we mean by "feminist"? That word . . . poses some serious problems. Not that we would want to end up by demanding a definition of what feminism is, and therefore, of what one must do, say, and be, if one is to acquire the epithet; dictionary meanings are suffocating, to say the least.[2]

Toril Moi considers this to be a defeatist position. To her, to name is to exercise power. The notion of conceptually rigorous definitions is *merely* constraining, is a fashionable dogma of post-structuralism. Jardine herself offers a definition of feminism. "Feminism," she writes, is generally understood as a "movement from the point of view of, by, and for women."[3]

By locating feminist criticism within "very precise political struggles and practices," Jardine does try to provide some specificity to this general position. Jardine views feminism as a movement by women which takes on different and very specific forms in different contexts. This definition has a bias of much Parisian feminism in the 1970s with the emphasis on *des femmes en movements.*

In Jardine's central neologism: *gynesis,* there is an interesting contradiction between her rejection of labels and definitions by naming her own textual discovery. *Gynesis* is the name for a textual process, which she describes in the following words:

> The putting into discourse of "woman" as that *process* diagnosed in France as intrinsic to the condition of modernity; indeed, the valorization of the feminine, woman, and her obligatory, that is historical connotations, as somehow intrinsic to new and necessary modes of thinking, writing, speaking.[4]

Focusing on the necessary blind spot, the repressed contradictions and paradoxical self-deconstruction of every discourse, Jardine labels this the "master-narratives," own "nonknowledge." "This other-than-themselves," she continues, "is almost always a 'space' of some kind, over which the narrative has lost control." This space has been coded as *feminine,* as *woman. Gynesis,* thus, is the process of putting woman or the feminine into discourse as the unknown other of every text. Traditionally, this has been represented as *negative* process, a process of patriarchal impression of the feminine. Here Luce Irigaray's *Speculum* can be referred. But what Jardine is offering can be called *positive gynesis*, the deliberate valorization of repressed femininity. This she finds first and foremost in French post-modernist theory produced by men where Lacan, Derrida and Deleuze participate in the process of *gynesis* in France.[6] Toril Moi, however, raises several questions regarding this theory of *gynesis*. Is *gynesis* possible within an explicitly feminist discourse? Or should we rather look for the silent exclusion or explicit circulation of the masculine in such texts. Is there not the danger of repeating the patriarchal exclusion of woman?

Present-day feminism is a historically specific movement, rooted in French Enlightenment thought (Mary Wollstonecraft) and in British liberalism (John Stuart Mill), and consequently wedded in deeply critical style to notions of truth, justice, freedom, and equality. Toril Moi offers a critique of post-feminism on the ground that it avoids taking sides. Post-feminism represents a particular development of one of the three conflicting discourses of feminism. In its eagerness to please the high priests of post-structuralism and post-modernism, post-feminism takes little account of other forms of feminism, and thus enacts a scenario of exclusion and delimitation? Toril Moi believes that only by attempting the impossible wager of constructing a materialist feminist theory, that includes the three feminisms, that the feminist criticism can be pushed forward past the political impasse of post-feminism.

Gayatri Spivak has made an admirable effort to develop a materialist anti-imperialist feminism which draws on the insights of recent post-structuralist and post-modern theory.[8] Spivak's textual strategy, for instance, is to make different discourses critically "interrupt" each other in order to bring each other to crisis. She does not leave high theory to men. She takes it over for her own feminist and anti-imperialist purposes. In a typical Spivak essay, the Marxist theory of surplus value, feminist debates on reproduction and the domestic mode of production, Indian critiques of imperialist ideology, and post-structural theories concerning the construction of the colonial subjects are all brought into conflict at the same time.

Karen Offen, in her brilliant scholarly attempt to define feminism, has grouped the different strands of feminism into two arguments: "Relational" and "Individualist."[9] The relational feminist thought proposed a gender-based but egalitarian vision of social organization. It mainly featured the primacy of companionate, non-hierarchichal, male-female couple as the basic unit of society. On the other hand, individualist arguments emphasized the individual, irrespective of sex or gender, as the basic unit. Relational feminism stressed women's rights *as women* in terms of their childbearing and/or nurturing capacities in relation to men. It insisted on women's distinctive contributions in these roles to the broader society. By contrast, individualist feminist thought emphasized more abstract concepts of individual human rights and celebrated the quest for personal independence, dismissing all socially defined roles. Though these two discourses are distinctly different, they are discernible as intertwined in feminist utterances. The interplay of these two strands can be seen in the later eighteenth-century British writer on women's rights, Mary Wollstonecraft, and then nineteenth-century American suffragist Elizabeth Cady Stanton. Wollstonecraft in her "Vindication of the Rights of Women" in 1792 showed a clear sense of women's role and responsibilities as mothers. Cady Stanton argued in 1869 that "because man and woman are complement of one another we need woman's thought in national affairs to make a safe and stable government" and later in 1892 insisted on woman's right to "her birth-right to self-sovereignity." The self-sovereignity was more a "moral imperative" rather than a "categorical absolute" in the thought of these two women.

The Anglo-American feminist tradition, however, advocated the individualist thought as the only "politically correct" form till as recently as 1970s. This strand placed political priority on enactment of the Equal Rights Amendment and on demolishing the gender stratified educational system and economy that disadvantaged women through occupational segregation. As the situation changed, this thought has come under attack. The claims for uncompromising self-realization perhaps causes the current resistance to feminism, especially among women who have chosen marriage and motherhood.

In France, the relational feminism led to the seemingly paradoxical doctrine of "equality in difference." The French theorists argued showing that equity is distinct from equality. The basic tenets were that there were *both* biological *and* cultural distinctions between the sexes, a concept of womanly or manly nature, of a sharply defined sexual division of labour, or roles in the family and throughout society following from that "difference" and that "nature" and of the centrality of the complementary couple and/or the mother/child dyad to social analysis. It combined a case for moral equality of women and men with an explicit aknowledgement of differences in women's and men's biological functions in society. Catharine Mackinnon has very aptly used the phrase "difference difference makes."[10] This "bi-valent" argument constitutes core of the present-day French feminist argument.[11] Temma Kaplan writes that the historical roots of both the modes of arguments are discernible in "female consciousness or consciousness of the rights of gender."[12]

In post-1968 French movement *pour la liberation des femmes*, the groups known as Psych et Po (Psychoanalyze et Politique) emphasized the centrality of biological *differences* between the sexes. Drawing heavily on Lacanian psychoanalytic postulates, this group argues that just this women's *difference* which lies essentially in a sexuality that has been repressed by patriarchal culture is the source of women's potential liberation.[13] The "feminism" has been totally repressed, they challenge existing language and culture through exploration of "women's language." Thus Psych et Po seeks to overthrow on the basis of these postulates the Western patriarchal culture by the emergence of female discourse. Interestingly, Simone de Beauvoir's arguments, existentialist environmentalist/position, which rejected "the feminine" as a purely cultural construct and rejected the social role implications of women's psychological difference, were in more harmony with tradition of individualist feminism. By positing the male model as its ideal type, by posing for women the transcendent act of "becoming" against the imminent stance of "being," Beauvoir set up a de facto trap whereby women are constantly faced with the threat of *démission*, or back-sliding in "being" of female passivity.[14] The avant-garde French feminists consider Beauvoir's type of feminism as male identified. If autonomy is seen to be purchased at the price of womanliness, these French women choose to reject the goal, insisting and prizing *la différence*.

Thus, today feminism must be viewed as a rapidly developing major critical ideology or system of ideas in its own right.[15] The concept incorporates a broad spectrum of ideas and possesses an international scope. Its developmental stages have historically been dependent on and in tension with male-centred political and intellectual discourse but whose more recent manifestations transcend the latter. In ultimate analysis, "feminism emerges as a concept that can encompass both an ideology and movement for sociopolitical change based on a critical analysis of male privilege and women's subordination within any given society."[16] As a philosophy of life, it opposes women's subordination to men in the family and society, along with men's claims to define what is best for women without consulting them; thereby offering a frontal challenge to patriarchal thought, social organization and control mechanism. The present-day feminist thought seeks to destroy masculinist hierarchy but not sexual dualism. It is necessarily pro-woman, but this does not mean that it has to be anti-man. This acts as a rebalancing factor between women and men of the social, economic and political power within a given society. It is viewed as a humanistic philosophy. It still remains a political challenge to male authority and hierarchy in the most profound sense. But today the theorists in describing its ultimate vision prefer the word "transformational" to the term "revolutionary."

Karen Offen's dualistic distinctions—individualist versus relational feminism—have not been fully accepted by critics like Ellen Carol DuBois[17] and Nancy F. Cott.[18] DuBois contends Offen's concept mainly on the ground that the "account is based strongly in the history of French feminism . . . but she uses a great deal of material from the history of American and British feminism." Her main objection is to Offen's reading of Elizabeth Cady Stanton as a relational feminist. On the other hand, Nancy F. Cott objects to Offen's inclusive use of the term "feminism" to account for the relational point of view. To Cott, the term basically denotes "individualistic, liberal and rights-conscious."

In her answer[19] to the above criticism, Offen stands by her view of finding relational aspects in Stanton's feminist thought. She also stands by her definition of "feminism" including "relational feminism" because we do not have an equally effective alternative term for the issues and problems of women. Offen refers to NOW activist Jo Ann Evansgardner who suggested to replace the term "feminism" with "socracism" and which did not evoke any enthusiastic response. Offen says that the term "feminism" lives on because it is "the most powerful term we have at our disposal and that we should use it knowledgeably, taking into account its transnational historical provenance and its varied implications across time and place. It allows us to get a better fix on the overall picture of sexual difference and sexual domination and, possibly, to design a better contemporary politics."

Virginia Woolf wrote in 1929: "it is obvious that the values of women differ very offen from the values which have been made by the other sex." There is a moral vision inherent in the feminist thought. Theorists like Susan Sontag believe that there is a congruence between women's subjective experience of oppression and the objective realities of war, imperialism, and the technological destruction of the environment. Contemporary theorists hold that this situation prevails because masculine destructiveness correlates to a denial of the female.[20] Susan Sontag strongly felt that "Virginia Woolf was altogether correct when she declared that the fight to liberate women is the fight against fascism."[21] The feminist thinkers perceive masculine psychology as a primary factor in female subjugation and the destructive military imperialism that dominates world politics.

The situation can be countered when women turn their world into a subject and a cultural ideological source. The study of what constitutes women's world, its culture and values, they feel, should be a major area of feminist studies. Women have fundamental respect for the contingent order, for the environmental context, for the concrete, everyday world. They willingly adopt a passive mode of accepting the diversity of environmental "voices" and the validity of their realities. Women appear less willing to wrench that context apart or to impose upon its alien abstractions or to use implements that subdue it intellectually or physically. Such vision promotes an ethic that is non-imperialistic, that is life-affirming, and that has a reverence for the concrete details of life. The British philosopher and novelist Iris Murdoch has articulated such an ethic in her works. This ethic emerges out of the structures of women's experience. The primary condition of powerlessness makes them hyper-sensitive to their surroundings to survive. Women have been able to carve out a separate space of their own. In domestic sphere also, the fundamental "interruptibility" of women's projects contributes to a sense of personal vulnerability to environmental influence, fostering a sense of being bound to chance, to circumstance, of not being in control of one's world.[22] They consequently develop a consciousness of flexibility, of relativity, of contingency.

The primary aspects of housekeeping, child-rearing and economic production for use contribute further to the construction of a female epistemology. Katheryn Allen Rabuzzi in her monumental work[23] finds that women's fundamental experience in the domestic sphere is one of repetition and waiting. Unlike the traditional male experience of linear historical time through the quest, the home-bound woman experiences time as a stasis—either as perpetual repetition or "eternal return" or as a pattern of passive waiting. From the point of view of the Western male questor, stasis is a negative experience but Rabuzzi urges that the static waiting pattern may be seen as "simply another mode of being" and may imply rootedness of a positive sort.[24] Out of this women's mode emerges a sensibility that is a positive alternative to the masculine mode of questing and conquering. Responding in this way to the whim of the moment is markedly different from imposing your will on time. The passivity so induced is that of a light object thrown into the water; it is not the object that determines its direction but the movement of the water. "This is different from the assertive striving more typical of the masculine temporal mode, questing." Like Rabuzzi, Sara Ruddick in her important article "Maternal Thinking" focuses upon the positive modes that emerge from the maternal role; these modes, she proposes, must become the basis of a new public ethic.[25]

Mothers are forced into an intense awareness of the reality of the child. Ruddick does not confine "mothering" to biological parenting but to all forms of maternal, caretaker roles. Teaching for example, can be so experienced. "Maternal thinking" grows out of "maternal practice," which requires responding to the reality of the child, an Other who demands preservation and growth. Because so many of the factors involved in this process are beyond her control and because she realizes that excessive control may defeat the purpose of growth, the mother must adopt a relatively passive attitude, which Ruddick describes as waiting mode. It is a "holding" attitude, one that "is governed by the priority of keeping over acquiring, of conserving the fragile, of maintaining whatever is at hand and necessary to the child's life." She contrasts this attitude to that of scientific thought which is similar to Rabuzzi's distinction between feminine waiting and masculine questing. The recognition of the priority of holding over acquiring distinguishes maternal from scientific thought, as well as from the instrumentalism of technocratic capitalism. "To recognize excessive control as a *liability* sharply distinguishes maternal from scientific practice."[26]

In a recent article on feminism and science, Evelyn Fox Keller contrasts contemporary scientists Barbara McClintock's attitude with the aggressive manipulation of nature proposed by Francis Bacon.[27] McClintock evinces a feminine mode when she speaks of "letting the material speak to you" or of allowing it to "tell you what to do next." She does not believe that scientists should "impose an answer" upon their material; rather they should respond to it and retain an empathetic respect for it. Keller suggests that feminine modality points to "a science less restrained by the impulse to dominate." Observance of feminine modality can give a positive direction to science. Azizah al-Hibri hypothesizes that prehistoric men came to envy women's reproductive powers, a means to immortality. To establish his own sense of superiority and to carve his own avenue to immortality, the male turned to production accepting it as an imitation of reproduction. He channelled his energy into technology transcending his condition. Like Ruether and other existentialists, al-Hibri sees that the establishment of the transcendental male self meant the domination of an other, the female and feminized nature. Al-Hibri says that not only women but other "others,"—black, red, Jew, Arab, native etc.—must rebel in order that a feminist, humanist revolution be accomplished. The "male has to come to terms with his own being"—he must face the fact that his obsessive technological imperialism is rooted in a fear and denial of the feminine, rooted in his own sense of masculine inadequacy.

Developing the moral implications of Ludwig Wittgestein's thesis, Simone Weil and Iris Murdoch believed that in the social world people tend to resort to the use of commonplace paradigms out of moral weakness. Murdoch proposes that the way out of this epistemological trap, this conceptual net, is by a moral effort, a redirection of the will to see what is other than oneself. Rosemary Ruether similarly calls for a renewed "ecological consciousness," an ability to enter into reciprocity with the other to acknowledge the validity, the reality of the "thouness" of the other's being.[28] Robin Morgan proposes that the new feminist moral vision is in many ways analogous to the vision of reality offered by the new physics. She sees feminism as "crucial to the continuation of sentient life on this planet." It is the key to our survival and transformation. The reason she offers is that women have over the centuries developed an ethic that is appropriate to the world view that is emerging out of the new physics: they see in terms of relationship and in terms of environmental contexts. Moreover, women have been the custodians of humane values for centuries. Their primary value is a reverence for life. This ethic must become the governing world ethic.[29]

Feminist thought is "humanist" thought, and I conclude with Virginia Woolf's *Three Guineas*, which she structured around three causes; first, to prevent war by helping a pacificist society; second, building of a women's college; and third, establishing a society dedicated to helping women to enter the professions. For her the three causes are interrelated and might help to prevent war and to eradicate fascism. She notes that women have never made war, "scarcely a human being in the course of history has fallen to a woman's rifle; the vast majority of birds and beasts have been killed by you, not us."[30] Virginia Woolf proposes an outsider's society that will encourage the development of a women's ethic that is holistic, anti-militaristic and life-affirming. Such an ethic, contemporary feminist thinkers urge, must become the basis for a new public morality for the constitution of a left-handed world.

In the 1980s, feminism emerges as a thought system, a point of view to reorganize the world realities, a positivist holistic approach to life, a step towards sanity in human relationship, and perhaps the only mode for preservation of very human existence on this planet.

NOTES

1. Toril Moi, "Feminism, Post-modernism, and Style: Recent Feminist Criticism in the United States," *Cultural Critique*, 9 (Spring 1988), pp. 3-22.
2. Alice Jardine, *Gynesis: Configurations of Women and Modernity* (Ithaca: Cornell University Press, 1986), p. 20.
3. *Ibid.*, p. 15.
4. *Ibid.*, p. 25.
5. Luce Irigaray, *Speculum de l'autre femme* (Paris: Minuit, 1974).
6. Alice Jardine, *Gynesis*, p. 27.
7. Toril Moi, p. 19.
8. Gayatri Chakravorty Spivak, *In Other Worlds: Essays in Cultural Politics* (New York: Methuen, 1987).
9. Karen Offen, "Defining Feminism: A Comparative Historical Approach," *Signs*, 14: 1(Autumn 1988), pp. 119-57.
10. *Ibid.*, p. 139.
11. The term has been used by Elizabeth H. Wolgast, *Equality and Rights of Women* (Ithaca: Cornell University Press, 1980), p. 16.
12. Temma Kaplan, "Female Consciousness and Collective Action: The Case of Barcelona, 1910-1918," *Signs*, 7:3 (Spring 1982); pp. 545-66.
13. Dorothy Kaufmann-McCall, "Politics of Difference: The Women's Movement in France from May 1968 to Mitterand," *Signs*, 9:2 (Winter 1983), p. 285.
14. Helene Lamoure Eisenberg, "The Theme of Demission in the Works of Simone de Beauvoir" (Ph.D. Dissertation., University of California, Berkeley, 1978).
15. Karen Offen, p. 150.
16. *Ibid.*, p. 151.
17. Ellen Carol DuBois, "Comment on Karen Offen's 'Defining Feminism: A Comparative Historical Approach,'" Signs, 15:1 (Autumn 1989), pp. 195-97.
18. Nancy F. Cott, "Comment on Karen's 'Defining Feminism: A Comparative Historical Approach,'" *Ibid.*, pp. 203-5
19. Karen Offen, "Reply to DuBois" and "Reply to Cott," *Ibid.*, pp. 198-202, 206-9.

20. Josephine Donovan, *Feminist Theory: The Intellectual Traditions of American Feminism* (New York: Frederick Unger, 1985), p. 172.
21. *Ibid.*, p. 171.
22. Michelle Cliff, "The Resonance of Interruption," *Chrysalis*, 8 (Summer 1979), pp. 29-37.
23. Kathryn Allen Rabuzzi, *The Sacred and the Feminine: Toward a Theology of Housework* (New York: Seabury, 1982).
24. *Ibid.*, p. 151.
25. Sara Ruddick, "Maternal Thinking," *Feminist Studies*, 6:2 (Summer 1980), p. 348.
26. *Ibid.*, p. 350.
27. Evelyn Fox Keller, "Feminism and Science," *Signs*, 7:3 (Spring 1982), p. 599.
28. Rosemary Redford Ruether, *New Woman: New Earth* (New York: Seabury, 1975).
29. Robin Morgan, *The Anatomy of Freedom: Feminism, Physics, and Global Politics* (New York: Doubleday, 1982), pp. 282-84.
30. Virginia Woolf, *Three Guineas* (New York: Harcourt, Brace and World, 1963), p. 6.

Feminist Critical Theory
A Search for New Paradigms

SUDHA P. PANDYA

> What happens when a new work of art is created is something that happens simultaneously to all the works of art which preceded it. The existing monuments from an ideal order among themselves, which is modified by the introduction of the new (the really new) work of art among them. The existing order is complete before the new work arrives; for order to persist after the supervention of novelty, the *whole* existing order must be, if ever so slightly, altered .

In this extract from T.S. Eliot's celebrated essay "Tradition and the Individual Talent"[1] we find his concept of literary tradition and the relationship between the literary works of past and present is promulgated. While one may not agree with his idea of "order," what he says about a new work of art is applicable to some extent to a new approach in the field of literary criticism.

Feminist criticism is, essentially, a new way of reading/thinking about literature. It has lost its capacity to shock and has been accepted inside the critical canon as a valuable approach to literature. The history behind its success reminds one of what F.R. Leavis wrote in "Retrospect" to *New Bearings in English Literature*. It illustrates how "when resistance to the new thing collapses, the readjustment is effected . . .

and the world made safe again."[2] The word "safe" would be better substituted by "sane," some feminist critics would argue.

To find out how it was done, one has to take a detour into the evolution and development of feminist criticism. From its very beginning, it has been intertwined with political events. Feminism emerged as an important force in the Western world in the 1960s. The earliest feminists were women who were active members of Civil Rights movement, who protested against the Vietnam war and struggled for the abolition of slavery. The sexist attitude of their male colleagues who swore about equality brought them closer—to form all-women groups. They realized that the strategies used to oppress the blacks were similar to those used to keep women subservient. An urgent need was felt to acknowledge the necessity of viewing women as a separate group. This revolutionary feminism was a political necessity to fight racism, sexism, capitalism and patriarchal society.

The same awakening spread to the reading of literature. Feminist criticism emerged as an off-shoot of the Women's Liberation Movement, sharing its polemical force and activist commitment. Its central hypothesis was, and is, that gender is a crucial determinant in the production, circulation and consumption of literary discourse. Literary criticism and literary theory have traditionally been guarded male-dominated areas. It was taken for granted that the representative reader, writer or critic of literature was male. The feminist criticism protested against this exclusion of women, this misogyny, and the movement provided the impetus. As Elaine Showalter puts it:

> It was through the women's liberation movement that we began to draw connections between our own work and our own lives, to note the disparities between the identifications and ambitions that had attracted us, along with thousands of other women, to the study and teaching of literature, and the limited and secondary roles granted to fictional heroines, women writers, or female scholars.

> Feminism spoke to our lived and our literary experience with the fierce urgency of a revelation or a Great Awakening.[3]

Radical thinking often finds a haven in the academy. Very often these women were creative writers and academicians who asked fundamental questions about the depiction of women in literature and why so few women writers survived to become part of literary tradition. Soon it became an intellectual movement charged with the excitement of violating existing patriarchal/sexist paradigms and discovering a new field of vision. Some pioneering works that stimulated this movement are Virginia Woolf's *A Room of One's Own* (1927), Simone de Beauvoir's *The Second Sex* (1949), Mary Ellmann's *Thinking About Women* (1968) and Kate Millett's *Sexual Politics* (1969). Virginia Woolf has always fascinated feminist critics who find her much ahead of her time in her thinking about women. She is hailed as the mother of the movement by most. Some like Showalter accept her historical and representative importance but find it a serious limitation in her that she had no first-hand experience of what she wrote about, that as a privileged woman in society she lacked the negative experience which is necessary to be able to feel for or think about the problems of women.

Showalter advocates a reading of Woolf which is detached from the narrative strategies she employs. In her thought-provoking book *Sexual/Textual Politics,* Toril Moi formulates a more positive approach to reading Woolf, suggesting a "Derridian and Kristevian" reading, as an alternative. The elusiveness of Woolf's writing, the steadily shifting perspective of her style which is interpreted by Showalter as a denial of authentic feminine states of mind—anger and alienation—is to Moi a deliberate deconstructive form of writing: "one that engages with and thereby exposes the duplicitous nature of discourse."[4] Virginia Woolf's famous concept of androgyny which to Showalter is a flight from fixed gender identities is to Moi a rejection born out of a recognition of their falsifying metaphysical nature. In deconstructing the binary opposition of masculinity and femininity, of sexual identity, Woolf is doing something authentically feminist.

Simone de Beauvoir's *The Second Sex* is espoused to socialism but is based on Sartre's existentialist philosophy. Her main argument here is that women have always been thought of and treated as an object for men—as men's other—relegated to secondary roles, and denied individuality and responsibility. These assumptions dominate social, political and cultural life to such an extent that women have come to believe in them, accept them and enact them in real life. Thus women become what they do because society expects them to be so. To quote her now-famous statement, "One is not born a woman; one becomes one." The basic tenets of her argument are generally accepted by all, but British feminist criticism, in particular, is more immersed in Marxist ideology than its American and French counterparts. Besides gender, class also becomes a preoccupation in such literary studies.

Mary Ellmann argues in her book that Western culture employs a very obsolete and ridiculous sexual mode of thought and discusses the insidious effects of thinking by sexual analogy. It is generally believed that women, as readers, critics or writers can only be weak and passive whereas men are always strong and active. She advocates an effort to resist and subvert this mode of thought. Like Germaine Greer's *The Female Eunuch* (1970), this book abounds in irony as a means of doing this. It is not surprising that Ellmann finds a model in Jane Austen who uses wit and irony with great deftness. Because it does not have a vein of explicit anger, usually believed to be the fundamental feminist emotion, some feminist critics have been biased against this work.

Kate Millett's *Sexual Politics* can be regarded the first major book in U.S.A, with this slant. It is characteristically a combination of detailed analysis of literary works and political argument. Her approach necessitates destroying the prevailing assumptions to pave the way for feminist thinking. In a raw, polemical style, she traces the history of women's symbolic oppression, from the myth of Pandora through the prose of Henry Miller. On one hand, like many other feminist critics, she posits a reaction to New Criticism by insisting that a work has to be placed in its socio-cultural perspective to be understood fully. On the other hand, she foreshadows the "return of the reader"—the acceptance that the reader is dependable, not the text or the author. She describes sexual politics as the method by which one sex seeks to maintain and extend its power over the other subordinate sex. She attacks D.H. Lawrence, Henry Miller, Norman Mailer and Jean Genet for carrying sexual politics to literature. Millett goes on, in her book, to extend her scathing criticism to Freud and the psychoanalytical theory derived from him.

These books greatly influenced what is known as Images of Women criticism—the first phase of feminist writing which focuses attention on women as readers. It discards the historic and anti-biographical New Criticism as well as Formalist criticism, insisting on the importance of reading a work as an experience of the reality presented therein. Writers, both men and women, who create "unreal" female characters are in for harsh strictures. Feminist readings have no pretensions of being value-free, dispassionate or universal. But there is a conviction that they are necessary and important—as one way of reading a text, which is also fully conscious of its leanings and limitations. This insistence on the realtionship of literature to personal experience lends an autobiographical, or even confessional tone to this kind of writing. Sandra Gilbert compares the beginning of feminist critical awareness to a conversion experience:

> . . . most feminist critics speak . . . like people who must bear witness, people who must enact and express in their own lives and words the revisionary sense of transformation that seems inevitably to attend the apparently simple discovery that the experiences of women in and with literature are different from those of men.[5]

This phase is marked by a preoccupation with exposing the misogyny of literary practice reflected in distorted and stereotyped images of women in literary works. Women are rarely presented as women and realistically. Very often, either woman is portrayed as a selfless, self-denying, sacrificing, compliant angel—a symbol of purity and beauty; or else she is presented as a monster—the villain, victimizer, devourer, predator—as one who like Eve instigates man to do things which ultimately ruin him, as one who frustrates man's attempts to make a better life.

Women characters are given no positive roles even as house-makers. Such misrepresentation, literary abuse and textual harassment of women in literature is exposed by the feminist critics. The connections between the social and literary mistreatment of women are drawn and the exclusion of women from literary history and criticism is challenged. Vigorous feminist questioning on these lines led to a reappraisal of old classics and the result is a changing atmosphere of literary response. A well-known example is the opening part of Hardy's *The Mayor of Casterbridge.* As Lawrence Lipking observes, "Something peculiar has been happening lately to the classics, some of them now seem less heroic, and some of them less funny."[6]

The other branch of feminist criticism deals with women as writers. The need to study them separately may be labelled anti-egalitarian but to these critics it is an urgent political necessity to combat the patriarchal strategies employed to keep women as the misrepresented and muted lot. Here the focus is on women's writing, with the conviction that there is a continuity, a coherent tradition, of women's writings that "women writers had a literature of their own whose historical and thematic coherence as well as artistic importance was obscured by the patriarchal values that dominate our culture."[7]

Nina Baym, while writing a book on Nathaniel Hawthorne came across Hawthorne's complaint to his publisher about the "damned mob of scribbling women" who he believed were affecting the popularity and sales of his works.

Bent upon finding out who these women writers were, who were probably outselling Hawthorne in his own day but were virtually forgotten, Baym undertook painstaking research. It led to the rediscovery of dozens of novels which may not be the best that the age produced, nevertheless have representative value and were some of the most popular books of that period. The conclusion arrived at by such feminist critics is that women's writing has suffered immeasurably under a masculine value system. Even conventional concepts of literary merit are often biased since they priorize men and consider what women write as insignificant and forgettable.

The efforts of the feminist critics resulted in a massive recovery of almost forgotten women writers and also re-reading of literature by women with a view to understand the evolution of the "female aesthetic." Anthologies, histories of literature and college syllabi have all been since forced to incorporate more women writers to be able to give a balanced picture of the creative output of any period in literary history. Four books which are now accepted classics of feminist criticism were largely responsible for these developments. They gripped the minds of women scholars and students, and represent the specific approach of Anglo-American feminist critics, in so far as they believe that it is society and women's interaction with it that shapes women's different perception of the world.

Patricia Meyer Spacks in *The Female Imagination* (1975) characteristically discusses Kate Millett and Mary Ellmann's path-breaking books. She considers Millett's account of psychoanalysis in her book as one of its strong points. Her more important observation is about Ellmann who, according to her, uses a distinctive feminine discourse apparent in the narrative strategies employed by her. She examines the common themes in women's fiction as products of a particularly female experience. Ellen Moer's *Literary Women: The Great Writers* (1977) may have nothing new or illuminating for the present-day writer or reader. But in her conviction that women ought to be viewed and studied as a distinctive group, she is a forerunner in the field. Elaine Showalter in her book *A Literature of Their Own* (1977) calls women's writing a subculture. However, what has alienated women writers from a sense of collective identity is the "transience of female literary fame." Women writers popular in their life-times seem to vanish without trace from the records of posterity. She traces the evolution of this "subculture" from the times of the Brontës to the present day. The development is outlined by her, very convincingly, in three stages:

1. *Feminine:* The phase of imitation of the prevailing modes of the dominant tradition.
2. *Feminist:* The phase of protest against the standards and values, in favour of autonomy.
3. *Female:* The phase of self-discovery, of a search for identity.

Besides this pioneering work of practical criticism, Showalter has also significantly contributed towards giving some theoretical base to feminist thinking and is therefore often grouped with other theorists like Annette Kolodny and Myra Jehlen.

In *The Madwoman in the Attic* (1979), Sandra M. Gilbert and Susan Gubar present a study of the nineteenth-century women writers claiming that their works which have been read through centuries as very unproblematic have deeper levels of meaning, waiting to be explored. Creativity was considered then, a fundamentally male quality. There were stereotyped images of women in the writing by men—of angels, as women who are selfless, docile and passive—or of monsters, as women who are not so. As victims of the "phallocentric myth of creativity," women writers could not present the real woman and often conformed to the patriarchal standards imposed on them. The main argument of the book is that the women writers of the nineteenth century overcame a debilitating anxiety of authorship and through their work managed to both conform to and subvert patriarchal literary standards. In order to be able to present a true female voice, they assault and deconstruct the stereotyped images of women.

Thus the mad woman like Bertha Mason in *Jane Eyre* is the author's "double," an avatar of the writer's own self, mirroring her own anxiety and rage—the "female schizophrenia of authorship."[8] This characteristic is, according to Gilbert and Gubar, common to all the nineteenth-century novels studied in the book and is also very conspicuous in twentieth-century fiction by women. The argument is extended by Susan Gilbert in a later essay on Milton where she not only identifies Milton as the "inhibiting Father" of the female literary imagination but also sees in his portrait of Eve, Milton's unwitting homage to female creativity with which writers like Charlotte Brontë and Mary Shelley must have identified.

I have here confined myself to Anglo-American feminist criticism—as a specific approach and not as dependent on the critic's nationality. However, to give a picture of the internal debate and variety within the field, it is imperative to look at the other strands also. The most innovative and fertile writing on the problems of women's writing and criticism can be attributed to the French feminist critics, best represented by Helene Cixous, Luce Irigaray and Julia Kristeva. Borrowing heavily in vocabulary and theory from post-structuralism and Marxism, they have moulded their ideas to suit their own concerns. The post-structuralist challenge to the authority of the literary canon is assimilated in their own attack on patriarchy and call for the inclusion in the canon of more female-authored books. They employ the Lacanian concept of "absence" to rescue the concept of a female writing difference. The theoretical base having been provided by Lacan, Derrida and Barthes, attacks are mounted on "patriarchs" like Plato and Freud. Despite their internal differences, the French feminist critics believe that female subjectivity is derived from women's physiology and bodily instincts. They are convinced that if women are to discover and express who they are, they must begin with their sexuality and their sexuality begins with their bodies. They urge the woman writer to ally herself with everything in the culture that is muted, unrepresented and marginalized in order to subvert the existing systems that repress feminine difference. Abounding in brilliant and extensive use of puns, neologisms, coded allusions, typographical breaks, *l'ecriture feminine* suffers, however, from its major proposition that women's biological makeup dictates how they think, read and write, which has the danger of leading to very reductive readings.

Feminist criticism has also come under fire from some of its own branches. It can be assailed as heterosexist, homophobic, racist or guilty of "cultural imperialism," Lesbian feminist critics like Bonnie Zimmerman challenge the heterosexist assumptions of Anglo-American feminist criticism. Black feminist critics, on the other hand, believe they have suffered from the "racism" of white feminist theory. What they ask is, "Men have constantly spoken for women. Is it right that women now should take up that masculine position in relation to other women?" And we also have the kind of writing done by Gayatri Chakravorty Spivak, a Third World Marxist feminist critic. She attacks the theorist of the world, Marx, and the theorist of the self, Freud, for their incomplete and erroneous propositions. At the centre of her attack is Freud's theory of pain which is presented as being outside the idea of normality and health. Spivak argues that Freud did not know enough, that for a woman pain exists within the concepts of normality and productivity. Her strictures against Marx revolve around her observation that women's role as agents in the theory of production is neglected by Marx.

What seems most timely and valuable in her work is her warning against the "over determinants":

> We must . . . remind ourselves, our positivist feminist colleagues in charge of creating the discipline of women's studies, and our anxious students, that essentialism is a trap. It seems more important to learn to understand that the world's women do not all relate to the privileging of essence, especially through "fiction," or "literature," in quite the same way.[9]

Warning against the trapping of an essentialist bourgeois feminism, Spivak makes a case for a Third World feminist criticism which will have its own concerns, priorities as well as its own means of dealing with them.

Considering the fact that there are all these various strands within feminist criticism, it is understandable and probably welcome that it has not arrived at any one theory, acceptable to all. The internal debate and acceptance of mutual disagreement on fundamental theoretical questions is the basic strength of the movement.

NOTES

1. Thomas Stearns Eliot, *The Sacred Wood: Essays on Poetry and Criticism* (London: Methuen, 1969), pp. 49-50.
2. Frank Raymond Leavis, *New Bearings in English Poetry: A Study of the Contemporary Situation* (Harmondsworth: Penguin Books, 1972), p. 159.
3. Elaine Showalter, ed., *The New Feminist Criticism: Essays on Women, Literature, and Theory* (New York: Pantheon, 1985), p. 5.
4. Toril Moi, *Sexual/Textual Politics: Feminist Literary Theory* (New York: Routledge, 1988), p. 9.
5. Sandra M. Gilbert, "Life Studies, or, Speech after Long Silence: Feminist Critics Today," *College English*, 40 (April 1979), p. 850.
6. Lawrence Lipking, "Aristotle's Sister: A Poetics of Abandonment," *Critical Inquiry*, 10 (September 1983), 79.
7. Elaine Showalter, p. 6.
8. Sandra M. Gilbert and Susan Gubar, *The Madwoman in the Attic: The Woman Writer and the Nineteenth Century Literary Imagination* (New Haven: Yale University Press, 1979), p. 78.
9. Gayatri Chakravorty Spivak, *In Other Worlds: Essays in Cultural Politics* (New York: Methuen, 1987), p. 89.

Problematizing Feminism

JAIDEV

I am sick of being the victim
of trends I reflect
but don't even understand.

The above lines are spoken by Kate, "an affluenza-stricken American," in a recent feminist play by Jane Wagner.[1] Kate finds her life extremely boring and the reason behind her boredom is that she has been reflecting trends which she does not understand at all. She comes to realize that instead of her using them, it is the trends which have been using her all along. Her naivete has been useful to the trend-setting, trend-selling, manipulative system. Indeed, any sophisticated system today operates not by a direct and visible exploitation of people but by making them retain an illusion of freedom and free choice, by making them willingly give into its imperatives, and by subtly ensuring that they do not see that they are dupes or victims. Kate's anxiety is a first step towards recognizing her position in the system whose trends hold her in thralldom.

This paper is made up of random thoughts on feminism for the Third World and in justification it can only plead an anxiety which is qualitatively similar to Kate's. The anxiety is rooted in my suspicion that instead of developing a genuine, need-based feminism which is so obviously needed in our country, we might simply be reflecting or buying a trendy feminism which is little different from many a multi-national consumer product. Another basis for my anxiety is that many of us assume that any novel by a woman must needs be a feminist text. My observations are drawn on the basis of a comparatist reading of half a dozen novels by women novelists, three from the West and three from India: *The Golden Notebook* by Doris Lessing, *Surfacing* by Margaret Atwood, *Beloved* by Toni Morrison, *The Day in Shadow* by Nayantara Sahgal, *Ek Thi Anita* by Amrita Pritam, and *Chitkobra* by Mridula Garg.

Feminism is a global and revolutionary ideology and as such calls for a definite stance, a set of firm, exacting attitudes. The ideology is political because it is concerned with the question of all questions, the question of power; it is revolutionary because it is against the status quo. Predictably enough, feminism is viewed as a threat (once it becomes something more than a laughing matter or gossip theme) by forces which have stakes and interest in the status quo. These forces are not only sexist but can include economic, political, religious, racist, neo-colonial, and even multi-national ones. Connections stop nowhere, and a feminist, rather than staying naive, would be considered paranoiac *a la* the unnamed heroine of Atwood's *Surfacing*. There cannot be a significant feminist gain without the entire system registering tremors and taking steps either to absorb the shock or else neutralize it. The system-preserving forces can be daring and ruthless in their attempts to curb revolutionary tendencies, but these forces can also be very imaginative and innovative. They can manufacture an imitation feminism to counter the genuine one. They can also try to corrupt the latter from within. All is permissible.

Of the various methods used by the system to contain or counter feminism, the two most important are: the strategy of trivializing and fetishizing feminism, and the strategy of making feminism too involved, jargon-ridden, and abstractified. Its revolutionary urge is sought to be bogged under an avalanche of reflexive and self-begetting cliches and concepts, and these are all introduced for a deflective purpose. The first strategy reduces feminism to a mere trend, a consumer item or fashion. The system appropriates feminism by first allowing some unspectacular concessions and then tailoring (read: distorting) it so that it is devitalized and loses all its potential for destabilizing the system. The strategy can be called castration by canonization. Derrida's deconstruction has been more or less neutralized in this way in America, so that one would be justified today in enquiring of a deconstructionist if he is a simple deconstructionist or an American one, for the two are different species altogether. The second strategy has been in use against Marxism in America; many brilliant scholars are busy adding by thousands the basic terms and concepts one is supposed to master before trying to relate Marxism to society or political systems. Marxism thus becomes too specialized. This strategy is now being applied against feminism as well, if one goes by the number of new-fangled and curious notions, concepts and paradigms that have suddenly erupted. Feminist research is turning into an industry, and so micro and fine are the subjects being tackled that one is in danger of forgetting that feminism is meant to address itself to real people, real problems, etc. This fast-expanding feminism is part of what has been called the post-modernist condition, and perhaps a few words on this condition will be relevant.

Feminist literary theory has begun to invade our consciousness in the wake of post-structuralism. The movement differs radically from the traditional approaches of literary criticism in that it does not emerge from, or even address itself to, literature in practice. Post-structuralist literary theory usually evolves from the semiotic logic. Literature as it exists does not have to prove the theory right. It is enough for a post-structuralist that literature can be written according to the literary theory. Such a premise seems depressing because it expects literature to learn from theory. In any case, several post-structuralists are feminists and naturally therefore they are busy creating a feminist aesthetics, a feminist literary theory which, out of politeness, is supposed to illumine past texts but which actually will be fulfilled only in expressly-written texts for theory. It seems it is necessary to consider the implications of much of the feminist literary theory. For example, it is not at all clear how female time is different from male time. The former has been characterized as involved and fluctuating, while the latter is linear and forward-going—as if Faulkner and Garcia Marquez were not men! The female sentence is supposed to be tentative, open-ended, desiring continuity rather than snapping communication; female reality is individual-oriented, not collective or societal. This last concept has been shown to be at work in Lessing's *The Golden Notebook* which, I think, is the most collective and societal of all English novels of the 1960s, and which, according to its author, was intended "to give the ideological 'feel' of our mid-century."[2,3]

The three western novels are all feminist texts, and they have their value as such, but none of them upholds the idea of a female syntax or a female time. The vision, the style (which isn't merely a linguistic matter) and the feel are inescapably female—but none of these is reducible to clear intellectual concepts. This seems to me a very happy state of affairs. For the day any philosopher is able to formulate precisely what is inalienably female about a sentence structure or a theme, we will begin to see men trying to appropriate them by clever imitations. The point is that it is quite possible for a misogynist to write a thoroughly anti-female text while still using each and every specific nuance and trait of feminist literary theory. This mania for specifically female traits would not cause anxiety if it were merely a scholarly matter. The feminist approach in literary criticism cannot be a mere academic matter; it has to be part of feminism which is a political ideology. The kind of hair splitting the feminist literary theory seems to generate cannot help the cause of women. The status-quoist forces will naturally promote such a situation, for so much dangerous energy is being dissipated in deciding the sex of a particular kind of sentence and so on. Even when this kind of theorizing is well-intentioned and honourable, one has to see whether it furthers the cause or obstructs it. In any case, going micro and fine-grained might add to our existing knowledge but might also widen the gulf between men and women, might promote sexual separatism. The real beneficiaries will be the status-quoist forces, for this denotes a success of their second strategy. Worst of all, this kind of separatism is a form of biologism, something feminism should not endorse. The best feminist texts rise above gender. For example, the moral of Atwood's *Bodily Harm* is: to be weak and powerless and violable is to be woman. Given power, a woman will be a man.

Another problem with this quest for quintessential female traits relates to its political implications. To be fair to all such seekers, they are probably motivated by a desire to discover and stabilize woman's identity. She must have some things which are essentially her own. Humanism or human traits are not enough, because all through history these have denoted attributes wholly in possession of men. There are two ways of tackling this obviously most unjust situation. One is to become aggressive and militant and ask for secession—what is mine, so keep your hands off! The other way is to seek to put an end to the unjust interpretation of the term human and redefine it so that it accommodates woman and her traits on an equitable basis. This is what co-existence and love are about.

Meanwhile, people should be educated about the extent and depth of sexist biases and distortions introduced by unequal distribution of power. Identity becomes available both ways, but when achieved in the first way, it might be a mere fetish, for it might have little contextual solidity. Indeed, such an identity will again be very favoured by the forces of the status quo, for in gaining this identity the whole society will have been divided along sex lines. How can one think of work for class solidarity, if the family itself is already engaged in a civil war? Granted that the all-too-many divisions we have today in our society, divisions along regional, racial, communal, class, and other lines are men's doing, still feminism has to oppose splits and fragmentations. Otherwise, power might perhaps change hands, but there will be no revolutionary change. Too much of microism and polarity (books for women, by women, about women?) is likely to be merely deflective, for the real aims of feminism are upstaged and all energy is spent in fighting against a particular syndrome of power instead of getting concentrated on the power and its redistribution. This separatism is political and aimed at preserving the status quo by deflecting the victim's energy away from the right object and against each other.

The men in Anna Wulf's life, all fail her, all prove exploitive, opportunistic or worse. Experiencing men raw as she does, she probably does not understand the pattern behind their monstrosities. Her husband is a victim of man's image of man: hard, cold, rational and analytical. Another similar victim is Richard, Molly's husband. For the rest, Anna's lovers are all victims of insecurity, be it class-based as with the doctor-lover or ideological as with the American lovers. Her most-missed lover is from the working class and loves security too much, and the American lovers are all filled with fear, for their leftism has rendered them unwelcome at home, what with the McCarthy era and witch-hunting. Of course, Lessing's heroine is used badly by men, but she is not just a free woman; in her own way, she is the most intelligent of the whole lot. She knows men are bad, but then one cannot do without them, and so one has to be reconciled to being a "boulder pusher," a Sisyphus-like figure except for this crucial fact that with each attempt the level of consciousness does rise if only very slightly. Men are bad, but if they won't help themselves, women have to act to redeem them, hoping that the effort will be shared by some more mature men as well.

The Golden Notebook is very much against splits and fragmentations, even when they can be justified, for sexual separatism is viewed by Lessing as a form of insanity, in spite of her tolerance for homosexuality. It is not at all by chance that Anna's writer's block is lifted by a man who is helped equally by her. Her novel's first line comes from the man and she gives him the first line of the novel. She rejects the battlefield view of man-woman relationship, and it will only be a vulgar, superficial male pig who will feel great because all through Anna aches for a man's body. Indeed, what the book is suggesting is that if any man does not ache for a woman, then there is something rotten and diseased about him. And even when her lovers prove to be rotten, she does not want to dump them, she would rather prefer that they get healthy. This is feminism at its most sane. It pleads for the health of all men as well as women, so that together they can act to free the world of oppression, apartheid, exploitation and bullying. Anna knows the traits which are evil in her men, but she treats these not as their essential traits but as traits which men acquire for the purpose of degrading both themselves and women, once they are seduced by the lure of power.

Atwood's *Surfacing* similarly takes woman as an existential condition, the condition of being powerless and manipulatable. Since power is centralized in the hands of men, they feel nothing wrong in destroying her dignity or her creativity. The fake husband of the unnamed heroine exploits her innoncence and convinces her that she should not mind compromising her artistic integrity since there haven't been any important women artists in history, the implication being that women should not even aspire to greatness. Then, he makes her agree to terminating her pregnancy, since he cannot marry her, the implication being that without a husband for its father, a woman has no right to have a baby. She sheds these manly notions, but in the process she also comes to develop a deep empathy for the flora and fauna of her Quebec island which too is being mutilated by power-holding groups, called Americans. The heroine discovers that woman is not indicative of a particular sex, but includes in its definition all those who are powerless, vulnerable, rapable—men, trees, animals—anyone that is a victim. Fellow-travelling for men should be allowed, not as a concession but as a necessity for organizing the weak against the strong:

> May be it was true, I leafed through all the men I had known to see whether or not I hated them. But then I realized it wasn't the men I hated, it was the Americans,

> the human beings, men and women both. They'd had their chance but they had turned against the gods, and it was time for me to choose sides. I wanted there to be a machine that could make them vanish, a button I could press that would evaporate them without disturbing anything else, that way there would be more room for the animals, they would be rescued.[4]

The Americans represent power and *Surfacing* again and again makes it clear that any meaningful feminism has ultimately to face up to the problem of unequal and unjust distribution of power. It is of course necessary to fight against sexist biases and discriminations, but the focus should still be on their root cause, namely an unjust distribution of power. There is no point in losing the support of all those groups whose battle too is with inequalities.

Toni Morrison's recent novel, *Beloved,* is a profound book because it refuses to simplify things. It is a very touching feminist text, dealing with the ultimate nuances of an ex-slave and her relations. The most humane things about the book are its refusals to subscribe to stereotypes. The whites are wicked because as slave-owners they are profiteers, and in fact even when they are gentle, they are gentle because they know they can exploit the blacks more through gentleness. In this pattern of exploiter-victimizer, sex is not the issue. Between themselves, a stranger black girl and the heroine's daughter who too is black can have a very shifty, beautiful but also difficult relationship. Beloved, the stranger, has a hold on the heroine, Sethe, and at once a power relationship develops. Then, we are told about another Denver, a white freak, who had saved the heroine while she was in labour pains and also running for life. The white Denver had not only helped her escape but also acted as a midwife so that the heroine was able to deliver her female child, the daughter Denver. And of course the most unforgettable and heart-warming scenes in the novel relate to a slave Sixo and his Thirty-Mile girl, another slave, who works thirty four miles away. Sixo and she use their Sundays for running towards each other so that they may be together for a few minutes. Sixo is shot dead after he and some other slaves plan an escape, but even while dying Sixo wails, "Seven-o, Seven-o," thus warning off the Thirty-Mile girl.

The whole problematics of social relations is summed up in the conduct of a white teacher who used to beat Sixo in spite of the fact that the latter was right: "School teacher beat him anyway to show him that definitions belonged to the definers—not the defined."[5] The definers are the power-wielders and they are pitiable, too, because they do not realize how badly power has distorted them: "it wasn't the jungle blacks brought with them to his place from the other (livable) place. It was the jungle white folks planted in them. And it grew. It spread. In, through and after life, it spread, until it invaded the whites who had made it. Touched them everyone. Changed and altered them. Made them bloody, silly, worse then even they wanted to be, so scared were they of the jungle they had made."[6] The common point in Morrison, Atwood and Lessing, as also in several other distinguished female novelists, is that they all believe in feminism but do not wish to be reductive or simplistic in their assessment of the human predicament.

A criticism based on good, sane feminist novels seems to me to have greater validity than an extravagant literary theory which sinks or sails only with semiotic logic. The feminist literary theory as it seems to be developing under the aegis of post-structuralism may be well-intentioned but somehow appears to be more amenable to the pressures of the system. The system can reduce it to a mere commodity and reduced to a commodity it can build a factitious, over-specialized mystique around itself.

In fact, this danger wouldn't bother one much except for one major reason: feminism commodified, tamed and fetishized serves as a trend for home consumption, but sooner or later it also becomes an export item, especially in the countries where there is a section of the population willing to cherish everything Western, including Western insanities. The market logic which brings Pepsi Cola cannot leave feminism alone but must result in a flooding of our culture counters with feminism. And why not, when there are already keen collaborators (with their clear stakes in the status quo) as well as keen consumers? Culture sells here (and all culture is Western, of course), if not as culture *per se,* then as the free gift for promoting the sale of other, more important wares. Cultural pacts are a prelude to arms sale deeds, etc. Culture is business, just as lovely libraries and dirt-cheap textbooks are part of a larger business deal.

Kate in Wagner's play is naive, but whole nations can be naive as well. Without detracting from the value of the good work being done by several feminist groups in our country. I would like to suggest that given our bourgeois fondness for all Western trends and fashions and also given the conversion of feminism into an international best-seller, we need to avoid becoming feminists just because it is the in thing. I am anxious because so much of our urban bourgeois culture is pastiche culture, a bizarre combination of motifs, details and trends adopted without discrimination or understanding and stapled together to show off our foreign connections.

Pastiche culture is a mockery of culture and it exults in exhibitionism and fetishes. Pastiche culture is ugly because it seldom connects with people, alienation being intrinsic to it. One is not at all impressed by someone who can spit out fifty lines of Kate Millett, Germaine Greer or Marilyn French, but who cannot understand the language of a woman from a nearby village. Our universities are today so heavily alienated from the rhythm of our people, these are such bastardized and pastiche places, that one does not put too much faith in trendy campus Marxism or Feminism. It is very necessary for us to have feminism in this country but then this feminism has to be authentic, rooted and context-bound. One does not mind if our feminists are not too clever or good at quoting Western critics or weaving intricate post-structuralist cobwebs. These do not really matter. The concept of feminism is nothing mysterious. And one must never borrow or buy any Western details for the simple reason that these details are context-bound, context-specific. A pastiche feminist is likely to go all out trying to transpose Anna Wulf's patterns on to an Indian woman. This clearly wouldn't do. The patterns are irrelevant here. Anna Wulf does not seem to be aware of or need any neighbours. In India, neighbourhood is a central fact of our social life. Similarly Anna Wulf can stay alone and keep a man as a paying guest without anything happening to her against her wish. She can depend on a machinery of law and order. Can a female divorcee here be as confident? Pastiche in our country has become a prestige item, but we should learn to do without it. Pastiche feminism, to improvise a dialogue from Wagner's play, can make lib stand for libido, instead of liberation.

Naiveté characterizes people who seek to live by pastiche patterns. A different kind of naivete underlies all uncritical, over-enthusiastic celebrations of novels which are written by women and, instead of heroes, have female heroes. The concept in such novels is the same, only it has been embodied in a female figure.

Mridula Garg's *Chitkobra*[7] is a good case in point. The heroine, Manu, is free, experimental, brave in her job, but the problem with her characterization is that she is constructed at a fantasy level in a more or less total socio-cultural vacuum. She is a pastiche, a discordant and pointless medley of motifs from Lessing, *Love Story* (whose smart dialogues are imitated here at a Bombay-film level), Kafka, Lawrence, Philip Roth's *The Breast* (which is imitated for deliberately titillating purposes, especially on pp. 111 ff.), and so on. This is Women's Lib as an exercise in fantasy, in superlative sex. Its politics and ideology are both vulgar and superficial, for they remind us of her foreign connections and prototypes, her Indian connections being entirely absent. Of course, the heroine is a poetess and writes a vulgar satire on 15 August, but you do not create social conscience for a heroine through such petty, cosy gestures. It is all a put on and there is no clear or firm idea or stance behind the book.

Such decadent books (*Uske Hisse Ki Dhoop* is another)

are bound to be a liability for Indian feminism because they degrade consciousness instead of raising it. Equally discouraging is *Ek Thi Anita* by Amrita Pritam. It has less desire to appear foreign-looking (except in a rather pointless use of Camus's *The Plague* for suggesting the heroine's state of mind—just because she has dreamed of an extra-marital affair and a quite confident, poetical handling of the theme of the double) but it is a typical sob-stuff, sentimental and determined to turn the heroine an exceptional being.

It is typical both of *Chitkobra* and *Ek Thi Anita* to foreground all that is exceptional and romantic and asocial in the heroines so that they can have no social reference or conscience. Both are reductive characterizations; they are working women, but we know little about their professional aspects, or, for that matter, about their parents, brothers, sisters, other relations. They live in a very small familial world—the husbands are necessary because the themes are related to extra-marital loves. Fetishization and exhibitionism are all in all. One heroine uses smoking the stub left by her lover as an objective correlative of her desire to kiss him. One wonders if this is any improvement on our Bombay films. The other heroine asserts her liberation by drinking and talking of orchids and de-realizing the whole world for the sake of her lonely, sick sex fantasies. This is not the kind of stuff of which a meaningful revolutionary stance can be made.

Sahgal's *The Day in Shadow* is little better than either of the two novels, except for the fact that it does have two characters, both reductive and vulgar, who talk and reflect on politics, and two others who more convincingly represent the rising business and industrial class. The book is in English and is extremely conscious of its possible market in the West, and therefore goes out of its way to denounce Marxism, Russia and the left, as if these are plagues. But this paranoiac-opportunistic aspect apart, it is a bad feminist book because it depicts woman as victim and yet simultaneously it recommends that woman stay dependent for all practical purposes on man. It is amazing how polarization is naively accepted as the eternal law. A woman won't talk politics, won't know where she is signing, won't object when the man who has been asking her to be independent, arbitrarily announces that he is going to marry her, won't question the mystifying nonsense of her lover about Hinduism and Christianity when her own predicament is clearly not religious but economic. She accepts so very abjectly the definitions of woman which men have worked out and indeed she doesn't mind when her good lover calls her daughters "the litter." She should still be acceptable as a realistic portrait of a trapped, exploited, indoctrinated woman who hasn't even begun to see that she is a victim. But how do we rationalize the author's naivete in letting the male lover get away with his all-too-manly handling of the heroine whom he loves but also patronizes a little too much? How do we rationalize Sahgal's own refusal to tell us how many daughters "the litter" is supposed to comprise, or what their names are?

Sahgal diminishes her women about as much as men diminish them. This is not really baffling, for it is part and parcel of the way women are exploited by men that they, the victims, speak the language of men, indoctrinated as they are. And they speak and think like men want them to, even when they are independent. This shows how difficult a task feminism has in our country, but it also shows that most novels written by women in this country are anti-feminist, pro-male. So a course on Indian women novelists, while it appears to deal with "a literature of their own," is not necessarily a feminist course. A feminist novel for India is not a novel which a woman will write just because she is a woman and knows how to write. It will be written by one who has understood a woman both as a woman and as a person pressurized by all kinds of visible and invisible, external and internal forces, by one who is not carried away by fetishes but who is mature enough to see that it doesn't do to bark irresponsibly and stupidly that Hinduism and Christianity "had to be joined—united in an ocean of strength if (India) was to combat the genius of Marx."[8]

If Jane Austen, George Eliot and Emily Bronte were not feminists then the task of a feminist today is going to be more difficult than theirs—this task includes their task plus something more. For us here in India, it is tempting to say, well, these are our feminist writers as if making do is all that matters. No, we should insist on a true feminist novel for India, encourage our young ones to prepare for this, hope for one, but we should not issue false certificates. It is a lesser disgrace to admit that so far we do not have a book comparable to *Middlemarch* or *Surfacing* than to be found inventing ideological similarities between, say, Atwood and Anita Desai.

Naivete and sentimentalization—these are the two trends in our responses that have generated much anxiety in me about feminism. Some of my anxiety is due to the market logic, becoming more and more apparent in India, thanks to the arrival of multinationals and the growth of capitalism; this logic is bound to promote feminism and a deflective micro-specialization. I have nothing against introducing courses on our women novelists. This is only necessary, but should we necessarily also fetishize them? The teacher has to bring a certain amount of understanding of politics, history, culture and social and economic system. In addition, this feminist teacher has to know how to resist the text and to read what the text is trying to convey subliminally. In other words, the teacher, especially in the Third World, has to be political, has to be a purposive deconstructionist. This approach would pay dividends in reading even such an anti-feminist writer as Jonathan Swift or T.S. Eliot. It is, in short, necessary to read politically both women's and men's novels. In fact, reading novels is to be part of a larger programme involving reading politically thousands of messages which flit across our consciousness day in, day out in our social existence. For, ultimately the feminist approach in literary criticism has to be part of a most comprehensive agenda called feminism.

Finally, as teachers, we can explain to our young students some of whom might grow into writers, how a proper feminist novel should be written. We might also explain that too many of our fairy tales, folk tales and myths are anti-feminist, and that they are anti-feminist even when they worship women as deities, and these therefore need to be rewritten or re-interpreted. There are absences, erasures and gaps in our epics and these can be filled in by feminist writers. As students and critics, there is need for us to read feministically not just women's but men's texts as well. And there is need to revise the list of canonized texts because canonization involves power factors. It is also necessary to legitimate the teacher's emphasis on sexual politics in the classroom by introducing a similar emphasis in the examination papers. Young students especially should be encouraged to know more of the unromantic, marginalized India and learn not to bring any sentimental or naive expectations to bear on it. India is not beautiful but is often very sordid and petty, but it is only here that feminism or humanism can have any possible significance for us. The difficulty of acting here is genuine, but action here is surely more valid than any of those imitative, pastiche gestures like smoking or drinking which one does not even enjoy but reflects and enacts just because they are as fashionable as Pepsi Cola.

NOTES

1. Jane Wagner, *The Search for Signs of Intelligent Life in the Universe* (New York: Harper and Row, 1987), p. 53
2. Doris Lessing, Preface to *The Golden Notebook* (Frogmore: Panther, 1973), p. 11.
3. Suzanne Hall, "Feminist Writing: Some Twentieth Century British Women Writers: Hopes and Achievements," *Literature Alive*, 1 (September 1987), pp. 1-14.
4. Margaret Atwood, *Surfacing* (New York: Warner Books, 1983), p. 181.

5. Toni Morrison, *Beloved* (New York: Alfred A. Knopf, 1987), p. 190.
6. *Ibid.*, pp. 198-199.
7. Mridula Garg, *Chitkobra* (Delhi: National, 1976).
8. Nayantara Sahgal, *The Day in Shadow* (Delhi: Vikas, Bell Books, 1973), p. 201.

The True Voice of Endurance: A Study of Rukmani in Markandaya's *Nectar in a Sieve*

C. T. INDRA

I

In feminist criticism, the unilateral condemnation of partiarchy has gone out of fashion; the recommendation of an exclusive feminist poetics (as against androgyny) propounded by the matriarch of feminist criticism Elaine Showalter also seems to have lost its prestige. There is a steady recognition of the reality of man-woman relationship in the field of women's studies.

Indian feminists tended to isolate the Sita archetype perhaps because it suited their social goal aptly—the stereotype of the oppressed, meekly accepting wife which they said was more a creation of chauvinist patriarchy than anything natural. But there was not much said about Savitri who fought for her husband's life by outwitting no less a person than Yama. May be because she was still loyal to the old-fashioned idea of fidelity to the spouse. It may not be all the time wise to adopt an ideology or a mode of interpretation which has sprung from Western cultural matrix and which suits its context. Take, for example, the Derridean deconstructive approach which thinks in terms of binary opposition and suggests that it always implies the subordination of the second element. This may be true of the English pair Father-Mother. We have only to recall the pair *mata pita* in any Indian language and not in Sanskrit alone, to disprove the argument that secondary place implies subordination. Derrida's formula cannot be simply applied in toto to our situation.

I am aware that ideology is one thing and the prevailing social reality is another. "Actual behaviour is likely to be more varied than is suggested by social myths or stereotypes, and the relation of the ideology of woman to social reality remains difficult to measure."[1] Although female subculture calls for an exclusive study and in fact offers an attractive prospect, we require a more inclusive notion of history which is "based on the recognition that women have always been essential to the making of history and that *men and women* are the measure of significance."[2]

A study of the mutual or interactive aspect of public and private life, society and family, and work and home enables us to understand better the role of woman in all these spheres. The new history should avoid both the "heroic models" and the "models of oppression" and concentrate on the complexity of women's past. This enables us to transcend the tension in feminist scholarship today between the celebration of the "female" and the advocacy of "androgyny." Judith Stacey recognizes no doubt that the tension is productive when she says: "Instead of celebrating the feminine, we need to retain a vital tension between androgynous and female-centred visions. We need to recognize contradiction and to apply a critical perspective that distinguishes between giving value to traditionally female qualities and celebrating the female in a universalistic and essentialist manner."[3]

II

With these few basic observations we may proceed to examine the voice of the female protagonist in Kamala Markandaya's *Nectar in a Sieve.*[4] In fact, the choice of the novel which is neither "recent fiction" nor a feminist piece of writing is perhaps unwise. If anything, the heroine seems distressingly close to the detested archetypes of the suffering

Hindu woman, docile, submissive. On a closer look, however, it will turn out to be a misreading. We can even construct an affirmative feminist poetics from a concentration on the protagonist, a poetic which may be complementary to the "gynocriticism" of Elaine Showalter. I am aware that the novel is more often than not read as a critique of industrialized society and as a paean of rural India (vide its subtitle "A Novel of Rural India"). In its apparently pristine simplicity and pastoral setting it seems to suggest idyllic happiness. But that is all only on the surface. This novel is nothing if it is not a paean to human suffering.

Let us recall that the novel is in the mode of first person narration, almost cast in memory. The tale of Rukmani and Nathan, and through them the story of the changing life-style of the village, is told by Rukmani. It is an unmistakably female voice, an aged woman's, but not shaky. In fact, it is filled with compassion and tenderness for a boy who is not her own son, who is affected by leprosy. The old woman starts reminiscing in the evening of her life.

What is it that marks out Rukmani as an interesting narrator? She has a firm grasp of details, a phenomenal memory, the capacity for an imaginative rendering of atmosphere, a stark austere vocabulary, a respect for others who crossed her life, and the detachment of a dramatist. The story is in fact told almost in a linear manner from her marriage to Nathan till the present. It is not innovative in any sense. It is the intelligence of her mind and integrity of her personality that make the narration engrossing. Rukmani is not an educated woman, but she is not an illiterate. She has been taught to read and write by her father and that accomplishment invites the derision of the women-folk in the village where she settles down after her marriage. She is sensitive, but not to a fault, as in some feminist works. Her most prominent feature is her serenity and sense of balance in direst situations. The rare exceptions when she becomes a slave of passion are when she is provoked by the adulterous Kunthi and again when she attacks her daughter Ira in the dark, mistaking her for Kunthi who might have come to steal the precious little rice secretly stored underground during one of the worst periods of drought. Rukmani becomes possessed with jealousy when Nathan himself confesses to having committed adultery with Kunthi in his youth. It is a trait which humanizes her, but does not debase her essential goodness nor does it put the family in a painful, irreconcilable situation. Rukmani is too balanced to allow this one moment of lapse on the part of her husband to vitiate her judgement of him. We can only imagine how another modern feminist-protagonist in her place would have ruined the family peace and her own peace over this.

Rukmani's relation with the white doctor Kennington—called Kenny—is an instance of her progressive and liberal approach to the problems of life. When she finds that she has some gynic trouble, she meets her mother's doctor Kenny who treats her. She bears several children after that, and she develops a feeling of kinship with him for the rest of her life. She does not, however, choose to disclose the truth to her husband because she knows that as a man, he may feel hurt in some way. She would not wish to upset Nathan. It is not fear or deceitfulness but a calm appraisal of human nature touched by genuine conjugal love. Later when her only daughter returns home rejected by her husband on account of her childlessness, Rukmani once again makes bold to approach Kenny. Predictably, she does not disclose this to Nathan. When the daughter takes to prostitution to feed her starving youngest brother Kuti, she conceives and delivers an albino baby. Even Rukmani is disturbed by the conjunction of misfortunes, but Ira shows a surprising calm, even joy. Rukmani too learns to cherish the baby. The question of petty morality is transmuted by the sanctity of affection. Ira, surely owes her wisdom to her mother.

Dire poverty and cruel starvation do not dehumanize either Nathan or Rukmani. When the impatient sons are understandably affected by the disastrous consequences of drought, the parents are able to withstand the strain with remarkable forbearance. In fact, the whole family soon becomes a picture of resilience. It is in such situations that we realize the value of the conjugal amity between the couple. Nathan is a gentle soul bound to the soil, alive to the individuality of his wife and children. Hence even provocative situations do not lead to confrontation. Frustration is transmuted by faith in life and human nature. Rukmani cherishes her husband's sterling qualities as a man which have mitigated her own suffering to a large extent. She stands by him when the crop withers in the drought. She supports him with loving labour when the harvest is rich. Her will is strong, but it is not discordantly assertive. There is "a daily beauty" in their lives, in prosperity as well as in adversity. This does not imply any sentimentality on the part of the author. In fact, their hunger and physical suffering are gruesome. But they cannot break their spirit.

What is the secret of this triumph? It is in the affinity of Rukmani for the land and its fertility. She is the archetypal mother earth searching for Persephone and rejoices when she finds her. The mother and the daughter form a fine parallel creating a matrix of matriarchy for the members of the family to belong to. Ira in her turn becomes Ceres waiting for the appearance of her own child. Even when the land seems to let them down, such a phase of deprivation is temporary. With all its barrenness and fertility, the land pulls Rukmani's soul to itself. In fact, it gives a centripetal motion to her life. It accounts for her spirit of survival. It teaches her *endurance.* This spirit of endurance is not stoicism as is practised in the West, a spirit of resignation. But it is significantly Indian, nay, Wordsworthian, for it is *titiksha*, endurance tempered by love which does not succumb to frustration nor does it end in bitterness. [We may recall Wordsworth's Michael.] The beauty of the novel lies in the spirit of *titiksha* which the husband and more so the wife exhibit. When distorted this quality may dwindle into mere reconciliation and passivity condemned by Indian feminists. Rukmani and Nathan go all out to beat fate; they are even willing to be displaced from the cherished land, but they will not succumb in a spineless manner. Their heroism is not brittle.

As the novel proceeds, the couple wander toward a dirty town in search of their son Murugan. It is Rukmani who emerges more and more dynamic, positive, not buckling at the worst of blows. Not only that, she sustains her husband when his body, will and spirit, start giving way. The peregrination of this aged couple in the city, stripped of their possessions and identity, is a moving image not only of poverty but of heroism in the midst of existential despair which is the lot of the many underprivileged in India. Experience of hardship chastens them, refines them further, winnows their souls which become translucent. Rukmani in fact progressively attains to a clarity of perception, a lucidity of the soul. She does not become hardened as a diamond but mellows as a ripe fruit. She becomes the fulcrum of the family. In this, she is not merely role-playing. She invests the role with a profound sense of personality and life.

III

Rukmani grows gracefully from a girl into an old woman. In her long life as a woman, she meets with a whole gamut of experiences. It is remarkable that none of them—even the most harrowing of them—does not distort her soul's inclination toward light. She never allows herself to sink into an amoral world. She deals with her husband and children showing respect for their individuality. Elaine Showalter has complained that women writers have often lamented about woman's lot in society instead of offering a positive way out of an impasse. Let us briefly see how the author of this simple novel manages to depict a different female consciousness.

The concentration in the novel is exclusively on the woman's feelings and thoughts, her sufferings and struggle. But the tale does not become on that count solipsistic. Her reality neither diminishes nor succumbs to an outer reality. The reality of the village—the neighbours, the sense of community, the threat to their life-style by the setting up of the tannery—impinges on her consciousness duly. Two of her sons, Arjun and Thambi, leave for Ceylon to work in tea plantations. Another son Raja is murdered. The final ordeal of Nathan and Rukmani working in a stone quarry in a nameless, alien town for a year and more in the hope of returning home is equally graphic. It is there that they learn a lot from the young orphan boy Puli confronting undaunted the hard fact of existence. For Rukmani, it brings about an expansion of consciousness, saving her from the dangers of solipsism. It releases her ego. In the whole of the novel, most of the experiences which are tragic lead the heroine to this expansion of personality. She grows in stature.

Rukmani has equally valuable subjective experiences as a woman. Her relation with her husband is supreme. Not only does she have the proverbial Indian wifely fidelity to her husband and solicitude for his welfare, she is alive as a person and not an automaton performing duties. In fact, she experiences a moment of ineffable beauty in a rare sexual union during Diwali. In that primordial communion with her husband, she conceives her last child, though rather late in life. For Nathan too, it is a profound enhancement of self. They taste the joy of a consummation which is precious. Rukmani's friendship with the English doctor Kenny does not infringe upon her marital integrity. The author does not contrive to create a promiscuous situation between the two, for that would be alien to their personalities. In fact, Kenny builds a hospital and takes over the only surviving son of Rukmani, Selvam, and thereby sustains the battered family. There is a vague rumour in the village about Rukmani and Kenny, and Kunthi tries to blackmail her during drought to get rice. Rukmani's most difficult period is when she carries her last child Kuti, for her barren daughter resents her mother's pregnancy. Rukmani conducts herself with tender understanding. One of the possible moments of humiliation for her self is when she tries to dissuade Selvam from joining Kenny's venture on the pretext that there will be none to till the land. She has to take into account what "villifiers" (112) would say—that Kenny offers a position to Selvam in return for the clandestine relationship with his mother. It is a very tough moment for her as an honourable woman and mother and she naturally hesitates to talk about it. But her son shows a surprising nobility of spirit, assuages her fears and reassures her of his faith in her. In a village set-up, this nobility of the mind and this concern in the youngster is touching. Rukmani is vindicated not by any social code but by her son's faith in her.

As a mother Rukmani is admirable, although it must be stressed that Nathan's generosity and sensitivity as a father make him even a better parent. They bear the separation and loss of some of their children valiantly. The lot of their only daughter, rejected by her husband, forced into prostitution by starvation, giving birth to an albino, is a matter of deep grief for both of them. But Rukmani learns from her daughter's quiet tenacity and sustains her.

Kamala Markandaya has managed to give full play to a woman's self cast in a relatively unadventurous social milieu and that is a remarkable achievement. The conception of Rukmani as an integrated personality—she is not the Victorian "angel in the house" whom Virginia Woolf made fun of—is not a gesture of courtesy extended to convention by the author but a reality made possible by the nature of the culture in which she lives. She proves that within the traditional role, she can accommodate her other roles as a human being; and not through alienation and self-laceration, but through expansion and communion a deeper self-knowledge can be attained.

NOTES

1. Gayle Greene and Coppelia Kahn, eds., *Making a Difference: Feminist Literary Criticism* (London: Methuen, 1985), p. 18.
2. Gerda Lerner, *The Majority Finds its Past: Placing Women in History* (New York: Oxford University Press, 1979), p. 180.
3. Judith Stacey, "The New Conservative Feminism," *Feminist Studies*, 9, 3 (Fall 1983), p. 575.
4. Kamala Markandaya, *Nectar in a Sieve* (1955, rpt., New Delhi: Jaico, 1988).

Woman as Possessor: A Reflection of Markandaya's Anti-Patriarchal Rage and Divided-Consciousness in *Possession*

RAMESH K. SRIVASTAVA

It is interesting to note that Kamala Markandaya in *Possession* has portrayed the character of Lady Caroline Bell diametrically opposed to the women in some of her other novels. In *Nectar in a Sieve*, the protagonist Rukmani has so much of proverbial humility, monumental patience and an untiring devotion to her husband that his illicit relationship with another woman, the vagaries of weather, the onslaught of the tannery, and even the deaths of her sons fail to evoke an angry remark, let alone a protest, from her. She remains a perfect specimen of an Indian wife conceived and idealized by the patriarchal society and its authors. Nalini in *A Handful of Rice* is also so submissive that she puts up with the mercurial whims, impractical dreams and occasional outbursts of Ravi's anger, though her mother Jayemma is somewhat dominant over her "mouse-like" husband. Lady Caroline Bell in *Possession* seems to belong to an altogether different category created possibly out of Markandaya's opposition to patriarchal traditions as also of her intention of giving an allegorical garb to a political theme of the British domination of India.[1] Consequently, Caroline turns out to be a monstrous creation of a woman[2] whose instinct and ambition to possess—living beings as well as lifeless objects—become the main concern of her life. Her nature and activities give an impression that by inverting the sex-roles, Markandaya has thrust the traits of a patriarchal male tyrant into Caroline's personality.

A possibility exists that Kamala Markandaya had written *Possession* (1963) under the impact of the feminist movement in Europe, particularly in France, before it had gained momentum in the U.S. What is to be seen is, first, how the feminist movement and anti-patriarchal rage could possibly have influenced Markandaya in shaping the women characters, particularly Caroline of *Possession*, in whom the traits of the patriarchal value system condemned by the feminists have been imposed under different garbs as if for perpetuation, and, secondly, how they in Markandaya create a divided-consciousness.

In *Sexual Politics*, published nearly a decade after Markandaya's *Possession*, Kate Millett points out that patriarchy "subordinates the female to the male or treats the female as an inferior male."[3] In being oppressed, weak and masochistic, such women can be compared to the negroes in the U.S. and the working class anywhere. In *Possession*, the stereotyped sex-roles have been reversed to make Caroline as the oppressor and Valmiki as the oppressed. If there is any character in the novel who is to be associated with the coloured people, it is Valmiki. In the eighteenth and nineteenth centuries in the U.S., the whites bought the negroes as slaves and treated them as possession. When criticism against the ill-treatment of the negroes had risen, the whites had found and condescendingly doled out recognition of their talents in music, painting and sports for public consumption as an evidence of treating them with dignity and honour even when they were physically and economically seduced and exploited. There is a close resemblance between the plight of the negroes in the U.S. and that of Valmiki who with his dark skin is bought, his talent in painting recognized, while he serves as a sexual partner for the white Caroline[4] who goes around in many countries arranging the public exhibition of his paintings.

Sandra Gilbert makes uses of the metaphor of literary paternity in considering the text's author a father, "an aesthetic patriarch whose pen is an instrument of generative power like his penis."[5] The role of women is confined to be passive and as sexual objects in order to please men's minds or bodies. Toril Moi believes that the patriarchal traditions imposed certain social ideals and standards on women.[6] Those who conformed were termed feminine but those who failed to do so began to be called unfeminine and unnatural. Since women under patriarchal traditions have been victims intellectually, emotionally or physically, Elaine Showalter suggests that the attempts of gynocritics should be to illuminate every aspect of women's writing in a male-dominated society.[7] The female authors experience an anti-patriarchal rage which gets reflected in their writings. The themes, subjects, characters and situations created by female authors out of this rage are bound to be different from those by male writers in a patriarchal society. For Toril Moi, the feminist writing has "a discernible anti-patriarchal and anti-sexist position[8] which is what can be seen in Markandaya's Caroline—a possible consequence of this anti-patriarchal rage.

In the character of Lady Caroline Bell, Markandaya has transformed the patriarchal suppressed woman into a domineering and tyrannical possessor and an active victimizer of an adolescent male. She is independent of and even dominating over other men as well. If Caroline possesses Valmiki by money and strength, Anasuya does the same by her kindness and sympathetic understanding and Ellie and Annabel by their youthful charms. In *Possession*, it is a woman's world in which the male is manipulated, purchased, commanded, exploited and taken around like a pet. Of all the women characters in the novel, Caroline is a model of anti-patriarchal stance and her traits are associated with male members in patriarchal cultural construct. She has none of the traits conforming to "predefined patterns of femininity," such as, "sweetness, modesty, subservience, humility."[9] It is Valmiki who is sweet, modest, subservient and humble. Caroline, on the contrary, is active and victor, crude and harsh, domineering and arrogant. If seen from the feminist view, Caroline is victorious for having emerged out of cultural obscurity in which she was thrown for many generations by patriarchal society. Markandaya has made her "visible" so much that the male members like Jumbo, Valmiki and the Swamy are overshadowed.

Selden refers to Aquinas's theory that the "form is masculine and matter feminine" and that "the superior, god-like, male intellect impresses its form upon the malleable, inert, female matter."[10] Contrary to the theory, it is Caroline who considers herself and is, in certain respects, superior to Valmiki and his father, the headman and the Swamy. It is she who gives form, shape and design to Valmiki and his art. Having come from and going finally to chaos and wilderness, Valmiki is feminine. To use Selden's terms, it is not the "waiting ovum" of Caroline that lacks identity and is given by Valmiki's "sperm as the active seeds" but vice versa. Here the ovum is daring, independent and individualistic; the sperm conforming, panic-stricken and sheep-like which passively awaits "the journey into the unknown"[11] which is what Valmiki's cave is.

Raman Selden points out five areas in which woman under patriarchal value system was considered inferior to man but under feminist value system, she has been shown as stronger of the two. They are: (1) biology, (2) experience, (3) discourse, (4) the unconscious and (5) social and economic conditions.

Biologically, a woman's body has always been considered inferior to that of man and many times no more than a mere womb. For feminists, however, her biological attributes are superior to those of men because she has certain life-experiences, such as, ovulation, menstruation and parturation denied to men. Caroline has certain traits of nature which make her biologically stronger, even superior to Valmiki. Being thirty-two, Caroline is maturer of the two. She has a dazzling white skin, good looks, silken, pale-gold hair as opposed to Valmiki who is dark with none of Caroline's transcendent loveliness.

Domineering, self-centred and with condescending attitude to Indians, Caroline has the courage to go to a South

Indian village for illicitly-distilled liquor called *arak*, but decides to abandon it for a more intoxicating simpleton. The possessed here is a male and the possessor a woman, considered an object of possession in patriarchal culture. With a feeling of triumph over the goatherd, Caroline's face glows like that of a witch and can be associated with her psychological parallel in Lady Macbeth. She plays the same role, at least in parts, in the destiny of Valmiki that the witches do in that of Macbeth. Like them, she is a sorceress who foresees the artist in Valmiki.

Markandaya has made Caroline quite confident and biologically powerful in her capability of possessing Valmiki even though Anasuya's uncle calls Caroline "erratic" and her mother "a bit wild."[13] Successfully outwitting others, Caroline puts "her arms around the boy as it were taking possession of him in full view of his family," (20) implying her victory over the resisting parents, the headman, the Swamy—the authority figures of this patriarchal society. Her act of taking other possessions of the headman—a palmyra fan, a fly-whisk, some cheroots—symbolically suggests that for her no difference exists between living beings and lifeless objects. After taking possession of him with her "inherited arrogance" and considering herself "his guardian," Caroline then employs her full powers by denying the freedom to Valmiki and by snatching the guardianship from the Swamy who for Valmiki was like his father, mother and friend. She reduces the Swamy as well as his Valmiki to passivity associated with women in patriarchal society.

Caroline's sense of possession gets a jolt when Valmiki begins to like Ellie, though she hopes that his temporary affair with Ellie might be cured in the same way she had managed to cure his feelings of homesickness by forging a letter from the Swamy. On the other hand, the anguish of the possessed Valmiki is juxtaposed by the soldiers's forcible "possession" of Ellie in the camp as also by the wailing of Valmiki's chained monkey. As Valmiki was clumsily dressed for Caroline, the monkey is ludicrously jacketed for Anasuya. By keeping him unschooled, alienated and in odd clothes, Caroline makes sure that none would take a fancy for him and he would remain confined to her. It is a symbiotic relationship in which she parasites on a parasite. Like Valmiki, the monkey is a pet. Valmiki is tired of his pet but Caroline is not. Both Valmiki and the monkey were bought for public shows, exhibit respectively their paintings and antics, and are cheered, jeered and cajoled by their respective audiences. The monkey becomes a dear "little" creature that clings tightly to Valmiki's neck as does Valmiki to Caroline's.

The words, images and expressions used for Valmiki only strengthen Markandaya's anti-patriarchal rage. By stripping Valmiki of his human traits and ties, she reduces an important male character to a fool, a toy, a nugget for which she can take a fancy at one time and discard at another. With arrogance and power, Caroline considers others as "little" and uses this expression for the education authority in England, for Ellie, for Valmiki and even for Anasuya.

The projected arrival of the Swamy in London causes some flutter to her even though he poses no threat directly. With the confidence of a master-player, she gets rid of the Indian cook who had forged the Swamy's letters for Valmiki. After the Swamy's arrival in England, Valmiki remains in Caroline's house but under the Swamy's spiritual sway. In voicing her opinion that the Swamy should not have been allowed in England, she means that spiritualism is a threat to her plan of physical and materialistic possession of human beings. To use Harish Raizada's words, "the conflict between the Swamy and Caroline for the custody and control of Val truly becomes symbolic of conflict between Indian spiritual values and Western materialistic civilization for the possession of Indian."[13] For Meenakshi Mukherjee, the conflict is "between possession and renunciation, between wealth and fame on the one hand and freedom and obscurity on the other . . . the spiritual East encountering materialistic West."[14] When Valmiki finally does go back to India, she wishes to reclaim him as an object under her possession.

The second focus of woman's superiority, as considered by Selden, is experience. The experiences of a person—rich or otherwise—have been considered sufficient grounds of superiority and inferiority of one person on the other. Men are mobile; women confined to home, and hence lacking in experience particularly of rugged areas, government, politics and war. In patriarchal value system, these experiences made men superior, women inferior. Markandaya, out of her anti-patriarchal rage, has made Caroline superior to all male members—Valmiki, his father, the headman, the Swamy and Jumbo in terms of certain experiences. Her visits to India and to other European countries make her superior to Valmiki whose world was confined to a village and a cave. It is Caroline who guides and chaperons Valmiki, arranges his visits and exhibits while he follows her passively—a role assigned to women in patriarchal value system.

Caroline's act of taking Valmiki around in 1949 from England to Switzerland and then on to France, Italy, Greece and the Nile delta, happened to be largely with the intention of denying education to Valmiki, the way it was made a taboo for Indian girls in patriarchal societies. By introducing him to various people, she makes him more experienced before the exhibition of paintings is held. She directs a raw Valmiki as women were in patriarchal societies ("you tell her, Val," 181) but now he is a "finished article, free of further refining." (181)

Discourse is considered to be the third instrument of man's domination over woman. Men's domination of discourse had trapped women in a male-perceived truth. In patriarchal value system, woman's language is considered inferior to that of man for having certain weaknesses and uncertainties, and bordering on the trivial, the frivolous, the personal and the emotional. In contrast, the male utterances are stronger. In the use of language, Caroline is patronizing, domineering, strong and commanding. She orders men and women around, and keeps them under her sway. It is she who teaches Valmiki the use of English. Dominated by her discourse,

Valmiki gets reduced to the traditional place of the woman in patriarchal society. By a Freudian inversion, masculine traits have been projected on to Caroline.

Caroline many times speaks to the narrator with forthrightness and insolence. On the revelation of the forged letter, Valmiki becomes upset and she calls him "a guttersnipe," "a silly little fool" and "the dreary little zombie that you used to be." (146-47)

Her act of sabotaging the efforts of the divisional education officer for educating Valmiki is to put a check on the better communication with people which might have meant a threat of his moving out of the orbit set for him by Caroline. Hence her small doses of lessons in English and denial of additional information and, consequently, his illiteracy and isolation and dependence on Caroline.

The fourth focus—the process of the unconscious—has been provided by the psycho-analytic theories of Lacan and Kristeva. Some feminist writers have associated the "female" with encouragement to a free play of meanings and prevention of closure. Without believing in a female unconscious, Virginia Woolf feels that women would freely develop their artistic talents as a consequence of their achieving social and economic equality with men.[15] In *Possession*, Caroline may have developed no artistic talents because of her economic and social superiority but can be said to have managed a subversion of male values and taken a revenge on the male's dignity in possessing an adolescent dark boy through a reversal of the conventional patriarchal sexual roles. Obviously, Markandaya's anti-patriarchal rage makes her challenge male authority and value system through Caroline who unconsciously is outside the male definition of female. Being self-opinionated, she considers herself as benefactor and manager of Valmiki while unconsciously aiming at something else. The wine reveals in her, what Anasuya feels,

> the sexuality latent in move and counter-move, in gesture and inflection and laughter.

> Were they one flesh? Were the rumours I had heard in India more solidly based than I, lulled by her series of love-affairs, imagined? The thought hammered at me again as I saw her white arm encircle him, holding him as if he were hers; and then memory stirred, and I remembered this was just how she had held him long ago when he was a boy, and she was establishing her claim to him as plainly as if flag in hand she were registering property rights. This stance once suggested, there were other reassuring props: the disparity in their ages, the differences of race, above all their long association and close peculiar relationship which would bring an unpleasant whiff of incest to a carnal union between them.
>
> What I did not take into account was strength of purchase and the terrible overpowering craving for possession. (110-11)

Here Caroline's sense of possession over Valmiki is as strong as of Chillingworth tyrannizing over Dimmesdale's and even Hester's personalities in *The Scarlet Letter* and different from the association between Ellie and Valmiki who happen to be of the same age and who, being rootless, had joined together against the hostile world for the assertion of their respective identities. Their relationship is based on love; Caroline's on her craving for possession. Anasuya comments on the nature of her relationship to Val:

> My protege— "my ward"—even "my pupil": these labels, with their imprecise ratios of age, she was willing to accept; but never one which I floodlit with the possibility of narrow calculation the fourteen years difference between Valmiki and herself. (160)

Even in Valmiki's speech, Anasuya notices the kind of affectionate playful talk associated with newly-married couples and a sign of union now "set in the calmer pattern of harmonious cohabitation." (182) And Caroline becomes different too.

She does not yearn and burn for sex but is transformed into

> a new and tender Caroline, rich from mating, filled with her secret knowledge, bearing on her, the soft bloom of a woman taken voluptuously to bed, loins appeased with the urgent flow, body and blood nourished with the seething impregnation. Except that Caroline was not only possessed, but had also taken in possession. (183)

When Annabel begins to dance with Valmiki, Caroline regrets teaching him this art because it benefitted "a rival" and terminates the party. In Caroline's subsequent parties, Annabel does not find a place. Anasuya tells Annabel that Caroline feels Valmiki belongs to her and she cannot let him go: "People don't easily give up what they think are their possessions." (198) In order to maintain relations with Annabel without hurting Caroline, Valmiki thinks of maintaining relations with both. During nights, it is Caroline and Valmiki; by day, it is Valmiki and Annabel. The male member is under the possession of two women—an inversion of what Draupadi in patriarchal society was to five Pandavas.

The fifth factor which Virginia Woolf also includes in her analysis of women's writings is sociological and economic conditions. The feminists, particularly those with a leaning towards Marxism, try to relate changing social and economic conditions with the changing balance of power between the sexes. Valmiki is economically weak whereas Caroline is rich, with landed estates and money, having "descended from a long line of men who had ruled India in the days of the British Raj." (3) Since she has enough money and property for which people work, she has "got to roam farther and farther, like an animal in search of salt-lick that gives savour to living." (3) The absence of money and social position makes Valmiki timid and submissive. The goatherd has "got nothing, nothing of anything that he ought to have." (9) The fact of Caroline's money power is clear when Anasuya comes in the last cave and finds in it a ruby ring, a small column of gold sovereigns, and some uncashed cheques which could be considered "symbols all of power and influence" (230) that Caroline wielded after possessing him and which Valmiki no longer needs. The economic and social position of Caroline makes her domineering, arrogant and oblivious of human relationship and feelings. Caroline dismisses Anasuya's worry about Val's adjustment in London by saying that the city is full of foreigners like him. This lack of concern is pronounced so casually, so coolly and with so much of confidence that Anasuya is startled.

It is also to strengthen her sense of possession that Caroline condones Valmiki's use of peculiar, ill-fitting clothes. By keeping him unschooled, alienated and in odd clothes, Caroline makes sure that none would take a fancy for him and thereby ensures her possession. However, Valmiki is conscious of his plight and her attitude and says that if she does not want him, he could go back "to Swamy, not hole in stone like belly-lizard." (54)

While discussing the opening scene of Hardy's *The Mayor of Casterbridge* and the sale of Susan Henchard along with her daughter, Elaine Showalter points out that the tragedy occurs because of the constraints of Mrs. Henchard's womanhood. Mrs. Henchard is passive and cannot control events but must adjust herself to them.[16] Though Valmiki is male, exactly the same thing could be said of him. Like Susan Henchard, he is passive. Constrained by his economic and rural conditions, he accommodates himself to his sale by his parents to an outlandish female stranger in the same way as Susan Henchard had to an unknown male buyer. The sale of a timid boy in the beginning of the novel, like that of Susan Henchard, makes one suspect that the novel is the result of Markandaya's anti-patriarchal rage. *The Mayor of Casterbridge*, showing the sale of a woman, was written by a male novelist and *Possession*, dealing with that of a male, written by a female. The redeeming feature in Hardy's novel is that Michael Henchard was drunk and repented his act of folly after coming back to his senses; Caroline, on the other hand, is regrettably in her full senses and her crime becomes more daring, vulgar and serious because her intoxication of possessing a boy increases day by day. Elaine Showalter writes: "Patriarchal societies do not really sell their sons, but their daughters are all for sale sooner or later." India has a patriarchal society but significantly the object of sale is not a female but a male. If Hardy "wished to make the sale of the daughter emphatic and central,"[17] so does Markandaya make the sale of a son. If Henchand is a woman-hater, Caroline is a man-possessor.

Conceding for a moment that Markandaya was projecting a new image of woman, anticipating or responding to gyno-critics's idea of developing new models based on the study of female experience, Caroline turns out to be a rather clumsy projection. Markandaya clothes her in ill-fitting masculine traits which may conceal her feminine self for a moment but the result is something unnatural, unconvincing, peculiar and even monstrous. She turns out to be a terrible Mother figure enacting the primal scene of filial incest. In this sense, she can be associated with Kali and Medusa. By giving Caroline the patriarchal persona, the "feminine" in her has been reversed and this ultimately leads her to demonization—which is what the feminists have been fighting against in the male.

This raises a question if the character of Caroline is to be taken on its face value? Her monstrous character cannot be an ideal for women novelists, more so when Markandaya in other novels and even within this novel has female characters most of whom are ideal or at least common, more so because they subscribe to patriarchal values. Is it possible then that the character of Caroline originated not so much from Markandaya's anti-patriarchal rage as from anti-feminist rage? It could also have originated from a sense of horror after seeing the monstrous creations of the feminists. Whatever the reasons, the creation of the women's world in *Possession* does give the impression that Markandaya has within her a divided-consciousness which finds reflected in diverse women characters.

One possible reason could be that Markandaya wrote the novel more as a therapy and less in rage because she as an Indian woman must have been in "possession" of an English husband in London. Showalter significantly refers to this divided-consciousness of the patriarchal woman:

> We are both the daughters of the male tradition, of our teachers, our professors, our dissertation advisers and our publishers—a tradition which asks us to be rational, marginal and graceful; and sisters in a new women's movement which engenders another kind of awareness and commitment, which demands that we renounce the pseudo success of token womanhood, and the ironic masks of academic debate.[18]

Kamala Markandaya seems to have this divided-consciousness between the country of her birth and that of her marriage; between the influences of the male professors and writers, on the one hand, and her feminine wishes, feminist ideology and a female desire for assertion, on the other; between being subservient and docile according to Indian patriarchal culture and the desire for equality and assertion as prevalent in the West; between the pleasure of erasing her personality, identity and self for husband as Indian housewives have been known to do and the desire to show to the world as well as to her husband what even an Indian woman can be and achieve. As a consequence, this divided-self of Markandaya comes out in various women characters of other novels, particularly in *Possession.*

Even Caroline's character shows this divided-consciousness. Though she has been made a domineering possessor and an arrogant victor, there are occasions when she is made to realize that her victory over Valmiki remains partial, culminating in love-hate relationship between them, as she herself confesses: "We go out of our way to meet, and we squabble each time we do. It's a sort of love-hate relationship . . . like the kind Britain and India used to have." (70) Anasuya, who has none of Caroline's domineering traits, comes out better as a victor in helping Valmiki come out of Caroline's clutches and to go to India. It is Anasuya whom Caroline calls a "Winner."

The divided-consciousness of Markandaya is also obvious in the character of Anasuya who is closer to the patriarchal concept of woman and feels ill-at-ease with the feminish monster in Caroline. Her sense of shock at Caroline's possession is so much that she considers her erratic, bizarre and her activities preposterous. For Anasuya is the Good Mother and can be associated with Hera, Parvati and Saraswati. Unlike Caroline who has a condescending attitude to others, she is companionable and has kindness for others, particularly for the poor. She is, what Caroline calls her, a "gentle Hindu limb" surviving with difficulty in the "jungle of English man-eaters." (107) As opposed to the physical possession of Valmiki that Caroline has, Anasuya "possesses" his heart. Caroline puts flesh on his bones but Anasuya feeds his starved soul. Caroline reduces Valmiki's identity to that of a machine; Anasuya raises it to that of a human being. Valmiki's admirable activities make him a "diamond" around Caroline's neck but who, without them, is reduced for her to nothing— "no more than a small insect in a small crack in the ground." (55) Anasuya, on the other hand, considers Valmiki an individual and gives due weightage to what he is.

Anasuya, the narrator, is also a women as possessor but in a different way. Being a writer and a journalist, she captures certain objects and persons in her books and can be identified with Markandaya. If Anasuya succeeds in freeing Valmiki from Caroline's possession, it is Markandaya who has really done so because she is the father of her own text—"owner/ possessor of the subjects of his text."[19]

The divided-consciousness in the character of Anasuya makes her a eunuch because she carries, like Caroline, the superficial garb of male without having traits inside. H.M. Williams considers her character "flawed" and her sexuality possibly lesbian but "enigmatic to the bitter end."[20] The free movement of Anasuya in Indian village and abroad, her education, the nature of her profession put her in the category of male, as Caroline is, but her passive role in the sale of Valmiki and her inability to resist what she herself considers bizarre and preposterous make her weak and passive, cold and sexless as were traditional women in a patriarchal society. Such situations and characters in the novels of Markandaya have only a surface semblance of reality as can be compared to those eggs that are edible "and look just like live ones but never hatch."[21] Caroline, Anasuya and their creator Markandaya similarly look as much women as Indian eunuchs do till one scrutinizes them closely.

Caroline's womanly jealousy for Annabel and Ellie makes her feminine. In Anasuya, Ellie and Annabel, Markandaya has given the traditional feminine traits—docility, passivity, non-aggressive, loving, self-sacrificing. If Ellie and Annabel are poetic inspiration, Anasuya is journalistic prose and Caroline hard-hitting satirical prose with its associative harshness and sting.

If Caroline had taken possession of Valmiki's body and Anasuya of his spirits, it is Ellie who possesses his poetic self, and becomes "his inspiration, his model, his success." (123) Like Ellie, Annabel too becomes a good companion of Valmiki being of the same age as Valmiki's. Being a threat to Caroline's role as a possessor, she is, however, subsequently eliminated.

The fact that at the end of the novel, Caroline has been shown with her waning powers of possession and that Valmiki succeeds in extricating himself from her tentacles and further that the male world has been restored its preeminence with the end of a woman's possession of male shows again as if Markandaya does not want the inversion of sex-roles. Valmiki's release and then his departure to wilderness may mean Caroline's defeat but it means life to Valmiki. He owes his existence to to wilderness ("The wilderness is mine") even if Caroline considers it "a waste." (228) At the same time, her act of linking her arm to Valmiki's symbolizes that she has not yet fully and finally reconciled to his withdrawal from her.

Having been out of the clutches of Caroline, Valmiki works neither abundantly nor abandons working but achieves "a middle stage of serenity." (231) What matters is that the male is no longer under the female possession. Caroline's domination had suppressed some of Valmiki's traits which begin to find natural expression again. His work begins to be characterized by hitherto-unknown quality of compassion and profundity. His art is no longer under the direction of Caroline in the driver's seat but finds a free expression. It is no longer art for materialistic gains—name and money—but for the glorification of his god. Valmiki's peace and satisfaction in the cave implies the defeat of the woman as possessor to which Caroline cannot quite reconcile. She says to Anasuya:

> Valmiki is yours now, but he has been mine. One day he will want to be mine again. I shall take care to make him want me again and on that day I shall come back to claim him. (232)

NOTES

1. Srinivasa Iyengar calls the story of Caroline and Valmiki "a parable of Colonialism, the passing of an empire, and the current insidious movement of neo-colonialism." Quoted by C.V. Venugopal, "*Possession:* A Consideration," Madhusudan Prasad, ed., *Perspectives on Kamala Markandaya* (Ghaziabad: Vimal Prakashan, 1984), p. 151.

   Harish Raizada in "East-West Confrontation in the Novels of Kamala Markandaya" considers *Possession* "as an allegory of the direction the independent India has to follow in its onward march to its progress" and Valmiki as "the symbol of the raw independent India for the possession of whose soul the formidable Caroline Bell symbolizing the Western civilization, makes an all out effort." *Perspectives on Kamala Markandaya*, p. 53.

2. H.M. Williams in "Victims and Virgins: Some Characters in Markandaya's Novels" calls her "a monster of possessiveness." *Perspectives on Kamala Markandaya*, p. 30.
3. Raman Selden, *A Reader's Guide to Contemporary Literary Theory* (Sussex: Harvester Press, 1985), pp. 131-32.
4. Harish Raizada comments: "The possession of an Indian as a lover has another advantage for in the post-independence period, India had come into fashion— 'Fashionable to know of India, fashionable to know Indians, fashionable to admire its art, fashionable to welcome its women and even, at a pinch, its men,'" *Perspectives on Kamala Markandaya*, p. 55.
5. Sandra Gilbert, "Literary Paternity," in Robert Con Davis, ed., *Contemporary Literary Criticism: Modernism through Post-Structuralism* (New York: Longman, 1986), p. 190.
6. Toril Moi, "Feminist Literary Criticism," in Ann Jefferson and David Robey, eds., *Modern Literary Theory: A Comparative Introduction* (London: B.T. Batsford, 1986), p. 209.
7. *Ibid.*, p. 216.
8. *Ibid.*, p. 220.
9. *Ibid.*, pp. 209, 10.
10. Raman Selden, p. 128.
11. *Ibid.*
12. Kamala Markandaya, *Possession* (Bombay: Jaico, 1963), p. 34.
13. Harish Raizada, p. 53.
14. Meenakshi Mukherjee, *The Twice-Born Fiction: Themes and Techniques of the Indian Novel in English* (New Delhi: Arnold Heinemann, 1974), p. 106.
15. Selden, p. 137.
16. Elaine Showalter, "Towards a Feminist Poetics," *Contemporary Literary Criticism: Modernism through Post-Structuralism*, p. 171.
17. *Loc. cit.*
18. *Ibid.*, p. 179.
19. Sandra M. Gilbert, p. 191.
20. H.M. Williams, p. 31.
21. R.W. Dixon, Quoted by Sandra Gilbert, p. 193.

Beyond the He-Man Approach: The Expression of Feminine Sensibility in Anita Desai's Novels

R. S. PATHAK

I

Anita Desai is one of those few Indian novelists in English who have tried to understand intimately the predicament of their female characters. She represents the welcome "creative release of the feminine sensibility" which began to emerge after the World War II.[1] Anita Desai is a novelist of considerable merit and has enriched the Indian novel in English in more ways than one. It is her thematic concerns and technical innovations that have been chiefly responsible for making her "a disturbing and demanding presence in Indo-Anglian fiction."[2]

Anita Desai is not a novelist whose predominant interests are social or sociological. She is, obviously, not pleased with the achievements of Indian women novelists for the simple reason that "they have been content to record and document"[3] and their interest in the psychological aspect of their characters has been, at its best, generally marginal. In her review of Amitav Ghosh's *The Circle of Reason*, she shows her disfavour for the novelists who take interest in "the 'outer' rather than the 'inner' world, preferring the social to the psychological novels."[4] Anita Desai herself has written excellent psychological novels, which she describes as "purely subjective." She confides:

> It has been my personal luck that my temperament and circumstances have combined to give me the shelter, privacy and solitude required for the writing of such novels, thereby avoiding problems a more objective writer has to deal with since he depends upon observation rather than a private vision.[5]

It is this "private vision" that she has tried to encapsulate in her novels. Her *forte* is the exploration of sensibility, and her writings reveal inner realities and psychic reverberations of her characters. Her main purpose in writing her novels is, to quote her own words in *Voices in the City*, to make us "see what the subconscious does to an impressionable creature, how much more power it has on them than sun and circumstances put together."[6] (229)

Anita Desai excels in delineating human relationships. The most recurrent themes in her novels are "the hazards and complexities of man-woman relationships, the founding and nurturing of individuality, [and] the establishing of individualism" of her characters.[7] Few Indian novelists in English have surpassed Anita Desai in psychological delineation of the protagonists. She tells one of her interviewers that as a writer she is "interested in peculiar and eccentric characters rather than everyday, average ones."[8] Her earlier novels almost invariably present the plight of introspective, hypersensitive women.

In another interview, Anita Desai denied to have deliberately tried to "incorporate" any aspect of "modern sensibility" in her novels. "Of course I do write of the contemporary scene," she is said to have added, "and therefore the characters must contain the modern sensibility."[9] The predicament of the modern man is, in fact, Anita Desai's predominant interest. It would be worthwhile to consider her novels from fresh angles. The present paper aims at analyzing in depth Anita Desai's delineation of feminine sensibility in her novels.

II

The recent decades have witnessed the emergence of a fresh awareness of woman situation, which has brought about an unprecedented shift in our appraisal of human condition. The veritable explosion of "linguistic Sexism" during the past decade has been hailed as containing "an ocean of interest."[10] The politicization of the sexism-in-language issue has insured its future prominence for a systematic study of the complex interaction of language, sex and gender. It is believed that ways of speaking and writing are intimately tied to ways of thinking and patterns of self-and-other-evaluation. Scott observes: "The mere fact that there are two sexes gives rise inevitably to two ways of perceiving human life: the 'us' of one view and the 'them' of the other."[11]

The importance of woman has been recognized in literature on various grounds. But she has rarely been defined as a subject in her own right. For centuries, the human experience has been synonymous with the masculine experience. The importance of woman deserves to be seen in the context of what Michael Foucault calls "rupture" or "discontinuity" in history. Alex Comfort has asserted the value of "the ideology of the whole human being looking at the whole universe."[12] Woman is wronged in a society dominated by male-oriented institutions and world-view, although she is the complementing principle to what Carl Jung claims to be the "psychic activity which transcends the limits of consciousness." When in determining the status and role of woman in the society "the ideal man posits opposite himself as the essential other: he feminizes it because the woman is the palpable figure of other."[13]

The discrimination and women's anomalous position have left indelible marks in the sphere of language also. Linguists like Stanley have posited a theory of "negative semantic space" for women. When women move outside their traditional roles of mother and wife, they say, they enter the semantic space "already occupied by the male sex."[14] Right from the beginning of their life, women are forced to feel dwarfed and acquire a highly circumscribed world-view. To quote Bolinger, "Women are taught their place along with other lesser breeds, by the implicit lies that language tells about them."[15] This unfortunate state of affairs has been responsible for many problems and confusions which women have been condemned to face.

It may be mentioned at the outset that while dealing with her female characters, especially their relations with men, their drives and responses and their sexual repressions, Anita Desai has made significant efforts to step out of the main current of narrative devices and linguistic techniques as developed by the masculine approach. She has tried to look at things essentially from the women's point of view. Although writing, for her, is not an act of deliberation, reason and choice and is primarily a matter of instinct,[16] Anita Desai is fully aware of the possibilities of her medium and seems to be making at times strenuous efforts to explore its possibilities. Her earnest attempts to break new ground have made her linguistically self-conscious. She keeps on trying to annex, like a resourceful poet, new verbal domains and integrate varying modes of perception and writing. Whether she succeeds or not in her efforts, one thing that is certain is that she is almost invariably eager to exploit various linguistic resources at her disposal.

While going through Anita Desai's novels, one feels that the novelist is at times irked by linguistic constraints and aims at transcending the limits of ordinary language.[17] It is worth remembering that in her review of Amitav Ghosh's book mentioned above, she, referring to Rushdie, approves of the "ungaily, ungrammatical language" which not only possesses "an earthly gusto and verve" but is also "peculiarly suitable to convey the Indian character and spirit, atmosphere and condition." Moreover, in an essay entitled "Flight of Forms," Desai says that a book, in its finished form, 'continues to live a life and spin a web of its own".[18] This is possible only with the help of the loom of language properly woven and presented.

Language mediates and moulds reality and is in turn moulded and coerced by the novelist.

III

Anita Desai's novels give an expression to the long-smothered wail of a lacerated psyche. They tell the harrowing tale of blunted human relationships. The fate of Maya, Monisha, Sita and Nanda Kaul reminds us of Mr. and Mrs. Ramsay in Virginia Woolf's *To the Lighthouse*. Maya, in *Cry, the Peacock* (1963), is married to an older man, a detached, sober, industrious lawyer. Temperamentally, the two are opposite to each other. An average evening for Maya is hardly more than a "quiet formal waiting." (7) Their married life is punctuated all along by "matrimonial silences" (12) and her husband's "hardness . . . his coldness and incessant talk of cups of tea and philosophy." (9) She is pained by the total lack of communication on his part:

> How little he knew my suffering, or of how to comfort me. . . . Telling me to go to sleep while he worked at his papers, he did not give another thought to me, to either the soft willing body, or the lonely wanting mind that waited near his bed. (9)

An ever widening gap in communication between the husband and the wife is felt throughout the novel.

In the very beginning of the novel, we become fully aware of Maya's hypersensitive and highly disturbed state of mind. Reacting to the untimely death of her pet dog, she rushes to the garden tap "to wash the vision from her eyes." (15) But her husband remains unaffected and would shrug her "words off as superfluous, trivial." (19) A restlessness always boils within her and the strangeness holds them apart. Maya feels "defenceless and utterly alone" in the company of the "bleak, comfortless figure" passing as her husband, (146) whereas this "gaunt, sarcastically silent intellectual" is always eager to pursue the thread of logic to its illogical end "slowly and steadily as a meticulous tortoise." (74, 208) Ultimately, Maya's psychic problems, aggravated by her infantilism, drive her to a kind of schizophrenia. She describes herself as "body without a heart, a heart without a body." (196)

Voices in the City (1965) presents an account of the odyssey of two world-weary young women doomed to reside in Calcutta, the "city of death." It explores in a convincing way the inner climate of youthful despair and is permeated by the existential *angst*. The novel is an exemplification of what Anita Desai called, in an interview with Yashodhara Dalmia, "the terror of facing single-handed the ferocious assault of existence."[19]

The novelist has delineated Monisha's psychic life at some length. She is ill-fated to militate against a corrosive emptiness within as well as without. Her relationship with her husband is characterized "only by loneliness" and lack of proper understanding. Married against her will to a "blind moralist," a "rotund, minute-minded and limited" official, who is addicted to quoting indiscriminately from Burke, Wordsworth, Gandhi and Tagore—all spokesmen of individual liberty,—she finds her life dedicated to a nothing,"—a life teeming with these trivialities, these pettinesses of our mean existence." (121-22) "Is it what is then, my life?" she asks, "only a conundrum that I shall brood over forever with passion and pain; never to arrive at a solution? Only a conundrum—is that, then, life?" (124-25) The oppressive lack of privacy, her sterility and her in-laws's suspicion, the absence of love and understanding in her life and the resultant loneliness within and without go to make Monisha a pathetic figure. Realizing that "There is no escape from it," she becomes a "sleepwalker, ghost, some unknown and dreaded entity." (146) She develops an incurable claustrophobia and commits suicide. She knows that it is "a choice between death and mean existence" and she does not take long to decide her course of action.

Her younger sister, Amla, who is an extrovert and possesses an exceptionally sharp sensitivity, seems to be taking, initially, all life in her stride. She decides to lead a gay life with the painter Dharma. But her "primeval joy" is short-lived and she also begins to realize the hollowness and futility of her life. She becomes "agitated as a moth," for "she had submerged herself in the aqueous swaying underworld of Dharma's art" without fighting her battle bravely. (261-62) Her precarious condition is conveyed by the novelist as follows:

> She knew that Monisha's death had pointed the way for her and would never allow her to lose herself. She knew she would go through life with her feet primly shod, involving herself with her drawings and safe people like Bose, precisely because Monisha had given her a glimpse of what lay on the other side of this stark, uncompromising margin. Yet she was unable . . . to think of the path or the jungle, of compromise or isolation. (256)

Sita of *Where Shall We Go This Summer?* and Nanda Kaul of *Fire on the Mountain* are definitely more experienced and mature than Maya, Monisha and Amla, but, viewed from a closer angle, this marital incompatibility and emotional maladjustment and the problems arising out of them in the case of Sita and Nanda Kaul are not much different. The later novels also present the essential tragedy of the loss of the truly human beneath the welter of impersonal social forces.

Where Shall We Go This Summer? depicts the aching void in the life of Sita by probing deeper into her life as a woman, a wife and a mother. A highly sensitive, over-emotional, middle-aged woman, already saddled with four children and expecting the fifth, she feels alienated from her husband and is not able to understand at times the behaviour of her children. Sita and her husband behave as if they were the denizens of different worlds. Not only the face but also his nature looked to her "usually as stolid as soundly locked gate." (34) He regards her behaviour as hardly different from that of a juvenile delinquent. Her high-strung sensibility and explosive emotionality leave their scar on her personality in the form of a "dry, worn face" and an "aged stillness." (17-18) Owing to her mental condition, she "continually broke apart into violent eruptions of emotions," giving frequently a "paranoiac show of rage, fear and revolt." (19, 32) Her physical and mental condition deteriorated each day so much so that "control was an accomplishment that had slipped out of her hold." (32)

Sita feels suffocated by the "vegetarian complacence," "insularity" and unimaginative way of life of her husband and his people. Such were her experiences that "she never got used to anyone." (48) The drama of Sita's spiritual impasse and her hopelessly bruised life is beautifully suggested by the novelist. Lines quoted by her from a poem by Cavafy reveal her moral dilemma: "To certain people there comes a day/ When they must say the great Yes or the great No." Sita is keen on saying her "great No" even if it "crushes her for the rest of her life." But she is made to feel again and again that she is hardly better than "a cripple without crutches." (93) She comes to the conclusion that her marriage and, in fact, all human relationships are just a farce. "Bored, dull, unhappy, [and] frantic," she is disgusted with "the tedium and ugliness of a meaningless life." (144-45) This unfortunate state leads her on to the "confusion, the muddle" resulting in a split personality. She is not able to decide as to:

> Which half of her life was real and which unreal? Which of her selves was true, which false? All she knew was that there were two periods of her life, each in direct opposition to the other. (135)

The temporal dichotomy corresponds to the psychic ambivalence of Sita. It is too much to expect from a person like her a typical behaviour of a normal sensible person.

The plight of two friends Nanda Kaul and Ila Das, who share many features with each other, has been explored by

Anita Desai in *Fire on the Mountain* (1977). After fitful fever of her youth, Nanda Kaul lives like "a recluse" in a sprawling house at Kasauli. She has been conceived of as "a charred tree trunk in the forest, a broken pillar of marble in the desert, a lizard on a stone wall" (23) with only one difference, viz. unlike them, she is capable of irritation and annoyance. Earlier, she had led a frantically busy life as the Vice-Chancellor's wife, looking after several children and grand-children and arranging for interminable get-togethers. But now she lives undisturbed by human company and cares "out of vengeance for a long life of duty and obligation." She prizes her privacy more than anything else. She is particular in keeping "herself religiously aloof, jealous of this privacy achieved only at the end of her life." (36) She has cut herself off from human concerns entirely and even the arrival of her own grand-daughter is treated as an unwelcome interference with the course of her life.

There is another intruder into the quietude of Carignano in the form of Ila Das. A pathetic creature, she is described as "an old animal that has been made to run before the hounds." (109) She was not nicely treated by life, and "All her life mobs had taunted and derided her." (110) Her shrill thanks, which were always forthcoming, were not different from "the cackle of an agitated parrot":

> It was this [parrot-like] cackle, this scream of hers, Nanda Kaul thought, that held all the assorted pieces of her life together like a string or chain. It was the motif of her life, unmistakably. Such a voice no human being ought to have had: it was anti-social to possess. (111)

But for a couple of brief spells of happiness, Ila Das's life has been miserable and unfortunate, as is clear from various references to it. Her struggle in life had tired her out and tiredness was writ large "like a grey web across that aged face." (120) Her spectre-like figure is, to Nanda Kaul, "that last little broken bit of a crazy life, fluttering up over the gravel like a bit of crumpled paper." (112) Ila Das is, again, referred to as "a child-sized and time-shrivelled creature" full of "deformities" (137) and as "the dry, shrivelled, starved stick inside the wrappings." (143) To make matters still worse, economic hardship never left her life. She herself ruminates: "I've had to go from pillar to post, trying to earn fifty rupees here and fifty rupees there, with not a room to call my own most of the time, and it's grown worse." (125) One can easily imagine the mental condition of such a person. She is "ashamed" of herself and regards her upbringing as responsible for her "absurd" life. The way of her life, we are told, "was full of hazards, full of hazards." (139) Its end was no better either. The man whom this social worker gave a very sane advice, "pinned her down into the dust and the goat droppings, and raped her." (143) The society thus extended to her the treatment which it reserves for those who try to go out of their way to change its ways and behaviours.

IV

Through her themes, characterization and images about confinement and lack of freedom, Anita Desai has raised pertinent questions regarding the status and role of women in society. The most crucial issue that she takes up for discussions again and again is the question of women's freedom. The traditional attitude of our society is contained in the following advice from *Manusmrti*:

> *pita raksati kaumarye bharta raksati yauvane*
> *raksanti sthavire putrah na stri svatantryam arhati*
>
> (The father looks after her during childhood, the husband protects her during youth, and the sons take care of her when she becomes old. The woman is never fit for freedom.)

Anita Desai's young women yearn for freedom. They are

irritated by the sheltered, over-protected life reserved for them and the condescending, discriminative attitude adopted towards them not only by the society but also by the family. Women are not treated at par with men, and the males are entitled to a privileged treatment everywhere. It is they who control the destiny of women. The freedom, which they can always take for granted, is denied to women. Even Maya, in *Cry, the Peacock*, who does not seem to be sufficiently mature and intelligent, is not unaware of this kind of treatment. She complains of being treated as "a wild beast on a leash," which induces in her "a humiliating sense of neglect." (201) Even towards the end of the novel, she is seen moving about "like a being that is hunted." (212-13) Maya's experiences in life are such that she comes to have the feeling of being "bruised and tired, not quite alive, not quite of today." (94) It is no wonder that during all these years her sense of helplessness deepens:

> I had not escaped. The years had caught up, and now the final, the decisive one held me in its perspiring clasp from which release seemed impossible. (95)

Maya is haunted by her unfortunate condition. She often takes her to be a figure out of dreams, "stifling, grey dreams in which figures stood speechless in the horror of ultimate realization, incapable of motion or release." (70) The release from a kind of life-in-death seems to be the only wishful hankering of Maya. "And I knew," says she again, "I should never again sleep in peace. For, God, now I was caught in the net of the inescapable, and where lay the possibility of mercy, of release? This net was no hallucination, no." (97) She welcomes the storm, which would give her "a sensation of flying, of being lifted off the earth and into the sunset, release from bondage, release from fate. . . . Release and liberty." (190) Maya is pained when she compares her lot with that of her brother, Arjuna, who is "set free" and enjoys liberty like "a young hawk that could not be tamed, that fought for its liberty." (134) This difference makes her all the more unhappy.

Monisha, in *Voices in the City*, who is far more intelligent and unfortunately circumstanced, is even more unhappy on account of the denial of freedom to her. She longs to thrust her "head out of the window" but the "bars are closely set." (114) Monisha's "silent agony behind the barred windows of her house" gets worsened and she is condemned to lead a "one-dimensional" life. (195, 135) Her father, her husband, his "impossible family," (207) and more particularly the aggressive mother-in-law, all are hostile to her individuality. Monisha possesses a rare intellectual propensity, but in due course her conscience "has withered and died away." (140) The crisis of identity that Monisha faces is really pathetic. As she herself says, she grows "smaller every day" and shrinks and loses "more and more of my weight, my appurtenances, the symbols of my existence." (143) The indocile circumstances seize her and turn her "inside out, giving her an eerie unreality." (148) She describes her plight in the following terms:

> Why am I so sad? Why am I so afraid? . . . They put me away in a steel container, a thick glass cubicle, and I have lived in it all my life, without a touch of love or hate or warmth in me. I am locked apart from all of them, they cannot touch me, they can only lip-read and misinterpret. (247)

The entire novel is littered with meaningful suggestions about Monisha's identity crisis. "I am all exterior," she says; and "I'm done with most things. . . . Very little is left now." (115) She is, ultimately, reduced to "a woman who keeps a diary." "Traceless, meaningless, uninvolved—does this not amount to non-existence?" she asks. (144) Commenting on Monisha's "absurd" existence, her brother Nirode remarks: "All this fighting to carve out a destiny for oneself—it's nothing compared to the struggle it is to give up your destiny, to live without one—of either success or sorrow." (191) The ideals of non-involvement and self-effacement are very good as philosophical concepts. But what people like Monisha really need is the essential congenial environment characterized by freedom for their development.

We find Sita, in *Where Shall We Go This Summer?*, desirous of being free and discontented with a woman's life. Her desire to be free is manifested in her fascination with the foreigner whom she meets on the roadside. She is ever eager to escape from her unhappy surroundings by slipping through the fisherman's net like her mother. Sita always has the feeling of being tied with a chain, which "can only throttle, choke, and enslave." (87) Her house "seemed so like a jail" to her, and "the barbed wire of prudence, caution, routine and order" only made her life "disorderly." (118) She develops a sense of being flattened, "stretched out so vast, so flat, so deep." (50) She feels "suffocated by their vegetarian complacence, the stolidity of the well-fed" members of her husband's family. (49) She violently reacts against petrified dullness of the mainland and her husband's house. She takes to smoking and wears "the garments of a demoralized washerwoman" which were "so limp, so faded, so bedraggled and ragged." All this she does with a view to creating "shocks and suspicions" in her husband's mind. (130) The novelist informs us:

> She never got used to anyone . . . in the first years of their married lives . . . she had vibrated and throbbed in revolt against their subhuman placidity, calmness, and sluggishness. The more stolid and still and calm they were, the more she thrummed, as though frantic with fear that their subhumanity might swamp her. (48)

In *Fire on the Mountain*, Nanda Kaul retreats to Carignano after allowing her husband to have a lifelong affair with another woman. She does not revolt openly like Sita, but feels that she could be "shipwrecked." (82) There is also Sarla of *In Custody*, whose aspirations have been shattered into pieces against the rock of harsh reality of life:

> The thwarting of her aspirations had cut two dark furrows from the corners of her nostrils to the corners of her mouth, as deep and permanent as surgical scars. The droop of her thin, straight hair on either side of her head repeated these twin lines of disappointment. (68)

Sarla's miserable, routine life, full of labour, "the shabbiness of her limp, worn clothes, or her hunched, twisted posture, her untidy hair or sullen expression" were integral parts of her humiliation. (193) Anita Desai's novels are, in a way, an advocacy for the legitimate rights and freedom of such unfortunate women.

Anita Desai's novels contain a significant quantum of social criticism in them. They highlight the traditional status of women in society and the dominance of male in it. Maya's helplessness is conveyed through the following one-line description: "She sat there, sobbing, and waiting for her husband to come home." (5) The life of ceaseless passive waiting has been evoked in all the novels. This kind of life has been referred to in *Voices in the City* as "lives spent in waiting for nothing, waiting on men self-centred and indifferent and hungry and demanding and critical, waiting for death and dying misunderstood." Another novel called *Clear Light of Day* also condemns indirectly "the sense of dullness and hopelessness that reigned over their house [and] took on an aspect of intense waiting." (47) The meaningless waiting and fruitless involvement act as the catalysis of their unrest. "A humiliating sense of neglect, of loneliness, of desperation" is not only Maya's fate but also the lot of most of Desai's women characters. Sarla represents the destiny of most of them:

> Sarla never lifted her voice in his [Deven's] presence—countless generations of Hindu womanhood behind her stood in her way, preventing her from displaying open rebellion. Deven knew she would scream and abuse only when she was safely out of the way, preferably in the kitchen, her own domain. Her other

> method of defence was to go into the bedroom and snivel, refusing to speak at all, inciting their child to wail in sympathy. (145-46)

In other novels also, the novelist has revealed glimpses of the repressed condition of women in society. The very first novel pertinently talks of "polite, if vociferous, old women in brown, friendly and every-day as bits of burnt bread." (192) Sita is particularly upset by "half-smiling" women folk of her husband's house— "chopping, slicing, chopping, slicing the incredible quantities of vegetables they daily devoured." To her, they are hardly different from elephants "eating grass, shifting from foot to foot, swaying their trunks, small-eyed, eating." The household seems to have only one problem to face and solve, i.e. that of food; "if meals were not being eaten, then they were being cooked, or cleaned up after, or planned." (48-49) This is an ideal atmosphere where one can vegetate if one wishes to do so. Excessive concern for eating is, incidentally, symptomatic of psychological hunger. Though Sita feels out of sorts in an atmosphere like this, other women of the merchant class would not mind it, one of whom has been mentioned in the following way: "a soft-fleshed, thick, jewel-embedded woman with nothing to say although her eyes roved over and scanned every detail of their room and seemed to absorb and put away details that she might later vociferously reveal." (48) The novelist is, obviously, not happy with this kind of behaviour on the part of women themselves.

Voices in the City is all the more explicit in exposing the traditional values circumscribing the life and role of women. Monisha's diary begins with the "reception arranged by the heads of this many-headed family." (113) When she forgets to proceed according to the prescribed rituals, she is surreptitiously pushed by her husband; she is

> propelled forward into the embrace of his mother who is all in white and smells of clean rice and who, while placing her hand on my head in blessing, also pushes a

> little harder, till I realize what it means, and go down on my knees to touch her feet. . . . Another pair of feet appears to receive my touch, then another. How they all honour their own feet! (113)

They do not, however, have any sense of respect or consideration for other's person. Monisha is treated as a marionette and is reduced to the status of a "small, shrunken shell." Her husband's inability to fathom her needs and the hard-heartedness of his family only aggravate her problems. Callously enough, they talk about her "organs, the reason she cannot have a child." (117)

Voices in the City provides an intimate peep into the habits and attitudes of traditional women. "They are all covered with many thick, slack layers of prejudice, convention, ignorance and reticence." (221) The life of these women is full of trivialities and pettinesses. Monisha's diary contains the following details about them:

> always Bengali women . . . follow five paces behind their men. They wear *saris* of the dullest colours, beige and fawn and off-white, like the female birds in the cages, and there is something infinitely gentle, infinitely patient about their long eyes, the curve of their shoulders, their manner of walking, which arouses, not aggressiveness in one . . . but a protective feeling. . . . I think of generations of Bengali women hidden behind the barred windows of half-dark rooms, spending centuries in washing clothes, kneading dough and murmuring aloud verses from the *Bhagvad-Gita* and the *Ramayana,* in the dim light of sooty lamps. (124)

The piteously helpless condition of these women, which does not allow them even minimum freedom for cultivation of their selves, is primarily responsible for all repressions and tyrannies heaped upon them. They lose their physical charm with the passage of time and come to have "faces like freshly baked bread." (165) There is no deeper purpose behind the life of these unfortunate creatures. We are pertinently informed: "relaxing after the strenuous exercise of the midday mean, . . . [they] plunged into the fire and steam of preparations for dinner. As they lounged about in the first-floor hall, some massaging oil into their heads, or combing their hair or cracking betel nuts between broad-bladed scissors." (243) Death winds up the threads of their life-long meaningless activities and sordid existence. They "anticipate death, as they do everything, with resignation. There is no dignity in their death as in the death of that proud and glorious beast, but only a little melancholy as in the settling of a puff of dust upon the earth." (125) The idea of freedom is simply inconceivable to these women.

It would be interesting to recapitulate the concept of freedom which some of these women have. Aunt Lila, in *Voices in the City*, represents them in this respect. She advises Amla to "take pride in your *independence*, in this wonderful liberty you have of choosing and undertaking a career." (149) Apparently, she appears to have the attitude of a woman who is all for women's emancipation. But in reality, her attitude to women and their problems is not different from that of the traditional men and women. Lila is not in favour of Monisha's mother keeping "away on her mountain top, too busy looking after her orchids to give a thought to, what her children are doing."(227) She is convinced that most of the problems of modern generation arise from an unbridled freedom given to women. She asks Amla: "I don't know what it is that has diseased your generation—the very freedom we fought for and gave you, perhaps?" (185) Again she says: " we won you your freedom, but what do you do with it?" (228) She swears by individual freedom and keeps on repeating the term again and again, but her pronouncements lack sincerity. This duplicity in behaviour can also be seen in Dharma's treatment of his wife and daughter.

This issue leads us on to the related question of male-dominance. When Aunt Lila remarked that "Our country belongs to its men," (149) she was speaking the truth. Fathers and husbands very often treat women as their property, which can be owned, controlled and disposed of the way they like. The roots of much of psychological inhibition and complex can be traced to the tyrannical family background. The novelist has repeatedly drawn our attention to the dominance of men over women in the society. For example, Gautama "saw no value in anything less than the ideas and theories born of human and, preferably, male brains." (99) He was happy in his "carmed circle of leisurely gentlemen, so comfortably, securely male." (103) Maya had no place in their company. To Arjuna, however, all such "gentlemen" were "lying, cheating hypocrites." (138) Nevertheless they continue to control the destiny of women. As compared to them, men are "so unquestionably safe, sound and secure." (204) Monisha's mother used to say, "Men? But what do they know of the matters of the heart?" According to Aunt Lila, "They know nothing of course, inadequate at that as at everything else, but they like to imagine they run everything, so women ought to just go on and let them imagine it while they get on with the *work*." (205) This, however, would not solve women's problems. To people like Dharma, married relationships are simply "the matter of loyalty, habit, [and] complicity." (235) But to women, these relationships define their very existence.

V

The repression, prohibition, exclusion and domination of Anita Desai's women characters can be analyzed in terms of the dynamics of the spirals of power-knowledge-pleasure. These join together to penetrate and control the individual's private pleasures, desires and behaviour. As Michel Foucault has pointed out, "Pleasure and power do not cancel or turn back against one another; they seek out, overlap, and reinforce one another. They are linked together by complex mechanisms and devices." These spirals are mutually reinforcing and are promoted by numerous interests. Power, for Foucault, is not "something acquired, seized or shared"; it is "an institution, and not a structure; neither is it a certain strength we are endowed with; it is the name that one attributes to a complex strategic situation in a particular society."[20] Anita Desai has conveyed her women characters's fundamental dependence on men through her lexicon and tropes of mastery, command and domination. Her women sometimes do attempt to assert their independence and self-sufficiency, but their quest for identity is thwarted at significant junctures. Some of them, like Monisha's mother, represent a "cold, frosty love of power—like a concealed fluorescent bulb." (215) Some of them do raise a cry of protest occasionally, but that does not change their lot.

Power and sex are two well-known deployments of inter-personal relationships. The latter is assigned an important place in Anita Desai's novels. The deployment of alliance comprises systems "of marriage, of fixation and development of kinship ties, of transmission of names and possessions."[21] Most of these have a constraining effect upon women. Foucault has referred to the Freudian endeavour "to ground sexuality in the law—the law of alliance, tabooed consanguinity, and the Sovereign-Father, in short, to surround desire with all the trappings of the old order to power."[22] No woman in Anita Desai's novels, however, not even Amla, has been fortunate enough to free herself from the shackles of femininity. Her male characters are invariably much older and follow the middle path of life. They represent the sovereign-father figure and his dominating authority. The women, on the contrary, are highly sensitive and over-emotional. They lost, during their early childhood, at least one of their parents. Emotionally starved, they develop a kind of fixation for the surviving parent. "Father! Brother! Husband!" cries Maya in utter need. "Who is my saviour? I am in need of one." (98) It is the figure of her father which continues to haunt her, although she tries to think of Gautama as "my guardian, my protector." (11) Gautama sums up her problems succinctly:

> You have a very obvious father-obsession—which is also the reason why you married me, a man so much older than yourself. It is a complex, that, unless you mature rapidly, you will not be able to deal with, to destroy. (146)

Sita and Nanda Kaul also remain under the constant spell of their fathers. An ex-freedom fighter, Sita's father was "so gentle, thoughtful, barefoot, dressed in homespun," whom she "respected, admired, and adored." (79) Later, he lived a mysterious life and evoked "a hypnotized kind of notice and regard." (89) Unlike Nanda Kaul's husband, her father was "an explorer, a discoverer." (85) The novelist draws particular attention to Nanda Kaul's, "absurd pride in being her father's daughter, her ridiculous failure ever to forget it." (141) If Maya, Sita and Nanda Kaul are governed by father-fixation, Monisha is under the gravitational pull of her mother. Nirode plainly reminds Monisha of her mother complex. (162) Monisha herself refers to "The problems mother presents to us all with her wide-flung and seemingly ageless love." (137) This obsession with the father/mother figure is chiefly responsible for these sensitive creatures's petulant dissatisfaction with life.

Closely related to this trait is the infantilism of these women characters. They all confess that their behaviour has not been much different from that of toy princesses in a toy world. Monisha, in her own estimation, is like "the lost princess of the fairy tale who sat somewhere in the deepest shadows of this forest, silent and unattainable." (200) Ultimately, she died "from an excess of caring, in a fire of care and conscience." (256) Sita, despite her maturity, leads "a lulled life, half-conscious, dream-like." (126) Even her daughter did not like her mother's "proclivity for drama, for theatre, for emotion." (109) When things did not go according to her wishes, she began to "kick up her heels and prance like a pony." (63) The novelist makes it a point to tell her readers that

> she had lived a strange life, an unusual life, that had the effect of making her withdraw into the protective chrysalis of childhood for longer than is usual for most. (63)

Nanda Kaul's life replicates the same pattern. She knew it well that "fantasy and fairy tales had their place in her life." (89) Even in her old age she is seen with Ila Das "reconstructing, block by block, of the castle of childhood." (116) Her gestures and actions speak of a childishness lurking inside her. Towards the end of the novel, we are told about it in precise terms: "She pouted, childishly. One might have said she had arrived at her second childhood if one believed in such things. She looked so exactly like a baby thwarted, wanting attention she did not get." (101) This world of make-beliefs serves her as tranquillizers:

> It was all a lie, all. She had lied to Raka, lied about everything. Her father had never been to Tibet—he had bought the little Buddha from a travelling pedlar. They had not had bears and leopards in their home, nothing but overfed dogs and bad-tempered parrots. Nor had her husband loved and cherished her like a queen. . . . And her children—the children were all alien to her nature. She neither understood nor loved them. . . . All those graces and glories with which she had tried to captivate Raka were only a fabrication: they helped her to sleep at night, they were tranquillizers, pills. (145)

Probably the most pathetic condition is Maya's. Right from her childhood, she regarded the world as "a toy specially made" for her, painted in her favourite colours and set to dance to her favourite tunes. (36) On account of her upbringing and pampering by her father, she had always been "a wayward and high-strung child." (53) Elsewhere she calls herself "a foolish baby," "a round-faced child" and "a wayward, trying infant, no more." (66) Her life, according to her, has not been different from that of "a painted butterfly." (94) To her husband, she is a "Neurotic. . . . A spoilt baby." (115) Significantly enough, her name—Maya—itself means "illusion," and it is the realm of fantasy that she prefers to dwell in. Her family background and readings have been chiefly responsible for her infantile behaviour:

> As a child, I enjoyed, princess-like, a sumptuous fare of the fantasies of the Arabian Nights, the glories and bravado of Indian mythology, long and astounding tales of princes and regal queens, jackals and tigers, and, being my father's daughter, of the lovely English and Irish fairy tales as well, that were read out to me by him. (43)

Anita Desai's women characters's attitude is thus controlled by fantasy. The fantastic is really allied to the "disexpected."[23] The conflict between the real and the fantastic makes the life of these characters all the more miserable. As for the necessity of the fantastic in their life, Sita herself offers an explanation: "If reality were not to be borne, then illusion was the only alternative." (101) The life of fantasy compensates for the harsh realities of life, which keeps on prescribing do's and don't's at every point. As Maya herself admits, her "childhood was one in which much was excluded, which grew steadily more restricted, unnatural even." (89) The life of repressions affects the very source of their thinking and behaviour.

Finally, Anita Desai deals with sexual repressions of her characters such as Maya, Monisha, Nanda Kaul, and Ila Das. The "deployment of sexuality," according to Foucault, is "a great surface network in which the stimulation of bodies, the intensification of pleasures, the incitement of discourse, the formation of special knowledges, the strengthening of controls and resistances, are linked to one another, in accordance with a few major strategies of knowledge and power."[24] Sexuality represents womanness and selfhood and is a significant aspect of a woman's experiences. Although Anita Desai has been extremely tongue-tied in delineating this aspect of her characters and there is very little "sextacy" or what Foucault calls the "hysterization of women's bodies," there are subtle references to intimate relations between the two sexes and complications arising out of them. A few examples will suffice. Maya, of all her women characters, is the one who is most aware of her body and its appeal. She is pained to find Gautama overbusy with his papers, giving no thought to her "soft, willing body." (9) She tries to enter Gautama's "securely male" world but is rejected. (103) Her reflections on the papaya tree tell us a lot about her plight:

> I contemplated that, smiling with pleasure at the thought of those long streamers of bridal flowers that flow out of the core of the female papaya tree and twine about her slim trunk, and the firm, wax-petalled blossoms that leap directly out of the solid trunk of the male. . . . Besides, if I could pleasure in contemplation of the male papaya, how much more food for delight in this male companion [Gautama], surely. And I melted with tenderness, my arms curled into an instinctive cradle. (92)

Maya finds Gautama's beam "especially tender, his attention especially loving" but what she itches for is an "open love." (39) Her wishes and desires, however, are thwarted. Gautama's behaviour is such that he appears to her "no more than a figure of granite . . . a mound of books that smelt faintly of mouldy rice and wisdom." (201) Even at the time of her dire need and emotional insecurity, he preaches to her an intellectual sermon like Angel Clare:

> This life you speak of, this little episode, this brief flash-in-the-pan, how insignificant and trivial it appears compared with this immortal cycle to which all humanity is bound, living or dying, and which turns without stop, without *point*, you might say. (122)

It is a pity that few people treat these sensitive creatures properly. They fail to realize the importance of their deeper urge in the form of "sex—where not union but communion is concerned." (104) It may also be noted that most of these women are childless or are alienated from their children. This fact makes their lives even more unbearable.

Anita Desai has thus presented in her novels the predicament of sensitive women characters, who find it very difficult to adjust in the present mechanical and urbanized set up. A careful study of the novelist's language reveals meaningful correlations between the psychic condition of the characters and the language used by them. Anita Desai's range is rather narrow. She is fully aware, as she told an interviewer, that "every human being's territory is really very small," and that all one can explore is "a very tiny section of this territory."[25] The novelist has nevertheless tried to do full justice to the characters and, despite all her limitations, has succeeded in her attempts. Elaine Showalter talks of the three phases of the emergence and growth of feminine tradition, i.e. the phases of limitation, protest and self-discovery.[26] Anita Desai's work is directly related to the third and the final phase. Her novels contain evidences of her awareness of various problems pertaining to women, which she has tried to tackle from a psychological point of view. The solutions presented by her may be muted or oblique at times, but the significance of her efforts can hardly be denied.

NOTES

1. A.V. Krishna Rao, *The Indo-Anglian Novel and the Changing Tradition* (Mysore: Rao and Raghvan, 1972), p. 50.
2. D.S. Maini, "The Achievement of Anita Desai," in K.K. Sharma, ed., *Indo-English Literature* (Ghaziabad, Vimal, 1977), p. 216.
3. Anita Desai, "Women Writers," *Quest*, 65 (April-June 1970), p. 43.
4. *India Today* (15 March 1986), p. 149.

5. Anita Desai, "The Indian Writer's Problems" in R.K. Dhawan, ed., *Explorations in Modern Indo-English Fiction* (New Delhi: Bahri, 1982), p. 255.
6. All textual references to Anita Desai's novels have been given parenthetically. The following editions have been used: *Cry the Peacock* (New Delhi: Orient Paperbacks, 1980); *Voices in the City* (New Delhi: Hind Pocket Books, 1965); *Where Shall We Go This Summer?* (New Delhi: Orient Paperbacks, 1982); *Fire on the Mountain* (New Delhi: Allied, 1977); *Clear Light of Day* (New Delhi: Allied, 1980); *In Custody* (London: Heinemann, 1984).
7. Raji Narsimhan, *Sensibility Under Stress* (New Delhi: Ashajanak Prakashan, 1976), p. 23.
8. Jasbir Jain, *Stairs to the Attic: The Novels of Anita Desai* (Jaipur: Printwell, 1987), p. 10.
9. Atma Ram, *Interviews with Indian-English Writers* (Calcutta: Writers Workshop, 1983), pp. 24-25.
10. B. Thorne and N. Henley, eds., *Language and Sex: Difference and Dominance* (Mass: Rowley, 1975), p. ix.
11. H. Scott, "Eastern European Women in Theory and Practice," *Women's Studies International Quarterly, 1* (1978), p. 198.
12. "The Ideology of Romanticism," in R.F. Gleckner and G.E. Enscoe, eds., *Romanticism: Points of View* (New Jersey: Prentice-Hall, 1970), p. 170.
13. Gaston Bachelord, *The Poetics of Reverie,* trans. Daniel Russel (Boston: Beacon Press, 1971), p. 35.
14. J.P. Stanley, "Gender-marking in American English: Usage and Reference," in A.P. *et al,* eds., *Sexism and Language* (Urbana: *National Council of Teachers of English,* 1977), p. 67.
15. D. Bollinger, "Truth is a Linguistic Question," *Language,* 49 (1973), p. 541.
16. Anita Desai, "The Indian Writer's Problems," p. 225.
17. Through the mouth of her characters, the novelist has given expression to her problems regarding an effective mode of communication. *Cry, the Peacock,* for example, contains this statement: "The things we leave unsaid would fill great volumes; what we do say, only the first few pages of introduction." (p. 105) In *Where Shall We Go This Summer?,* "Beginning to pace up and down, up and down, she (Sita) would train

to catch the precise language of this invisible unquiet." (p. 127) This is what, precisely, the novelist herself does.

18. Anita Desai, "Flight of Forms," *India International Centre Quarterly*, 10, 4 (1983), p. 419.
19. *The Times of India* (29 April 1979), p. 13.
20. Michel Foucault, *The History of Sexuality: An Introduction*, trans. Robert Hurley (New York: Pantheon, 1978), p. 93.
21. *Ibid.*, pp. 105-106.
22. *Ibid.*, p. 150.
23. See Eric Rabkin, *The Fantastic in Literature* (New Jersey: Princeton University Press, 1976), pp. 14-24.
24. Michel Foucault, p. 106.
25. Jasbir Jain, p. 14.
26. Elaine Showalter, *A Literature of Their Own* (New Jersey: Princeton University Press, 1977), p. 13.

"My life is my own": A Study of Shashi Deshpande's Women

P. RAMAMOORTHI

I

The culture that created a Sita and a Gandhari has denied existence to woman except as a daughter/ sister, a wife/daughter-in-law, and a mother/mother-in-law. The Hindu Society has denied woman the possibility of being a "SHE," a person capable of achieving individuation.[1] She is a non-person and as described in Raja Rao's *The Serpent and the Rope:* "Women should not be."[2] Man's relationship with woman is most often the bond that exists between a master and a slave. Woman is an object and she is essential to man because "it is in seeking to be made whole through her that man hopes to attain self-realization."[3] It is in such a culture, in recent times, that voices of dissent are heard. Shashi Deshpande feels embarrassed to be called a woman writer[4] and she is not very enthusiastic about the label feminist.[5] However much she may deny the influence of feminism in her novels, it is the core of her novels. Her heroines speak of Virginia Woolf's *A Room of One's Own* and Betty Friedan and it becomes quite obvious that the women she has created are feminists, if she is not one.

One of the primal and seminal concerns of feminism is to declare that a woman is a being. She is not an appendage of man. A woman is not the "other"; She is not an addition to man. She is an autonomous being, capable of, through trial and error, finding her own way to salvation. It is true that feminism in its early stages thought of Amazon-Utopias, an all-female world where man have peripheral functions.

The attempts to create "female enclaves" are extremist reactions but the recent trends in feminist literature are an indication that it is possible for a woman to live in the world where men also live. From the limited perspective of women's rights and suppression of women, feminist literature has moved a step ahead in the right direction—that of painting up, through a study of "feminine mystique," that whether it is woman or man, the world we live in is disintegrated and *all of us are alone.* Loneliness, one of the concerns of modern society, is not a disease, but a symptom of man's condition and this awareness is the first milestone in one's journey into oneself.

II

Shashi Deshpande's novels are concerned with a woman's quest for self; an exploration into the female psyche and an understanding of the mysteries of life and the protagonist's place in it. *Roots and Shadows* (1983), her first novel, but published after *The Dark Holds No Terrors* (1980) and *If I Die Today* (1982), marks the beginning of the quest of woman for her self. The theme is continued in her later novel *That Long Silence* (1988) and Deshpande's concern is the woman and her external quest. In an interesting interview, Deshpande reveals that all her characters are concerned with their "selves"[6] and they learn to be "honest" to themselves. Being true to one's self, not as being true in the sense that nature/culture demands of you, is the wisdom the Deshpande protagonist learns.

I intend to study *Roots and Shadows* and *The Dark Holds No Terrors* as novels of the woman's self-quest and hope to posit the view that women in these novels have established themselves as autonomous beings, free from the restrictions imposed by society, culture, nature and also free from their own fears and guilt; that women have reached a stage of understanding the fundamental truth: You have to find it for yourself.

Indu, the protagonist of *Roots and Shadows*[7] learns the truth about herself, dismissing all the shadows that she had thought to be her real self. The chimeras, that she has been chasing through her life, end with her realization that she is a writer: "That I would at last do the kind of writing I had always dreamt of doing." (205) This statement of Indu is her assertion of her will and self. She can no longer cheat herself saying that she will do things for the sake of Jayant, her husband. She shall not remain a doll or a puppet but she will take decisions for herself and affirm her being. As Simone de Beauvoir observes, "the more women assert themselves as human beings, the more the marvellous quality of the 'other' will die in them."[8] We need to know the chimeras Indu has chased to understand her final standpoint. Indu, a middle class young girl, brought up in an orthodox brahmin family, headed by Akka (the mother surrogate in the novel) "left home full of hatred for the family, for Akka specially" and she had sworn, "I would never go back." (20) Indu who had lost her mother at birth identifies, throughout the novel, Akka as the mother figure. She rebels against Akka, her world, her values and marries Jayant against the wishes of Akka. Akka said at her marriage, "such marriages never work. Different castes, different languages . . . it's all right for a while, They realize." (74) Indu comes back to her parental home after eleven years when Akka is in her death-bed and on Akka's death, becomes the sole inheritor of her property.

Akka, the mother figure in *Roots and Shadows,* is a domineering woman. She came home as a childless widow and treated almost everyone with her rule of thumb. She is the symbol of authority. Everything that happens in the house is to be approved by her. When she does not approve of an alliance, it is dropped. Till her death, "she had maintained her power, her authority over everyone." Indu is much in the same mould of Akka. That she becomes the inheritor of Akka's property establishes her identity as Akka's child. But Indu, in the beginning, refuses to accept her as a role-model and rejects

Akka's orthodoxy, rituals and carves a life of her own, hoping that by escaping from Akka she will gain independence and freedom to live as she pleases without the bounds of the family and the society which is symbolized by the house. Saru in *The Dark Holds No Terrors** has childhood scars. She hates her mother to such an extent that she says, "If you're a woman, I don't want to be one." (55) Saru's mother shows sexist/gender difference in her treatment of her son Dhruva and daughter. In one of the recapitulations, Saru records her conversation with her mother:

> "Don't go out in the sun. You'll get darker."
> "Who cares?"
> "We have to care if you don't. We have to get you married."
> "I don't want to get married."
> "Will you live with us all your life?"
> "Why not?"
> "You can't."
> "And Dhruva?"
> "He is different. He's a boy." (40)

He's different. He's a boy—these words establish the traditional Indian mother against whom Saru has to rebel all her life.

The childhood experience of watching her brother sink into water and die gives her a sense of guilt that she is responsible for the death of her brother. It is enhanced by her mother's words, "You killed your brother . . . why didn't you die?," which drive Saru to hate her mother.

Saru rebels against her mother by going to Bombay to study medicine. The hostel life is a kind of "rebirth" into a totally different world where you don't have to stay outside for "those three days, you are no longer an 'untouchable'; you can even talk about it; "'Oh, damn. I must change again. It's like a tap, that's what it is.'" (87) When Saru falls in love with Manohar, again she defies the authority of the mother:

> "What caste is he?"
> "I don't know."
> "A Brahmin?"
> "Of course not."
> Then, cruelly . . . "his father keeps a cycle shop."
> "Oh, so they are low caste people, are they?" (87)

Saru's marriage is a means to get away from her mother and her home. The departure of the heroine from the mother is the first step towards autonomy; for, the mother is the first pedagogue of the do's and the don't's on the woman. Marriage, the promised end in a traditional society, in feminist fiction becomes only another enclosure that restricts the movement towards autonomy and self-realization.

There are recurrent images of enclosure in *Roots and Shadows* as well as in *The Dark Holds No Terrors*. Indu constantly speaks of the dark room where so many women had given birth and one of her recurring dreams is the subterranean passage through which she escapes and boards a bus to reach a deserted barren place. Saru is reminded of a room whose doors are closed whenever she looks at her daughter, Renu. Saru, even when she comes back home, "felt herself enclosed." (12) When she enters into her room, she finds male clothes hanging on the wall and realizes that she has no room of her own. The feeling of being enclosed is associated with the mother's house and the protagonists want to escape from the enclosure, as revealed in Indu's dreams. The image of the enclosed walls suggests the suffocation these women undergo not only in their parental homes but the homes they have chosen as refuge. The "room" and the enclosed feeling also relate them quite often to mere objects and cattle where they have no light of their own. They do not belong to the room; they are merely an addition to it.

Shashi Deshpande's heroines reject rituals that are the vestiges of the past. In their rejection of their mother, they also discard the meaningless rituals like circumambulating the tulsi plant. Both Indu and Saru refuse to undertake such rituals which are meant to increase the life span of their husbands. The rejection is an indication of their autonomy and their capacity to see their lives independent of their mother/past. Indu and Saru tend to associate their mothers/mother-figures with the stereotype normally created by male writers—the stereotype of a mother who is passive in her suffering, who showers affection on the male child and who makes a lot of sacrifices for the sake of the family. These heroines shudder at some of the natural biological functions of the female (associated with the mother) and they have developed, from their childhood, an apathy towards their body. Indu does not have a child and she fears to have one. She tells herself, "The truth is, I will have no child that is not wholly welcome." Indu constantly fights against her womanhood because it was thrust on her gracelessly and brutally, the day she came of age. She was told in a crude way that she could have babies now. The disgust with which she speaks of the incident, reveals the traumatic pubertal transitions. Besides, the idea that she is "unclean" has been planted in her mind. She develops an aversion to the body and all bodily functions. Indu cannot understand how a woman could breastfeed her child in the presence of another human being. Saru too has similar frightful experiences. She has her painful middle-claas inhibitions (and one constant image the novelist uses is "like removing your clothes in public") and though she has had two children, Renu and Abhi, yet the maternal instinct in her is not focused. The Shashi Deshpande heroine is confronted with the problem of what the mother stands for and the only way out for her is to seek a new environment where the mother cannot exercise her will.

III

The parental home, a symbol of tradition and old world values has no room for the Shashi Deshpande heroine. She breathes the air of rituals that obstruct the growth of a woman as a being. Mother, the possible model after whom she must mould her life, looks a bad model and hence rejected. In their desire for freedom, they almost resemble Caliban. Indu and Saru seek through their marriage, a room of their own and autonomy.

The woman in order to achieve her freedom seeks marriage as an alternative to the bondage created by the parental family. She resents the role of a daughter and looks forward to the role of a wife with the hope that her new role will help her in winning their freedom. Saru's situation is explicitly described in *The Dark:*

> I had come away from my parents in a fever of excitement after the last battle. The die was cast, the decisions taken, my boats burnt. There could be no turning back. Then, this ridiculous anticlimax. (31-32)

The words, "battle," die cast," "decisions taken" and "boats burnt," indicate that the heroine has taken a momentous decision which only proves to be an anticlimax, like Caliban becoming the slave of Stephano and Trinquilo. Both Saru and Indu marry out of their castes and their second homes become the very prisons they had escaped. Saru is soon disappointed with her husband Manu, who promised to become another Shelley; she had imagined herself as Harriet. Saru is not only the breadwinner; she has also to provide the butter. She soon realizes that her husband is a sadist and the domestic discord sets in. Indu in *Roots* has learnt the "gift of silence" (36) from her marriage and she has also mastered the art of deception. As R. Mala observes, these heroines are also victims of "sexual paralysis."[10] Both Saru and Indu experience disillusionment in sex and suffer a silent sexual humiliation. Saru's extra marital affair with Boozie also does not lead to sexual fulfilment. Indu's relationship with Naren has a totally different significance. Their sexual situation forces these women to extra-marital relationship. What is significant about such relationships is that they suffer no guilt and they begin to evolve a new code of sexual ethics. Their path to individuation is marked by contacts with diverse experiences such as extramarital affairs. They experience a sense of sexual autonomy freeing themselves from sexual politics. Further, these heroines arrive at a realistic perception of love as physical instinct. Saru reveals:

> Love . . . there was no such thing between man and woman . . . only a need which both fought against futilely, the very futility turning into the thing called love. (65)

She pinpoints that the code word of our age is "sex" and not love. Indu ridicules the very word love: "I love a book, a word, or a sari, a curry, a dog, a child, a man." (97) The realization that love has no place in their world drives them to the extreme stance of seeing only deceit, treachery and betrayal, all around. They also begin to see how sex becomes a symbol of power and authority and marriage, another kind of enclosure. Marriage proves to be another trap and woman feels like a caged animal. Making enormous sacrifices on her profession, the protagonists begin to understand that marriage obstructs their growth as individuals. They see marriage only in terms of the dark rooms where terror awaits them. Saru feels as though "She had exchanged one pair of pinching, torturing shoes for another." (74) Marriage, like the parental home, seems to be "the chalked lines drawn by others" where Indu and Saru have to be carefully walking on them—one step, this side or that, will ruin their lives.

IV

"Nostros," the Greek word meaning return home describes aptly the situation of Indu and Saru. Fearing that their continued stay would stifle their progress in their road to self-understanding, they come to their parental homes, the home which they dreaded as teenagers. Their return home is a sure sign of their escape from sexual politics. Both *Roots* and *Dark* begin with the heroines returning to their parents's home and this beginning allows the novelist to use the cinematic technique of flashback.

Indu comes at the call of Akka and stays there till the house is disposed off. Saru comes quite unexpectedly much to the surprise of her father. The visit to the parental home is like the *rites of passage*, the home they discarded becomes the very place of refuge. It is once again in their parental homes that both Indu and Saru acquire real independence and maturity.

Indu learns more about Akka, her past, her concern and her suffering. Akka's traumatic married life had come to a close when she exercised her will in not allowing her husband's concubine to see him at his death-bed. It is here Indu learns not to judge others by her standards. Akka's house provides her with ample opportunities to know herself, her secret passions and the volcanic sexual explosions that she is capable of. It is here that she realizes what her roots are—an independent woman and a writer, and what the shadows are—a daughter, a mother and a commercial writer. She takes a firm decision regarding her job and life:

> there were other things I had to tell him (Jayant). That I was resigning my job. That I would at last do the kind of writing I had always dreamt of doing. That I would not, could not enrich myself with Akka's money. That I would, on the other hand, pay for Mini's wedding. (205)

She also learns to see life in a fresh light. While everyone is shocked at the idea of demolition of Akka's house, she sees the house itself as a bondage and trap:

> As a matter of fact, I felt neither mournful, nor desolate, but in a peculiar way, both light and free. Yes, the house had been a trap too, binding me to a past I had to move

> away from. Now, I felt clean, as if I had cut away all the unnecessary uneven edges of me. (204)

The house, a symbol of tradition and lineage, has its own pulls on people. Her uncle has developed attachment with the house and demolition of the house means the disintegration of the family; whereas Indu sees the house as a vestige of the past with its emotional control on people. She releases herself from the bondage of the house and no wonder that she feels "clean". The word "clean" and its opposite "unclean" are associated with freedom and restrictions.

The most remarkable revelation about Indu is that she learns to see her life independent of Jayant. What happened between her and Naren does not concern Jayant. She has no guilt about her sexual encounter with Naren but at the same time she decides not to tell Jayant about it: "That had nothing to do with the two of us and our life together." (205) This sheds a brilliant light on Indu's awareness of her autonomy and her realization that she is a being, and not a dependent on Jayant. The novel gains its feminist stance in Indu's exploration into herself but it also moves beyond the boundaries of feminism into a perception of the very predicament of the human existence. Indu moves on in her road of self-realization and the destination seems to be the point of comprehension of the mystery of human life. The champak tree in the house will be cut off, and there will be no trace of the tree at all, "not even a stump." Indu wanders back to her childhood days when the tree was a mystery, a wonder and full of aroma. Now, will it be non-existent? In that epiphanic moment, Indu negates the idea:

> No, there is no such thing. To accept it, will be to deny the miracle of life itself. If not this stump, there is another. If not this tree, there will be others. Other trees will grow, other flowers will bloom, other fragrances will pervade other airs.
>
> It was like being let into a great secret. I felt as if I was

> watching life itself . . . endless, limitless, formless and full of grace. (202)

Roots ends with affirmation of the individuality of Indu and also the principle of life which is endless. Through the image of the tree, Shashi Deshpande suggests that Indu has learnt to see not only her life full of possibilities for growth and grace (If not Jayant, another/if not this stump, another) but the very meaning of Life itself. It is with this total understanding that Indu decides to go back to Jayant. It may be mentioned here that at the end of the novel, Indu realizes that Akka is not a sadist. Indu has confronted her real self and she knows her roots; she need not be ashamed of her body and sexual needs; she has to decide what her job will be; she is capable of taking decisions not only for herself but for others too, and life does not come to an end with individuals, be it Indu or Jayant.

Saru in *Dark* also undergoes the arduous journey into herself and learns to free herself of guilt, shame, humiliation and she is also initiated into the mystery of human existence. The epigraph of the novel

> You are your own refuge
> There is no other refuge
> This refuge is hard to achieve *(The Dhammapada)*

gains its total significance when Saru realizes that the parental home cannot be a refuge. She understands that neither her father nor her husband Manohar can be her refuge. She is her own refuge. She has to overcome herself; she has to kill the ghosts that haunt her; she has to find her own way to salvation. The parental home initiates the protagonists into an understanding of the meaning of human life. Saru reflects on the human situation:

> All right, so I'm alone. But so's everyone else. Human beings . . . they're going to fail you. But because there's just us, because there's no one else, we have to go on

trying. If we can't believe in ourselves, we're sunk.(200)

Saru has gained the assertion of will and confidence in herself. She learns to trust herself. Saru, who had instructed her father not to open the door for her husband Manu, now tells her father: "And oh yes, Baba, if Manu comes, tell him to wait. I'll be back as soon as I can." (202)

Saru who ran away from her husband and children, who refused to meet her husband, is not ready to confront him. This does not mean that she will go back to her husband but it only suggests that she is capable of facing Manu and asserting her own rights and individuality. The casualness in her words, "Oh yes, Baba" and "as soon as I can," assert her individuality. She is no longer doubtful about her potential as a human being. She thinks of the sick child she has to attend and begins to diagnose the illness. The novel ends with Saru restoring herself the pride of her profession, a doctor.

It is to be noted that Saru, at the end of the novel, has come to realize that her profession as a doctor is her own and she will decide what to do with it. "My life is my own." She will no longer be a puppet. Her marriage is a shadow. She held on to the marriage because she did not want to prove her mother right. Only she can be her refuge. Everyone is lonely and that there is no cause for despair.

The movement of the Shashi Deshpande heroine from her parental home to the outside world, through education and marriage, does not really initiate them into a knowledge of the self. Their defiance of the mother does not ensure them the freedom they desire. Their return home, in the absence of the mother/mother figure only helps them realize their own selves. They had imagined that their mothers stifled their growth and so defied them. But when husbands began to kill the very roots of their existence, they defied their husbands and find a way of their own, rejecting all over-riding influences. Their fear of losing themselves in the dark mysterious universe is dispelled by their understanding that the "Dark Holds No Terrors" if one can believe in one's self and if one accepts the responsibility for one's life.

NOTES

1. The term "individuation" is defined as the need for autonomy and a self-identity and this is central to Johanna Kirkpatrick's thesis in her paper, "Women in Indian English Literature: The Question of Individuation." *Journal of South Asian Literature*, XII, 3 and 4 (Spring 1977), pp. 121-29.
2. Raja Rao, *The Serpent and the Rope* (Bombay: Orient Paperback, 1968), p. 359.
3. Simone de Beauvoir, *The Second Sex*, trans. H.M. Parshley (London: Penguin, 1972), p. 173.
4. Shashi Deshpande, "The Dilemma of a Woman Writer," *The Literary Criterion*, 20, 4 (1985), pp. 33-36.
5. "An Unpublished Interview with Shanthi," "Tradition and Modernity in the Novels of Shashi Deshpande," Appendix of M. Phil. Dissertation, M.K. University, 1989.
6. R. Mala, "The Predicament of the Indian Woman: The Heroines in the Novels of Shashi Deshpande: A Select Study," M. Phil. Dissertation, Pondicherry University, 1989, p. 132.
7. Shashi Deshpande, *Roots and Shadows* (Bombay: Orient Longman, 1983).
8. Simone de Beauvoir, p. 74.
9. Shashi Deshpande, *The Dark Holds No Terrors* (New Delhi: Vikas, 1980).
10. R. Mala.

Breaking the Silence: Shashi Deshpande's *That Long Silence*

SARLA PALKAR

"If I were a man and cared to know the world I lived in, I almost think it would make me a shade uneasy—the weight of that long silence of one-half of the world." This statement by Elizabeth Robins forms the epigraph to Shashi Deshpande's novel, *That Long Silence*,[1] announcing, as it were, the intention of this talented contemporary Indian writer to break the long silence that has surrounded women, their experience and their world. For a long time, woman has existed as a gap, as an absence in literature, whether Western or Indian. This is not only true of the fiction created by men, but also by women, who have mostly confined themselves to writing love stories or dealing with the experience of women in a superficial manner, creating the same kind of stereotypes of women which they find so reprehensible in the writings of men. Women writers have also often fallen a prey to that prescriptive feminist ideology of creating strong women characters. This doctrine becomes as repressive as the one created by male hegemony and represses the truth about the majority of their sisters and their lives.

Against this backdrop, Shashi Deshpande's *That Long Silence* promises to be a refreshing departure from most of the fiction written by women. Of course, one cannot claim that she is doing anything extraordinary. We readily recognize the middle class ethos and people that we come across in the novel. The novelist's contribution lies in the heightened sensitivity and the fresh insights that she brings to bear on the well-known types and situations. The action of the novel is triggered off by a crisis in a middle-class family. Mohan, the narrator's husband, in his pursuit of prestige and security, had indulged in certain malpractices, as a result of which he now faces an inquiry and may perhaps lose his job. Mohan is advised by Agarwal, his partner in the crime, to stay away from the office and his Churchgate flat till the storm blows over. Luckily for Mohan, the children are away on a tour with their family friends, and it all ends well, they need not even know about this disgrace. Mohan, therefore, decides that he and his wife Jaya would go and stay at the flat in Dadar. This flat had belonged to Jaya's maternal uncle. Jaya and Mohan had stayed there before shifting to a bigger flat in Churchgate. Jaya acquiesces to her husband's decision and accompanies him, albeit in silent resentment, to their present exile at the Dadar flat. It is here, in the intolerable period of waiting and rising hysteria, that the process of self-examination and self-criticism begins for Jaya. She is flooded by the memories of the past—her earlier life, her marriage with Mohan, the frustrations and disappointments in her seventeen-year-old married existence, her personal failures, all these begin to haunt and torment her. By her journey into the past, Jaya gets the guidance for her future. By the end of the novel, the crisis—a mere storm in the teacup—has been averted and everything outwardly appears to be as it had been. Except for what has happened to Jaya. Jaya can no longer be a passive, silent partner to Mohan. The novel ends with her resolve to speak, to break her long silence.

That Long Silence, then, traces Jaya's passage through a plethora of self-doubts, fears, guilt, smothered anger and silence towards articulation and affirmation. Suman Ahuja, while reviewing the novel in *The Times of India*, observes that Jaya "caught in an emotional eddy, endeavours to come to terms with her protean roles, while trying, albeit in vain, to rediscover her true self, which is but an ephemera . . . an unfulfilled wife, a disappointed mother and a failed writer."[2] Jaya, in fact, rejects the patriarchal notion of a unitary self or identity when she observes, "But what was that 'myself? Trying to find oneself'—what a cliche that has become. As if such a thing is possible. As if there is such a thing as oneself, intact and whole, waiting to be discovered. On the contrary, there are so many, each self, attached like a Siamese twin to a self of another person, neither able to exist without the other." (69) That is why the novel offers interesting cameos of so many other people, men and women, as they have become a part of Jaya's personality and her unconscious. Even her mother and her two grandmothers—though Jaya may not like to think of it—have imparted something of their own selves to Jaya.

Even a casual reading of the novel makes one conscious that Shashi Deshpande is not only writing about her female protagonist, Jaya, who is trying to erase a long silence and grapple with the problems of self-revelation and self-assessment, but, through Jaya, also about other women, those unhappy victims who never broke their silence. The author, in the first place, points out how our culture has often kept silent on the subject of women. For instance, at one point in the novel, Jaya discovers that she does not figure in the family tree that her uncle, Ramukaka, had prepared with great pains and of which he was so proud. When Jaya asks her uncle why her name is not included in the family tree, she is given to understand that she now belongs to her husband's family and not to her father's. But this is only half of the truth. Neither her mother nor her *kakis*, i.e., her uncles's wives, not even her grandmother, *ajji*, that indomitable woman, "who single-handedly kept the family together" (143) find a place in the family tree. Jaya, to her dismay, finds that her name and existence, along with those of other women in the family, are completely blotted out of the family history. The novel, as it were, is Jaya's protest against the kind of treatment that is given to women in our culture and her attempt to give another version of history from women's point of view.

That Long Silence is also a scathing critique of our social institutions like marriage or family, the way they stifle the growth and free expression of the individual. These institutions put the individuals into the slots like wife, husband, brother, sister, daughter, son, etc. and obstruct the free communication between human beings. This is what happens in Jaya's relationship with Kamat. Kamat was Jaya's upstairs neighbour at Dadar. He was a widower and his only son had settled abroad. He was a lonely man and had shown a lot of understanding and sympathy for Jaya. In fact, Jaya was more free and uninhibited with him than she was with her husband. But in our society, this kind of friendship between a married woman and another man is always looked upon with suspicion and disapproval. That is why, perhaps, when Jaya had found Kamat lying dead on the floor of his flat on one of her visits to him, she had panicked and left the place in silence. This incident underlines how marriage often drives people into impossible and awkward situations. Jaya cannot even stay and pay homage to her best friend in his death for the fear of ruining her marriage. She perhaps does her role of wife to a perfection, but fails as a human being.

Shashi Deshpande employs the first-person narrative and makes her central character Jaya tell her own story. Jaya warns the reader at the very outset that she is not the heroine of her story, nor is she talking about her isolated self. One may say that her preoccupations are man-woman relationship, marriage and family life. But the novel avoids the facile solution of putting the blame on man only. Both men and women are products of their culture and victims of the institution of marriage. It is as difficult for women to outgrow the images and roles allotted to them by their society as it is for men. For example, during her first pregnancy, when Jaya suggests to Mohan that he should do the cooking, Mohan is highly amused by the suggestion, because he thinks cooking is not a man's job. Later on, we discover that Jaya also shares her husband's viewpoint when she confesses to Kamat that the sight of him doing the cooking made her uneasy as she thought it was unmanly. Like Mohan, she too puts her children into the slots and feels disappointed when they refuse to remain there and contribute their share in creating the myth of a happy and harmonious family. It is only at the end, after her ordeal, that Jaya realizes her mistake and releases herself as well as her children from the slots into which she had put them.

In her anxiety to fulfil her roles of a wife and a mother, Jaya had not done proper justice to her own talents. Years back Jaya had made a good beginning as a writer by producing a story which had won the first prize and was published in a magazine. But Mohan's response to the story was most disheartening. He assumed that the story was about their personal life. He was apprehensive and hurt at the thought that the people of his acquaintance would think he was the kind of person as was the man portrayed in the story. No doubt, this incident had left a deep impression on Jaya's psyche and affected her career as a writer. She, therefore, can easily make her husband a scapegoat for her failure, but in her self-critical mood at the Dadar flat she refuses to have this easy way out. She reminds herself that even after her confrontation with Mohan she had continued to write—write under an assumed name (as women writers have often done under patriarchy)—but her stories had been rejected. Something had been missing from them, something had been censored out of them. According to Kamat, it was Jaya's anger, her strong passions. Jaya had tried to remind him—what actually she had learned from her husband in her first memorable argument with him—that a woman cannot be angry, that anger makes a woman unwomanly. She had also given the familiar excuse that women give, when they fail at anything, that they have no time for serious work because of their household duties. Kamat had reproved of this tendency in her: "I'm warning you—beware of this 'women are the victims' theory of yours. It'll drag you down into a soft, squishy bog of self-pity. Take yourself seriously, woman. Don't skulk behind a false name. And work—work if you want others to take you seriously." (148) Kamat was a hard critic and he would leave no escape route for Jaya. The real reason for her failure, he pointed out, was her fear. She was afraid of writing, of failing.

Jaya was in no mood to take such hard criticism. She had crawled back into her hole. She had resumed her career as a wife, as a mother. In the meantime, Mohan had suggested that she should write light, humorous pieces in the newspapers, what they called "middles." Jaya had then started her weekly column "Seeta" which had won the approval of the readers, the editor, and above all of her husband. "And for me," Jaya observes, "she had been the means through which I had shut the door, firmly, on all those other women who had invaded my being, screaming for attention: women I had known I could not write about, because they might—it was just possible—resemble Mohan's mother or aunt, or my mother or aunt." (149) Thus the novelist makes it clear that not only patriarchy has kept silent on the subject of women, but under patriarchy, women have also recoiled from telling the truth about their sex.

When Jaya finally comes out of her emotional upheaval, she has sorted out a few problems with herself. For the two nights that she has to herself, she puts down on paper all that she had suppressed in her seventeen years's silence. What she has written is evidently the novel that we are reading. The novel is mostly concerned with women like Kusum, Mohan's mother, and many other victims like them—victims of patriarchy and also of their own silence. *That Long Silence* puts into nutshell the history and evolution of women through four generations that Jaya has known and promises a better future for women.

What has Jaya ultimately achieved by her writing, by her getting all the ghosts that bothered her out of her system on to the paper? In Jaya's own words, "I'm not afraid any more. The panic has gone. I'm Mohan's wife, I had thought, and cut off the bits of me that had refused to be Mohan's wife. Now I know that kind of a fragmentation is not possible. The child, hands in pockets, has been with me through the years. She is with me still." (191) Bald statements like these plainly show that *That Long Silence* is a feminist critique written in the form of a novel. As Toril Moi remarks, "The principal objective of feminist criticism has always been political: it seeks to expose, not to perpetuate, patriarchal practices."[4] And this is what Shashi Deshpande also does through her text. At the same time, *That Long Silence* is also a self-critique. The important insight that Shashi Deshpande imparts to us through Jaya is that women should accept their own responsibility for what they are, see how much they have contributed to their own victimization, instead of putting the blame on everybody except themselves. It is only through self-analysis and self-understanding, through vigilance and courage, they can begin to change their lives. They will have to fight their own battles, nobody is going to do it for them.

NOTES

1. Shashi Deshpande, *That Long Silence* (India: Penguin, 1989).
2. Suman Ahuja, Review in *The Times of India* (8 October 1989), p. 2.
3. Toril Moi, *Sexual/Textual Politics: Feminist Literary Theory* (London: Methuen, 1985), p. xiv.
4. *Loc. cit.*

Feminism and Nayantara Sahgal's *The Day in Shadow* and *Rich Like Us*: From the Particular to the Ideological

PANKAJ K. SINGH

Although its publication coincided with the rise of Women's Lib in the West, Sahgal's *The Day in Shadow* is not a feminist novel. In fairness to Sahgal, it was not even intended to be one. It is a woman's novel and indeed has a whole lot of data which could have gone into the making of a legitimate feminist novel. However, its naivety at the level of ideology, its "innocence" towards the issues of power in a patriarchal social set-up, its disinclination to relate the heroine's predicament to a social order which unjustly and arbitrarily marginalizes women and assigns privileges to men—all these constitute "flaws" from a feminist angle. Sahgal's progress as a novelist, however, bears testimony to the fact that she has been moving towards a definite feminist position, so that the women's experiences do not merely provide data but are actually organized in such a way that they become an exercise in raising consciousness and a critique of society with its unequal gender roles and the power distribution involved in them. The present paper is an attempt to concentrate on *The Day in Shadow*, an early novel, and *Rich Like Us*, a more recent one, to highlight the growth of Sahgal's political and ideological understanding of woman's position.

The Day in Shadow gives a sensitive account of the suffering of a woman in Indian society when she opts to dissolve a marriage seventeen years old. After divorce, she has problems not only in coping with her own irrational fears and tensions but also with society which does not recognize a woman's identity apart from her husband's. A divorced woman is stigmatized for ever and she is curiously watched by others as if divorce were "a disease that left pock marks."[1] The mere habit of living with someone for many years makes it difficult for Simrit to accept the idea of living alone, all by herself. The frightening dream that she has gives us an idea of her inner disintegration where pain follows her like a shadow never leaving her even for a moment:

> She was clinging to a balustrade at the very top of the building, within reach of the sky, when her fingers were wrenched loose, one by one, and she was hurled to the pavement below. The queer thing was that no one took any notice of her fall. Cars and people kept going by. A deafening scream, her own, went on and on. . . . She picked herself up in panic and was relieved to find she did not fall apart. She held. She took a deep breath. . . . My skin is whole, not even a break or a split in it anywhere. It's the inside that has gone to pieces, and I'll just have to go along very carefully from now on. . . . The pain, a leper-like thing, detached itself from her and walked beside her to the end of the pavement, the end of the road and beyond. (50-51)

Outraged at the brutal implications of the "Consent Terms," Simrit feels very diminished and humiliated. The huge amounts of tax she will have to pay on an income she cannot even use are staggering and she feels she is an "over-loaded donkey. . . with its back breaking, and no one doing anything about it, not because they can't see it, but because it's a donkey and loads are for donkeys." (56) Woman is just a beast of burden. In the renewed anguish, while talking to Som's lawyer, she sees her life with Som as no different from her present one:

> Maybe she had always been an animal, only a nice, obedient, domestic one, sitting on a cushion, doing as she was told. And in return she had been fed and sheltered. (57)

The agony that the woman feels after divorce in Indian society springs directly from the private world of the author, in whose own life divorce was still a recent happening. Coming from the first-hand experience of the author, the description of Simrit's suffering has an intensity which can carry the reader along and which also gives the "impression" of the novel being a feminist text. However, the rest of the novel is far from being a feminist narrative.

Simrit looks like a "liberated" woman who has the courage to break a long relationship which has become meaningless with no sense of companionship or partnership between husband and wife. But she opts for divorce when already another male support is waiting for her outside marriage. The situation in fact is rather a fantasy. She steps out of the sheltered world of Som not to live a life on her own, in her own way but to step into the shadow of another man. She really does not have to struggle alone for survival, neither at the economic level nor at the emotional one which leaves woman even more disintegrated and vulnerable. In Indian society where men hesitate to marry even a widow with a child, what to talk of a divorcee, can we really find a man who will so readily embrace a middle-aged woman with huge economic liabilities and a host of children to take care of?

It is in fact the character of Raj that makes the novel, if not an anti-feminist text, at least an embarrassment for feminism. Despite some feminist sentiments expressed by him now and then, his total behaviour merely reinforces the patriarchal myth of man's superiority over woman. He does feel genuinely concerned about Simrit at times: "First it had been her husband. Next it would be her children. Woman for use had been the rule too long." (38) He seems to respect her independence and her individuality: "She didn't need a man for identity or status." (139) In his "conscious" generosity he can go a step further: "It was not a question of Simrit for himself—at least not until he had some sign from her. It was Simrit for *herself* he wanted, Simrit to forsake her shadows, and begin to live." (Emphasis added, 167) However, the patriarchal attitudes are so deeply ingrained in him that they have become a natural part of his personality. He constantly maintains a stance of superiority towards Simrit. Anything that Simrit says or does is inferior, faulty and unimpressive. She quotes something from Aurobindo but he is not "impressed." (34) His infuriating assumption is that Simrit has not lived simply because so far she has not lived the way he thinks life should be lived. He almost bullies Simrit with his intellectual superiority. Language, which can be "an arena for struggle" for two unequal forces, here becomes merely an instrument of patriarchal oppression, never giving space to "feminist resistance to oppression."[3] Raj either "explains" something to Simrit or says "severely" that she must know more about this or that, or he simply "orders." Simrit on her part accepts her inferiority: she "confesses" about her ignorance, even though a short while ago she had corrected Raj about the marble table-top; she is apologetic about not knowing enough about a thing like petroleum. Knowledge and language both become instruments of intellectual terrorism in the hands of Raj (Simrit was first attracted to Raj by his talk only and she continues to honour every statement of his, however superficial or biased it may be, as great or simply invaluable).

For all his claims of concern for Simrit, one wonders whether a person like Raj can understand or share her agony and tensions. Standing on the high pedestal he has chosen for himself, can he ever be a partner or companion to Simrit? Oppressed by her immediate problems, she says, "I feel so disorganized" (14) and the "angel" (in fact this is how Simrit sees him all along) from the heights drops a sermon on this country and the times, on things being not in their places. The point of suffering is blown aside by the wind of words.

The climax of Raj's chauvinistic attitude comes with his one-sided announcement of marriage before Ram Krishan. Raj who had claimed to retrieve Simrit for her own sake ironically does not even ask her about marriage, a decision even Simrit feels was supposed to be at least mutual. The need for marriage is actually more desperately Raj's than Simrit's who had already tasted this institutionalized relationship for too long to be tempted into another such bond so soon. Once this "sign" of love has come from Simrit, Raj, like any other male chauvinist, starts taking her for granted. And Raj's indoctrination in the patriarchal set-up with its unequal gender roles is so deep-rooted and so thorough that he finds nothing unnatural in this kind of commanding of woman.

The major flaw in the novel is a total absence of irony both in characterization and in the narrative. If only Raj's character were treated with irony, the paradoxes—his occasional feminist sentiments and his strictly patriarchal behaviour—in his character would have been resolved. It is Raj's unqualified elevation as hero in the absence of all irony that makes the novel totally ignorant of the power structure in the patriarchal set-up. Equally damaging to the novel are the lack of irony in the narrator's stance, and a ready acceptance by the protagonist of the uneven sex-assumptions in social set-up.

Simrit fails to see Raj's prejudices, biases, superficialities. She blindly adores him and feels exhilarated in his company: a smile from him "radiated an atmosphere of suppressed jubilation that lapped around her in waves." (7) Genuinely grateful to him she feels "Raj had uncarved her," (11) never for a moment suspecting that Raj might be only carving her into a shape he himself likes. She gets easily subdued under his over-confident postures. She is taken aback at the abrupt announcement of marriage, yet surprisingly no protest comes forth from her. The indoctrination of unequal gender roles promoted right from the birth, sometimes subtly, sometimes not so subtly, is so deep-rooted in Simrit as well that she too accepts the sex-assumptions as natural and even remains oblivious to any injustice inherent in them.

Simrit's over-dependence on Raj is a central paradox in the novel. In a novel that seemed to begin with a woman's decision to seek freedom, ironically it is man who constantly provides the norm, and woman's dependence on man is seen as something inevitable and natural. In a narrative full of ironic situations and characters, one is surprised by a total lack of irony from the author at any level. And it is this absence of irony which makes the novel so oblivious to sex-discrimination in power division.

The ending of the novel is particularly disappointing. Despite the sudden one-sided announcement of marriage by Raj, Simrit continues in her euphoric admiration of Raj, "Men like him were born to lead and educate." (236) She does not even realize that she who believed herself to be a woman who had "never accepted a world where men did things and woman waited for them," (6) has in fact once again become the one who will take orders. Only this time, the one to give orders may not be so directly opposed to her tastes and values as her first husband was. She in fact just passes on from one man's world into another man's. The resolution just affirms the status quo and the heroine's grateful acceptance of her lot (which implied from the author's point-of-view a happy beginning for the heroine) makes an artificial power structure look like a natural one. Apart from the fact of divorce, Simrit herself remains a stereotype submitting to the idea of male superiority and male dominance. Though the novel has data good enough to make a feminist novel, which should centrally concern itself with the issue of power, yet, in the absence of irony at any level, it remains a novel by a woman, about a woman, where contrary to woman's cause the status quo is uncritically accepted as some inevitable law.

In a more recent novel, *Rich Like Us* (1985), Sahgal has transcended the personal introverted world of *The Day in Shadow*. Here she takes stock of woman's situation in the patriarchal society more objectively where power is monopolized by men. The novel of course is not concerned only with feminist issues; its canvas is much vaster and texture thicker. Yet as far as the woman's experience is concerned the novel presents it along the lines of feminist ideology. Though even in *The Day in Shadow*, Sahgal had tried to make the narrative look more than merely a story of a particular woman by bringing in discussions on Hinduism and Christianity and by giving occasional glimpses of the contemporary political scene, yet the novel really does not go beyond the limited personal world of Simrit's problems, with the huge tax as a rather gross symbol of man's cruelty to woman. The accounts of the parliament and the petroleum ministry do not get integrated into the main narrative while the discussions on Hinduism and Christianity, apart from being naive, get coloured by the uneven positions taken by Raj and Simrit. In *Rich Like Us*, however, the personal and the political worlds are very skilfully integrated. Through shifting perspectives, Sahgal is able to weave diverse experiences into one comprehensive whole where nothing remains an isolated segment. Unlike *The Day in Shadow*, in *Rich Like Us*, the uneven division of power between the sexes is accepted neither as natural nor inevitable. Rather by framing the female experience in the broader political context of Emergency, the arbitrariness of power distribution in gender roles is further emphasized.

In the present patriarchal set-up, man is not merely the master of his own life, he also creates woman's destiny for her. With a wife and a newly born infant back home in India, Ram is still free to court Rose in England. When he realizes that he cannot use Rose as a pastime, he very deliberately and cautiously starts building an "emotional labyrinth"[3] around Rose, "erecting a world around her, drawing her deep into it, the door shutting, Rose inside." (41) But once he is confident that Rose is too deep in love to ever desert him, he candidly announces that he already has a wife and a son in India. Totally insensitive to Mona's anguish, he marries Rose in the same house, but a marriage which Rose never thinks legal or religious. Wives for Ram are things to be used and not discarded but kept aside for future needs if any he may have.

Mona is useful as the mother to his son Dev and as the manager of the household while Rose is good as a mistress-wife, always showering love and attention on Ram with not even a child of her own to claim her attention or time.

In *The Day in Shadow,* Som's cruelty towards Simrit was very obvious in the form of tax in the Consent Terms. But *Rich Like Us* builds around more subtle forms of persecution of women where the "blood" does not show even though the wounds may be much deeper. Ram's insensitivity to the suffering of both his wives is appalling, When Ram returns to Rose after spending the better part of the night with Mona, the restless and unhappy Rose protests that she cannot continue like this with Ram living with two wives. But Ram very complacently laughs off her agony as a joke, "Lord Krishna had three hundred." (60) To another retort, he good-humoredly replies, "Muslims can have *only* four at a time. We are more adventurous, even polyandrous." (61) Once he meets Marcella, he as lightly discards Rose as he had earlier discarded Mona. He does not even make any attempt at subterfuge. With absolutely no regard for Rose's feelings, he comes back home, "his footfall open and normal on the stair at three a.m.," (104) and then "in the utter stillness the thin sobbing sound of pure grief no one was meant to hear, froze Mona's tears in Rose's eyes." (105) More than anything else, it is their identical suffering which ultimately binds Mona and Rose together.

Another dimension of this not so visible form of persecution is that the victims, instead of hating the oppressor, start hating fellow victims. Needless to say how well such an arrangement suits the oppressor. The situation in which Mona and Rose find themselves is in fact a creation of Ram but it means endless agony for both, where ironically they start hating each other for no fault of either. While Rose endlessly wishes for Mona's death, simultaneously realizing the wickedness of such wishes, Mona takes the drastic step of attempting suicide, constant agony at times pushes Rose to the brink of madness. (98) Mona is dying of cancer but Ram does not have time even to listen about it. He is too busy listening to the woes of another European woman whose husband does not pay adequate attention to her. It is a dismal world where Ram proudly passes on his legacy to Dev. "A man has to get his experience somewhere" (181) is Ram's response to Rose informing him about Dev abducting girls from Miranda House and taking them to private rooms at the Ashoka.

The women in this novel are certainly more aware of the injustice done to them by man, but habit makes them a willing prisoner in this world of exploitation and injustice. It may not be entirely irrelevant here to repeat Beckett: "Habit is the ballast that chains the dog to his vomit."[4] Knowing fully well what Ram is, Rose, out of sheer habit, is still in a hurry to reach him when she is slowed down by the procession on her way back from Minnie's. Love becomes a trap for Rose and, despite her suffering within marriage, she just cannot bear the idea of divorce, after getting used to living with Ram all these years. This also explains why women accept the order of life created for them by men without any protest. Mona at one stage is given a separate flat to live as an "honourably retired wife" 163) and later Rose is also made to live separately for five years, without even having the benefit of a reason or an explanation. What sounds like benevolence— "it would be a separation, not a divorce," (201) Ram tells Rose—is actually selfishness to keep her available for use at his own convenience.

In this male world where men pass orders and women carry them out, where men create situations and women live them, the only hope for a woman is another woman. Their experiences being identical, women alone can understand each other. Even though the need for "sisterhood" or "sister solidarity" is not so strongly felt by women in the Third World in general, yet in the educated, urban middle-classes in India, the problems of women are still quite identical to those in the West.[5] Hence we find in Sahgal's world, which is essentially the urban upper-class, "sisterhood" is surely one way to cope with male aggression. Mona in the extreme of despair gets welded to Rose and they become "sisters." She has a desire to know more about Rose, about her parents, and to share her childhood memories. No wonder Mona on her deathbed looks constantly at Rose for comfort, for peace, for assurance about her son and daughter-in-law rather than the husband who is also at her bedside. And Rose in her hour of grief and loneliness banks upon Sonali for solace and help.

In this world, Sonali is the only woman who is free to live life in her own way. But she has to pay a heavy price to maintain her freedom. To live a life free from subjugation and subordination, she has to remain single all her life. Entering into a partnership with a man means submitting to him completely. Sonali had realized it early in her life when she saw her friend Bimmie turned into an "inanimate object" (56) with "manacled hands resting submissively in her red silk lap" (53) even on her wedding day.

A man's experience and a woman's experience are seen as clearly different in the novel. Ravi's division of responses to communism into two categories of Our Side and Other Side is simplistic, and makes Sonali reject:

> I think he said that because he was a man. He had never fought a battle for freedom, never been patted down firmly when his sap was rising, never had a sari throttling his legs, making walking in the wind and running to catch a bus a threat to life and limb, never had his mother set up a howl when he went and got a haircut. He had no idea what the simplest subjugations were all about. I, who did, had no intention of chaining myself to any doctrine when I had just lost some of my chains. (112)

This kind of sensitive and discriminating awareness about woman's experience is absent in *The Day in Shadow*.

The details of women's exploitation in the Indian society keep unfolding at several levels besides the experience of female protagonists. A number of male voices vehemently expose the violence done to the women who mattered so much to them, making the novel a far more intense and legitimate feminist text. For example, the words of Sonali's grandfather written in 1915 give poignant accounts of gruesome murders committed in the name of Sati, including that of his own mother. The sad realization of a grown-up son about his mother makes the plight of the woman more telling:

> She was a good wife, I used to think. But now I believe all wives are good because they have little choice. The nuns in nunneries are good. Little children in their cradles are good. The Hindu wife is a Hindu wife and can be nothing else. And it is not until we can take the goodness of women less for granted that we shall learn to value it. (143)

The narrative is full of reminders of injustices and violence done to women in our society, e.g. the armless beggar's account of the atrocities on women committed by the police and that of the disappearance of his own wife who, like many others, must have fallen prey to the lust of brick-kiln owners. And there is that almost choric voice of Keshav, Sonali's father, reminding of injustice done to women in India right since its mythic antiquity, with Sita as the archetype of the wronged woman. Unlike *The Day in Shadow* which almost naturalizes the arbitrary power division between the genders, *Rich Like Us* firmly rejects the arbitrary distribution of power, be it on the purely political level as it was during Emergency or on the inter-personal and familial level as in the gender roles in the society.

NOTES

1. Nayantara Sahgal, *The Day in Shadow* (Delhi: Vikas, 1971), p. 4.
2. Robert Stan, "Mikhail Bakhtin and Left Cultural Critique," in

E. Ann Kaplan, ed., *Postmodernism and Its Discontents: Theories, Practices* (London: Verso, 1988), p. 123.

3. Nayantara Sahgal, *Rich Like Us* (1985; rpt., London: Sceptre, 1987), p. 43.
4. Samuel Beckett, "Proust" (1931) in *Proust and Three Dialogues with Georges Duthuit* (London: Calderce Boyars, 1965, 1970), p. 19.
5. Maithreyi Krishna Raj, "Women and Cultural Change," in Karuna Mary Braganza and Saleem Peeradina, *Cultural Forces Shaping India*, ed. (New Delhi: Macmillan India, 1989), p. 187.

Female Perspective in the Fiction of Mulk Raj Anand

MINA SURJIT SINGH

> And the Lord God formed man of the dust of the ground, and breathed into his nostrils the breath of life, and man became a living soul . . . and he took one of his ribs, and closed up the flesh instead thereof; And the rib, which the Lord God had taken from man, made he a woman, and brought her unto the man. . . . And Adam said, this is now bone of my bones, and flesh of my flesh: She shall be called Woman, because she was taken out of Man. Therefore shall a man leave his father and his mother, and shall cleave unto his wife: and they shall be one flesh.
>
> Genesis (1:7, 21, 22, 23, 24)

The purpose of this Genesitic reference is not to embellish my piece of writing with a doctrinally authenticated account of man's status, but to lend credence to the position of man's female counterpart in the Adamic infrastructure and to emphasize the descensional course it has taken after Adam's banishment from the idyllic Garden of Eden. The women that inhabit Anand's world are all victims of a habitat where man is assigned the pride of place and thus allowed the socio-religious sanction of female relegation. If woman, as Adam christened his female counterpart, were to be interpreted as woe-man (with its all-too-obvious implications of temptation), then man's dominance would concomitantly assume the proportions of a Darwinian struggle and justification for survival.

What is attempted, then, is not a detailed examination of Anand's projection of feminine nature in all its multifacetedness but an analysis of womanhood in the specific context of woman in her societal trappings, the woman-woman relationship, the man-woman relationship which holds special focus and woman's attempts at emancipation.

In her individual capacity, woman is placed in the traditional socio-cultural milieu of a conventional Hindu society wherein she is projected and recognized as everybody but her vital self which remains unrealized, caged and humiliated beyond repair. She is inauspicious, a witch, a prostitute, a cow cowered into docility, but unelevated to sanctity. The cruelty and depravity is further aggravated by familial apathy and Lajwanti and her likes seem doomed to a life of abject human degradation. Anand's sensitive handling of the malady arouses a conscious awareness of this facet of Indian womanhood. The author initiates the narrative of *Lajwanti* on a note of terror with the hapless young girl Lajwanti, fleeing the advances of her tyrannical, pock-marked, brother-in-law Jaswant. Her plight/flight becomes the plight of hundreds of women similarly circumstanced, but what jolts one out of apathetic complacency is the unfathomed depth of mental subjugation and conditioned responses. While her conscious mind revolts at the prospect of her violation, subliminally she is still the depressed woman, fettered by convention. Her guilt at her conduct reflects in her vacillations: "She might have borne the humiliation. She might have given in to Jaswant. She could have closed her eyes. Her husband Balwant was away at college. Her benevolent father-in-law would not have known. And the mother-in-law, who wanted son's son, more than anything else, would not have worried, even if she had come to know." (*SS*, 87)

The story opens in a temper of urgency, one feels anything may happen, that the hounded Lajwanti may suddenly leap out of her imprisoned body and break the boundaries of her painful existence. Still, for all the violence and hope generated initially, one is left disappointingly convinced towards the end, that in the conflict of individual desire and stifling social convention, the individual is mercilessly sacrificed. The futility of Lajwanti's rebellion in the face of unobviated trauma strikes home ruthlessly, when in an attempt to drown herself, she realizes that "unfortunately for her she [is] a swimmer." (*SS*, 105) She can visualize no escape even in the darkness of death. (*SS*, 106) All through Lajwanti's chastisement, Anand focuses his reader's attention on the wildly fluttering caged maina bird. By natural implication, then, Lajwanti becomes prototypical of this pathetic image of Indian womanhood, shrunk to a half-size, a half-life.

It is disheartening to note that in the Anandian microcosm is also evidenced an inherent antagonism between the homogeneous female species. Aside from an odd occasion wherein a tortured Lajo might find temporary succour in the person of a Shrimati Dayal, the older woman is projected in the unfavourable light of being largely responsible for inhibiting the amelioration of the underdog. Contrary to expectation, the mother-in-law rarely fits into the widely acclaimed slot of surrogate mother and is, not unfrequently, witnessed conniving with males in their vital business of taming the shrew. Lajwanti's mother-in-law's major concern is the propagation of the male species, without constraint. Kesaro[2] smothers Panchi under a feigned maternal affection which smacks of incest, a hypocrisy which stands jarringly exposed under Gauri's sudden outburst, "If you have no husband, go to someone else, but do not lay hands on my husband! . . . Go, get out! . . . Evil woman! You want two husbands! Your own for beating you and mine for loving you. (*OW*, 97) Even the emancipated Miss Young considers Gauri sinful and tries to convert her. And, Gauri stands betrayed by the redeeming mother-daughter relationship too. Her mother Lakshmi, the one woman she could turn to for redress ironically barters her away for the price of a cow. Several are the instances that can be quoted, of this none-too-fictional female apathy. Mr. Gopi Goel's (*SS*, 273) arraignment of native adolescent tendency in the sweeper girl, Sajani, for blandishments, speaks for the inadequacy of her own relationship with her spouse. This somewhat vicarious older-woman stance assumes the proportions of a stock conduit for the frustrations of unfulfilled youth, relegated middle age and neglected superannuation within the parameters of the man-woman relationship.

As regards the man-woman relationship, the ironic contradiction in the Biblically conceived Adam-Eve union and the actualized association in fallen man's world is amply evident in the near-total lack of communication between his male and female characters. Anand's protagonists are all spirited young men seeking fulfilment, but what is significantly lacking in his men out on their self-realization trips is the need for a relationship with the other, another human being in the form of a female, for complete self-knowledge. This female principle or "anima" in Jungian terms is, "An inherited collective image of woman [which] exists in a man's unconscious with the help of which he apprehends the nature of woman"[3] and since there is a connectedness between man and woman in the nature of things, it is necessary to establish a relationship with this female counterpart. In the absence of such effort, his men remain hollow and his women unredeemed. His women are dumb, mute creatures caught in a concentrated struggle wherein the principal instinct is for survival in a predominantly male world, and hence incapable of even comprehending life's possibilities beyond the merely biological.

The initiative therefore lies with the male, who comprehensively fails. Panchi feels "like a bull going off to marry the little cow Gauri" (*OW*, 8) with a temperamental perversity that entitles him to the "prize of a girl—a girl whom he could fold in his arms at night and kick during the day." (*OW*, 5) Roopa has resentment, a spite against the whole world that her inner impulses always remained where they were, incommunicable even to her man. (*SS*, 270) The couched hypocrisy of Shri and Shrimati Goel's uttering is all too evident in Shrimati Gopi Goel's despondent thoughts on her relationship with her husband. "Could she restore between herself and him . . . the actuality of any connection now. At the end of her heart's echo, there was a sinking feeling that there had been no connection at all. Only he had taken her after their marriage as a kind of ritual," a ritual which, "had been repeated for five years, becoming completely mechanical, without the intervention of words—automatic, like the gestures of old puppets. (*SS*, 275)

"The Two Lady Rams" (*SS*, 244) is symptomatic of the social trend of infidelity which seems to have entered the souls of the privileged male class. Sir Jhinda Ram's replacement of the fifty-five year old Sukhi with the twenty-five year old Shakuntala, smacks of an obvious attempt to hold on to a fast disappearing youth and Sukhi's battle for her conjugal rights is no burlesque on female vanity but a pathetic scramble for an identity which hinges on masculine acceptance, in the face of scant else for reprieve. It is not my objective to highlight the much-acclaimed Anandian advocacy of humanism which manifests itself, in ample measure, in his sympathetic treatment of the underprivileged. I am, however, tempted to mention the celibate and compassionate Dr. Mahendra's magnanimous exoneration of the representative Dr. Batra, ascribing his philandering and variegated passions to the unfortunate situation of man in not being allowed to choose his own spouse. I quote, "I am not concerned with religion Miss Young. I am talking of what actually happens to people. Dr. Batra is probably suffering from the usual frustrations of our country-men whose marriages are arranged. As he cannot get satisfaction from his wife, he seeks this in other women. He may have offended you but he is to be pitied." (*OW*, 187-88) What would follow by natural implication, then, is an extension of the same sympathetic understanding towards women which, surprisingly or not surprisingly, fails to come forth. As such, pity seems to acquire the dubiety of privileged sanction.

On this dismal firmament of Indian Womanhood shines, Gauri, the brightest star on Anand's canvas, with incipient temerity culminating in a flash of brilliance which explodes the Sita myth[4] into a thousand fragments and redeems thereby, the female species through Gauri's symbolic emancipation on the road to Hoshiarpur. The leitmotif of *The Old Woman and the Cow*, developed against the background of a claustrophobic social culture, is movement and each conclusive phase of movement corresponds with a progression in Gauri's journey to emancipation. Wedded to Panchi, "the holy bull," Gauri, "the gentle cow" moves from Piplan Kalan to Chota Piplan, a movement symbolically coinciding with a considerable fall in her fortunes. Badgered by a nagging aunt-in-law, Kesaro, the couple move to a life on their own with the benevolent potter Rafique Chacha who offers them shelter. The couple, however, are not destined to live together in peace. The spoilt Panchi's personal weakness and erraticism compounded by the failure of the monsoons and the none-too-meek Kesaro's haranguing, result in Gauri's ouster from her husband's home on flimsy hypothesis.

This finds Gauri back in Piplan Kalan, now significantly altered by expected, mutual attitudinal changes. She is thus callously bartered away by a jealous and lecherous uncle, Amru, and a greedy mother, Lakshmi, for cash and the wiping out of mortgage on two houses and a cow, to the old and vulgar widower Seth Jai Ram Das in Hoshiarpur. It is here that the cow analogy reaches its highest transparency and this one gross transactional act initiates Gauri's metamorphosis from meekness to an enduring strength and power which forms the basis of a personal faith and religion. In Hoshiarpur, she is shifted from the Seth's house to Dr. Mahendra's hospital, with fever, and it is with this good soul's assistance that she is freed from the clutches of the old Seth who wishes to lend respectability to his lasciviousness by suggesting that she put on the customary "chaddar" and live as his wife. At the hospital, she has a foretaste of independence when she begins to help out with the nursing. Her exposure to the advances of the dissolute Dr. Batra, and the resultant break-up of the hospital, help her build up a resilience which sees her through the emotional crisis of being disclaimed, a second time, by her husband. The much wished-for reunion with Panchi is everything that Gauri desires, but unfortunately, Gauri significantly returns to Chota Piplan after sunset. Driven once again by personal inadequacy and viscous small-town gossip, the small-town Panchi tries to beat the now-big-town Gauri into a confession of infidelity, which, significantly, never comes forth.

We see Gauri suddenly rising in stature when she does not feel the need to prove her chastity to unchaste people. Suffused with a strength with which she refurnishes her lost dignity, she breaks out against all taboos with full-mouthed intensity and sadly but surely steps out onto the road to emancipation. While Gauri's return to Piplan Kalan severed her links with her maternal home permanently, her return to Chota Piplan drives the final nail into the coffin of her alliance with Panchi, whose second betrayal is more than she can forgive. Albeit the city with its multivalent ambience may not promise unalloyed happiness, nevertheless, it does offer hope of deliverance from Adamic cleaving, and the spurious righteousness of masculine hegemony disintegrates in the face of Gauri's new-found sense of freedom.

NOTES

1. M.K. Naik, ed., *Selected Short Stories of Mulk Raj Anand* (New Delhi: Arnold Heinemann, 1977), p. 85. Hereafter *SS*.
2. Mulk Raj Anand, *The Old Woman and the Cow* (Bombay: Kutub Popular, 1960). Hereafter *OW*.
3. Carl Jung, *Two Essays of Analytical Psychology* (New York: Meridian, 1956), pp. 200-1.
4. Meenakshi Mukherjee, *The Twice-Born Fiction: Themes and Techniques of the Indian Novel in English* (New Delhi: Heinmann, 1971), pp. 163-64.

Padma's Tragedy: A Feminist Deconstruction of Rushdie's *Midnight's Children*

CHARU VERMA

Padma is the companion, nurse, and audience of Saleem Sinai in *Midnight's Children.* She figures only in the narrational perspective of Saleem's narrative. She has no role in the "recalled" action of the novel. Her absence from the actional perspective seems to have been used as an easy pretext by critics for not concentrating on her character. The present paper is a feminist deconstruction of the novel and aims at highlighting the strategies used by Saleem the narrator to give Padma a short shrift. These strategies reflect certain attitudes and ideological positions which reveal this otherwise remarkable novel to be a very sexist text. A humanistic focusing on Padma involves resisting the thrust of the male text. But such a focusing enables us to notice several disturbing sexist biases both in Rushdie and his narrator-protagonist.

Deconstruction by definition requires a resisting reader. Most critics have read the novel exactly as it wishes to be read. Thus, *Midnight's Children* has been studied as an autobiographical novel, as a political and historical novel, as a technically virtuoso performance, and as a work in which realism and fantasy combine to form a mixed mode. Rushdie himself calls it "a book that discusses the relationships between history and private lives."[1] David W. Atkinson analyzes *Midnight's Children* as an "autobiographical novel, projecting grandiosely the 'macro-reality' of national concerns as an extension of the 'micro-reality' of self."[2] Corall Ann Howells calls the both "a self-consciously autobiographical fiction" which is explicit about "its interpretative processes and rhetorical strategies for reading and rewriting history."[3] Dieter Reimenschneider writes, "Salman Rushdie's *Midnight's Children* . . . is essentially concerned with man's quest for his identity."[4] Rushdie's use of magical realism has similarly been commended by several critics. William Walsh writes, "Its astonishing staple is composed of elements of magic and fantasy, the grimmest realism, extravagant farce, multi-mirrored analogy and a potent symbolic structure."[5] Meenakshi Mukherjee comments, "In its inclusive and extravagant sweep the novel gathers up fragments of history, memory and fantasy to create a contemporary legend out of a sub-continent."[6] Very few critics have discussed Padma, although Uma Parameswaram says that Padma "is many things within the novel, and certainly deserves a full length study."[7] There has not been a proper consideration either of Padma or the novel's sexist bias. The present paper concentrates on Padma, though it is felt that the sexist bias operates against nearly all the women characters in the novel. This bias works though arbitrarily marginalizing them. It makes the book look overly manly.

Feminist criticism has not yet succeeded in evolving a distinct methodology of its own. Toril Moi, Susan Gubar, Sandra Gilbert and several other feminist critics have been conducting sensational research on sexism in society and culture. Feminist criticism relies upon feminism, especially as it has been developing since the 1960s. Basically, the feminists oppose the male view of the universe: man, not woman—not even man plus woman—is the measure of things. Patriarchy established itself as a social constant and the male set himself as the human "norm." In reference to him, woman is the "other" and is constantly and wrongly diminished. Kate Millett in *Sexual Politics* calls it the "power nexus": Discussing Henry Miller's *Sexus*, she writes "a male assertion of dominance over a weak, compliant, and rather unintelligent female. It is a case of sexual politics at the fundamental level of copulation."[8] Sheila Mcleod in *Lawerence's Men and Women* describes the power nexus:

> Women's work has long been downgraded and devalued when compared to men's work, male muscular strength has been prized above the female capacity for physical endurance; men have been the owners of wealth and property, the wielders of authority, the holders of power, the achievers, the doers, the go-getters, while women have been barred from such apparently desirable positions or behaviours.[9]

Many distinctions along the sexual lines are artificially constructed for privileging the male sex. The distribution of sex roles highlights man as ambitious and woman as domesticated.

Padma is a victim of this male hegemonic view. Occasionally, she appears to be the reader's surrogate in the book, but the first thing to remember about her is—should be—that she is a woman. Her characterization is managed through two prominent strategies: strategies of absences and those of presences. In Padma's case, most presences are openly derogatory, while the inferrable positives in her being are simply absenced.

Padma is most presented in the narrative through her animal physicality. Saleem introduces her as "Padma—our plump Padma . . . sulking magnificently. (She can't read . . . Padma: strong, jolly, a consolation for my last days. But definitely a bitch-in-the-manger.)"[10] This exposition does not create a positive image of her, and it is followed by a still more damaging insinuation: "She attempts to cajole me from my desk: 'Eat, na, food is spoiling.' I remain stubbornly hunched over paper. 'But what is so precious,' Padma demands, her right hand slicing the air updownup in exasperation, 'to need all this writing-shiting?' . . . Padma snorts. Wrist smacks against forehead. 'Okay, starve starve, who cares two pice?' Another louder, conclusive snort. . . . Thick of waist, somewhat hairy of forearm, she flounces." (24) It is noteworthy that for one good detail (a consolation for my last days), several derogatory and diminishing details are piled up one after another. She is compared to a bitch, she cajoles, snorts; moves her hand updownup and so on. This suggests a temperamental reluctance on the part of Saleem to allow her anything more than a comic status. She is not only illiterate and ignorant but is ugly as well. She is described as fat, "thick of waist"—and "somewhat hairy of forearm." These are not at all pleasing details. Her simplicity is also held up against her.

Padma's functions reinforce her as a mere stereotype. She cooks food for Saleem, makes his bed, sulks when she is ignored and performs all Martha's tasks. Her functions are all taken too much for granted, devalued, marginalized, They are considered to be so petty as to deserve no notice or appreciation. Her honest, simple responses deserve to be refined by "the" man who claims that he knows better. Writing is Saleem's territory, and she is alien here. His writing activity and his manly "penly" preoccupation with say, history, time and politics, are arbitrarily privileged as if cooking or making bed were not at all important. She is good only as audience, a receiver, for Saleem is the giver. Saleem often mocks her for being silly, and tries to assert his dominance by saying, "I attempt to educate her." (38) Saleem, like Rushdie behind him, claims that he knows India, her people, politics, sociology. How is it that he should be content with describing Padma as an illiterate without also pointing to the socio-economic conditions which keep women uneducated here? This is clearly a case of sexual separatism. Roles, traits, qualities, profession, etc. are divided along the sexual lines. Cooking food, washing clothes, raising children are all woman's jobs; the world out there is regarded as man's area. Actually, these roles and jobs are merely different, not superior or inferior. But since man holds power, he elevates his roles to a higher level and degrades woman activities. Difference is not superiority or inferiority. Indeed, cooking food is no less essential than, say, contemplating history or writing autobiography.

Quite a negative mystique is built around Padma's desire

for Saleem. Saleem the desexed man cannot bring her any physical fulfilment, but then he, in his consciousness of his barrenness, reduces Padma to a mere bundle of sexual urges. It is insinuated that man is higher on the sexual plane as well. Saleem highlights Padma's "suggestive" sexual reference as though she were vulgar or a nympho-maniac. What could be wrong if Padma does feel sexually deprived? Saleem takes such a long time to admit to her that he is no good in bed. Padma has been duped into assuming that he must be physically fit; how could she guess the truth? It is very reductive of Saleem to see her only as a bitch in heat. He should be able to appreciate the sentiment behind her administering of the "magic" aphrodisiac herbs, all for her lover, but he feels outraged at such a waste of time. He cannot see the solicitude underlying Padma's venture, and it is dismissed as a manifestation of her heat. She is seldom appreciated. A woman even at her best is not trusted.

Padma's needs are emotional and empathic and it is perverse of Saleem to suggest that she needs only sex. The spontaneous manner in which she demands to be his bride suggests that sex isn't everything to her. In fact, she would be happy if Saleem could give her some good, loving moments, moments of sympathy and nearness, of caring and touch. But the "city boy" has no time for this stupid village girl. Her only sin is that she is wholly, soulfully in love with him and love has become her trap. For a traditional Hindu woman, the decision to stay with a barren, Muslim widower is simply radical. It is a testimony to her deep love for him. Given the possibility that Saleem is disintegrating and dying, the decision is overwhelming because of its courageous, decisive enormity. She seems to have sold out all her future for the sake of her love. Still, she is a mere utility object. Saleem desires warmth, care, food etc., and she is supposed to fulfil all his needs. But in return, she is treated as a bad liability by him, Saleem has no time to sit and reflect as to whether he is being just to her. It is difficult to justify his heartless, superficial compliments to her: "I don't blame Padma," when all along he is very prone to insinuating gratuitous comparisons, all to the disadvantage of Padma.

Saleem cannot forgive Padma's absences. He needs her and therefore takes her presence for granted, but then being a male he hates to acknowledge his need. This is double ingratitude. He diminishes her and exploits her, and still expects her to be grateful to him. It is highly creditable of this woman that she loves him and is ready to accept his inadequacies without condescension. It is to be remembered that unlike Saleem whose adventures have included visiting prostitutes and entertaining incestuous desires, Padma has solid moral and ethical values. Why then should she be treated with so much contempt? What has she done to merit persistent equation with dung? Why is she debunked as superstitious? Why are her sincere, sentimental speeches mimicked into a joke? What, on the other hand, is so special about Saleem that he should dismiss her affectionate attendant at his feet as a distraction or nuisance?

Although Padma is Saleem's constant companion and audience, interlocuter and critic, the moments of crucial decisions or intensity in the narrational perspective simply leave her out. The two most crucial "narrational" moments—his decision to begin the narrative in chapter I and his reluctance to come out with the emergency truths in chapter 29—do not include Padma. The strategy used at these intense moments is that a woman will be a nuisance, for no woman can understand man's deep agony. Therefore, Padma too cannot sympathize with Saleem. Hence her erasure at these points. One recalls how Grass's *The Tin Drum*, a major influence on *Midnight's Children*, begins by introducing Bruno, Oskar's keeper in the narrational perspective, and how much dignity Oskar awards to him by asking him to do a whole chapter of the narrative. Padma, by contrast, is consistently diminished. It is safe to assume that Saleem's narrative, like Saleem, believes that it can easily do without her: "Padma must take a back seat." (385)

Padma's portrait is composed more of gaps and absences

than of presences. Her absences relate to such crucial matters as her background, her past, her family, her social contexts. She seems to be characterized only as a footnote to Saleem the narrator, and is shown to have only a vacuum by way of her human contexts. She is given no independent, contingent identity, her past, her family, her story, all are crashed. She is negated when Saleem discusses politics or history. Her story is discardable like dung. Saleem ignores her, but we cannot and we should not. Saleem, in fact, goes three generations back to start his story and claims that in order to know him, we will have to swallow a multitude of lives; but he does not feel any need to perspectivize Padma in time or space at all. "Grieve for Saleem. . . ." (345) But what about Padma's tragedy? Where is Padma's past, where are her parents, her earlier locations, her adventures? Where is her story? They are all lost in the man's story which alone is considered worth telling.

How do we reconcile the above analysis with the textual fact that Padma is described as the lotus-goddess? Perhaps there is no paradox at all. All male dominant ideologies need to compensate man's actual degradation and exploitation of woman by doling out to her some imaginary, mystified space in which she is worshipped as a goddess. This mystified space is the opinion of her sex. This unreal space is a device to legitimatize her actual exploitation day in, day out. Padma's description as the lotus-goddess is no compliment to her, though she may think it is, because she is a willing dupe of the sexist politics of India. She is Saleem's despised other, usable, exploitable, disposable. She is, in other words, a mere commodity. She is not only a slave but also a perfect fool. It is disturbing to see Saleem making so much of his victimization and tragedy but simply marginalizing the tragedy that is Padma's. Since women constitute a half of India, Padma's tragedy finds its echo in this other India's tragedy. Padma's tragedy is no less terrifying than Saleem's but the narrative being phallocentric, her tragedy is wholly, though arbitrarily, appropriated by that of Midnight's son.

Padma is reconciled to male domination and is willing to change her name from Padma Mongril to Naseem Sinai. She is amongst those women who are men's women. She has internalized men's arbitrary characterization of women, and, in fact, behaves more like how men would expect her to behave than how she as woman can or should. We should not regard Padma as a model for Indian women. Even as it is, she is projected as a pathetic victim who does not exist as a free, self-willing actor, but only as her master's voice, without knowing it.

Midnight's Children has several virtues, but its sexist bias reveals an ideology which in the 1980s appears obnoxious and grotesque to all those who believe in the equality of sexes. Padma is a stereotype, overly-diminished image of woman in a man-dominant society; in this image, woman is marginal, while man's story is the story. Objectively viewed, Padma's story cannot be any the less important or tragic than Saleem's, but the latter effectively subsumes it within itself.

NOTES

1. Malvika Rajbans Sanghvi, "You Fight to Like Where You Live," *Indian Express, Magazine*, March 20, 1983, p. v.
2. David W. Atkinson, *Abstracts of English Studies*, 27 (September 1984), 2293.
3. Corall Ann Howells, "Ruby Wiebe's *The Temptation of Big Bear* and Salman Rushdie's *Midnight's Children*," *The Literary Criterion*, 20 (1985), p. 197.
4. Dieter Reimenschneider, "History and Individual in Anita Desai's *Clear Light of Day* and Salman Rushdie's *Midnight's Children*," *World Literature Written in English*, 23 (1984), p. 196.
5. William Walsh, "India and the Novel," *The New Pelican Guide to English Literature*, Vol. 8: *The Present*, ed. Boris Ford (Harmondsworth: Penguin, 1983), p. 257.
6. Meenakshi Mukherjee, "A Legend Out of a Sub-Continent,"

Indian Express, Magazine, March 20, 1983, p. v.
7. Uma Parameswaran, "Salman Rushdie in Indo-English Literature," *Journal of Indian Writing in English*, 12 (July 1984), p. 23.
8. Kate Millett, *Sexual Politics* (1969, rpt., London: Rupert Hart-Davis, 1971), p. 6.
9. Sheila Mcleod, "The Passion to be Masculine," *Lawrence's Men and Women* (1985, rpt., London: Paladin Grafton Books, 1987), p. 18.
10. Salman Rushdie, *Midnight's Children* (1981, rpt., London: Picador, 1982), p. 24.

Women's Survival and Struggle for Change in Veena Paintal's *An Autumn Leaf* and *Spring Returns*

ANITA SINGH

Veena Paintal, a lesser known novelist of the Indian English fiction deserves much more critical attention than what she has been able to receive so far. All her novels deal with various questions pertaining to women. This paper examines women's survival and struggle for change in Veena Paintal's novels with special reference to her two novels *An Autumn Leaf* and *Spring Returns*. An attempt shall be made to study the various aspects of feminism that were taken up by the novelist in her novels and to see how far she has succeeded in securing for the members of her sex their present enviable status in the family and society. Although she does not write with a conscious social purpose, yet her works have unconsciously contributed to the feminist cause, an expression of inner preoccupation and the modern ideal of building a male-dominance free society.

In all her novels, there is a striving on the part of the female protagonists towards arriving at a more authentic way of life than the one which is available to them. Through the different portraits of educated Indian women, mainly from the upper middle class, and examples of Indian marriages in her novels, Veena Paintal has tried to focus on the subservient status assigned to women and the need for these women to fight against the traditional expectations of society to become independent.

Veena Paintal writes about women fighting endless battles to survive. She has endeavoured to draw a pen picture of the Indian women, who are independent in every way but still remain slaves of society, customs, parents, husbands and children. Her novels are about the educated upper middle class women, stripping away the facade of chiffon sarees and cocktail parties to delve into their lives, personalities and particular individual struggles. She frankly uncovered the long standing inviolate world of women's instincts and natural yearnings for love and understanding. Her awareness of the need for women's emancipation is strongly demonstrated through her novels *An Autumn Leaf* and *Spring Returns.*

An Autumn Leaf published in 1976 is Veena Paintal's third novel, the first two being *Roshini* and *Link in the Broken Chain. An Autumn Leaf* presents a young woman capable of flouting convention and preserving her identity. As portrayed by the author, Charishma represents the educated Indian girl who plans to put her education to use by taking up a profession and achieving independence. Thus, in defiance of social convention, she does not wish to marry until and unless her ideal man comes along—simply because society expects her to get married by a certain age. She claims to be a misogamist and maintains that if at all she would marry, it would only be "the ideal lover," who would be her companion rather than her master. Veena Paintal rejected the view than a woman should regard her husband with prostrate adoration. She emphasized the dignified notions of mutual respect.

Charishma in this novel rejected the conventional procedure of marriage. "One thing I know and that is that I want to find my own man," she had said, "I don't believe in arranged marriages. In today's world they have little chance of survival. I have my own personality and my dreams. I refuse to be tied down like a slave to some rich man I don't even know and be treated like a piece of furniture."[1]

Charishma, endowed with fine intelligence and a keen sense of discernment, has her own view of conjugal life. She is against marrying one who will be fauning upon her all the time. She decides to marry Amit, the thirty-five year old brother of her friend Neeru and a Colonel in the Army. Fearing the disapproval of her parents, she commits a daring act by running away from home and living with Amit, though they are not legally married. Later, she yokes herself in conjugal relationship to an aging Amit.

Although she has self-control and shows an unruffled surface, a rift open in her sense of kinship with the man who had seemed like an answer to her dreams. Having had the information of his infidelity, she once again displays the ability for independent action by breaking up her marriage and giving up the fear of social censure. At this point a comparison can be made with the heroine of her first novel *Roshini*. It was the story of a typical traditional Indian girl. Roshini's dismal fate highlights the predicament of a woman who wants to achieve self-identity but is too feeble to escape from the interlocked alternatives of restrictive matrimony or unlicensed passion. Yet, Charishma apparently triumphs over this predicament. Bold and unconventional, she has always stood for treating woman with respect and equality. As she tells Amit, "You cannot have the best of both worlds, Amit. You've chosen your path, now stick to it." (106) It is the cry of a broken feminine heart on betrayal which shows the emotional intensity of her character. She firmly struggled for preserving her identity and self-respect and always strove for the basic honesty in relationships.

The same unquenchable ambition to fight her way towards independence and infuse her life with meaning is seen when she decides to leave Rohit with whom she had been staying after her break up with Amit. Rebellious against the oppression of women in a male-dominated society, she realizes that a spiritual relationship of equality cannot be achieved in a marriage.

When the novel ends, it is a very mature Charishma we see, a certain tranquillity descends upon her: "She filled her days with her children, playing with them, joining in their laughter, helping them with their studies. She had discovered a flair for writing and was kept busy penning articles, for the press." (159-60)

Charishma not only has the novelist's sympathy, she is used by her as a mouthpiece to voice her views on the woman question. Veena Paintal does not make Charishma a conventional non-entity. She is submissive, but at times quite impulsive. Her creator endures her with passionate moments of strength. It is from Charishma that we hear the novelist's protests against women's fate or unrest and dissatisfaction. We can very well call *An Autumn Leaf* a novel of the condition of women. Despite all obstacles, public prejudice and long established strict convention, the figure of the modern girl Charishma emerged as someone active and full of life, ready to help others and able to face difficulties without tilting.

Veena Paintal's next novel, *Spring Returns,* published in 1977, depicts the theme of a truly emancipated and strong woman who seems to have understood life and her own role in it and who can, by breaking away from her prescribed situation in life, change her life for the better. Tara, the heroine of the novel, exemplifies the liberated and awakened Indian woman with a will to shape her destiny.

Almost an orphan after the death of her mother at the age of six and her father's remarriage, Tara, had led a dreary, lonely and loveless life. At the age of sixteen she undertakes a training in nursing, thus equipping herself for achieving independence through the adoption of a career. But her father and stepmother get her married at the earliest to the nephew of her stepmother. Her protest against such a marriage is unheeded. It is after her marriage to Dalip that she realizes that he is a psychic case although the circumstances causing his psychic disorder were pathetic. Dalip's beloved Anjalika, who was carrying his child, had been forcibly married off to a rich prince, Kenny, and this had left a deep impact on his mind and during one of his spells of madness, he runs away from his home leaving behind Tara to fend for herself. Tara stays back with her in-laws, looking after them and supporting them financially. But her refusal to continue life as it comes to her is a manifestation of her rebellion. It is her way of saying thus far and no further. Her enterprise in running away from her in-laws's home is an attempt to rebel against the meaningless, death-like existence. She takes up work as a governess in Srinagar to give meaning to her life, and this is where she meets Kenny and is able to put an end to her so-called marriage. The novel ends on a happy note. Tara is released by Dalip, and Kenny and Tara get married. Prita, who is Dalip's daughter by Anjalika, goes to live with her father, much to his happiness and he recovers from his psychologically disturbed state of mind.

The depiction of Tara is therefore of a woman who uses her education to earn a living and become independent. She is capable of changing her circumstances if she finds them unsuitable and capable of facing new challenges and situation squarely and intelligently.

Tara, like Charishma, is an intellectual and accomplished woman with an eagerness to discover the latent possibilities of life and to know its truth. The two represent those generous, loving and unsuspecting women, who are faced with the problem of preserving their self, and in their struggle for survival in a male-dominated society, they, by breaking from the shackles of conventions and traditions, move towards freedom and wholeness.

NOTES

1. Veena Paintal, *An Autumn Leaf* (Delhi: Hind Pocket Books, 1976), pp. 20-21.

Sylvia Plath's *The Bell Jar*: Portrait of the Artist as a Young Girl

PASHUPATI JHA

Sylvia Plath's *The Bell Jar* is a highly controversial autobiographical novel and controversies related to its character-sketch are still alive.[1] Very much aware of the resultant reaction, Plath published the novel first in England, in January 1963, and that also under the cover of a pseudonymn—Victoria Lucas. Thus, *The Bell Jar* is slightly ahead of the pioneer feministic study of Betty Friedan, *The Feminine Mystique*. When Plath's novel was published in America in 1971, it soon became a sort of Bible for the school and college going girls there, because of its portrayal of a growing girl as a budding artist amid surrounding social obstacles. On the other hand, it was also branded as "a profile done in thick charcoal"[2] by a "bitch goddess,"[3] and the expression of "the basest ingratitude."[4] Plath's heroine herself says about the novel that it "would fix a lot of people,"[5] as it certainly does by painting with a rough brush almost all the people that come in the way of the heroine. *The Bell Jar* is a *bildungsroman*—a novel depicting the early emotional development of the protagonist, as well as a revenge play where the oppressed heroine rises from fear to fury and assumes the mantle of a "vengeful Diana or Kali."[6]

Esther Greenwood, the heroine of the novel, is both a "green wood"—an immature girl in the ways of the world, and a revenge goddess, a Lady Lazarus, and a shooting Ariel. She is a bright college girl of nineteen, just "breaking out of cramped adolescent cocoons."[7] Her ambition is to become a

Professor of literature as well as a creative writer of repute. But when she tries to write a novel, she fails utterly and does not proceed beyond few initial lines. She ponders then: "How could I write about life when I'd never had a love affair or a baby or seen anybody die?" (128) It is for this experience of life that she values her arrival in the open air of New York from the claustrophobic suburb of Boston, after winning a keenly contested guest-editorship of a fashion magazine. Pressures put on Esther by her ambitious mother and the middle-class social mores had already made her "a dissatisfied satisfier of other people's expectations."[8] Contradictory pulls of her inner creative urge and the outer social compulsion had turned her "tight and nervy as the top string of a violin."[9] So, the shift to New York seems to her a symbol of freedom, where she can see and feel the world in her own ways, unfettered by the prying eyes of envious neighbours. But New York proves different only in degree, not in direction. All the eager expectations of a stimulating and adventurous exploration of the mystery and magnificence of a great metropolis end in increasing ennui and alienation. When Esther is supposed to be having the best time of her life, enjoying a real whirl, and becoming envy of thousands of college girls who had tried but lost the magazine contest, she actually feels marooned among an impersonal, cruel, and crazy crowd.

Esther tries her utmost to arrest her drift towards growing isolation and fragmentation, her dangerous drift towards the tight enclosure of the descending bell jar. *The Bell Jar* of the title is a metaphor for this inclusive enclosure of the mind, the "emotional cul-de-sac,"[10] which distances the heroine from her surroundings and her surroundings from her. This stifling enclosure begins to suffocate her with its stale, poisoned air. With so much of artistic ambition within her, Esther would have anything wrong with her body than something wrong with her mind. Her first attempt to escape from the constricting wall of the bell jar is to strike intimacy with Doreen and Betsy—two of the other girls selected by the same fashion magazine. Doreen, a seductive, voluptuous vamp, draws her by her sophistication and ready wit. She watches Doreen, with fear and fascination, playing seductress with ever-willing Lenny Shepherd, a dandy disc-jockey. Doreen and Lenny dance, and bite each other in a frenzy of song, drink, and passion. Esther, isolated and unnerved, begins to suffocate in the company of such sex-maniacs, and leaves them abruptly in the midst of their hugging and "Jitterbugging." This experience proves unsettling for an uninitiated Esther, but worse is still to come her way. With a lot of persuasion and assurance, Doreen brings her next time to a counter club where she encounters Marco, a woman-hater. With his masochism and the gift of a diamond, Marco dominates Esther and makes her dance with him against her will. After the dance, he coaxes her to an open field and attempts to rape her by flinging her on the muddy ground. Although Esther escapes this rape attempt, it imprints an indelible distrust of the city on her mind. Then it dawns on her that Doreen's way, howsoever apparently alluring it may seem, is not hers to experience the permissive society.

Esther then turns to Betsy, the Pollyana Cowgirl straight from Kansas, symbolizing purity and innocence. But the party thrown by *Ladies' Day Journal* which Esther attends with Betsy ends equally disastrously because of severe food-poisoning. Thus, neither the marvellous decadence of Doreen nor the unsullied innocence of Betsy lead Esther away from her isolation and disenchantment. She returns from New York empty-handed and empty-headed. Although she has thrown to the wind all her expensive New York gifts, she deliberately keeps the dried-up blotches of blood on her cheek a reminder of her terrible encounter with Marco. Unsettling as the New York experiences are, Esther returns home expecting selection for a summer course of creative writing at Harvard; perhaps her creative engagement would be able to erase some of her past memories. But that is not to be, she does not make it to that course. This rejection shakes her from within, and Esther feels sullen and sunk down. Bereft of that creative writing course, her mother tries to teach her shorthand for mundane reasons. But this scaling down from creativity to mechanical work is naturally loathing to her and she refuses to learn shorthand after the first few lessons. She makes an attempt to engage her mind and decides to finish her honours thesis on James Joyce, but failure stares at her face here as well.

Thus, remaining at home is both worthless and irksome for Esther. it is disgusting for another reason as well. Her mother goes out for work and she is left alone to hear the jarring music of Dodo Conway wheeling her children around. Dodo Conway is her Catholic neighbour with six children and seventh anytime on the way. Children make Esther sick, particularly more so after her watching of a delivery in a hospital amid moans and groans and so many mechanical tools. Children, furthermore, mean marriage, and marriage does hardly figure anywhere in her scheme of things. The sensuous haze of marriage means giving up her creative urge and losing herself in her husband and children. The fate of Mrs. Willard's beautifully designed mat is a pointer to the predicament of female creativity. Although emotionally poles apart from her date's mother, Esther appreciates the artistic pattern of the mat made by Mrs. Willard from waste materials. But that exquisite mat is not meant for interior decoration as some object of art; it is rather used as a kitchen mat, soon to be soiled under the feet of Mr. Willard. This hints at how even the little bit of female creativity is crushed in marriage in which woman is always a loser:

> And I knew that in spite of all the roses and kisses and restaurant dinners a man showered on a woman before he married her, what he secretly wanted when the wedding service ended was for her to flatten out underneath his feet like Mrs. Willard's kitchen mat. (88-89)

Esther thus becomes quite apprehensive that an independent literary career will not be possible side by side with marriage. She vividly recounts the words of Buddy Willard, her lover, regarding the permanence of poetry. Buddy has called poems "dust," and assured her that she herself would feel like giving up poetry and artistic pursuit after the responsibility of marriage dawns on her:

> I also remembered Buddy Willard saying in a sinister knowing way that after I had children I would feel differently, I wouldn't want to write poems any more. So I began to think maybe it was true that when you were married and had children it was like being brainwashed, and afterwards you went numb as a slave in some private, totalitarian state. (89)

So, Esther discards altogether the possibility of her marriage, for she cannot risk her creativity. Instead of being a launching pad for the career of her husband, as Mrs. Willard thinks every woman should be proud of, Esther wants to shoot off in all directions herself. She refuses to be a mere object, a mere event in the life of a man. Like the persona of the poem "Ariel," she imagines herself a "phallic man" who "would be the penetrator of the space, not the space itself."[11]

But such an independent bold plan can hardly be accepted by the middle-class society of suburban Boston. Mrs. Greenwood, Esther's mother, does not understand and appreciate the real aspiration of her daughter. She is always on Esther to preserve her virginity at any cost and remain clean for such a clean bachelor as Buddy Willard. Social compulsions are such that, for some time, they mould the mind of Esther in favour of virginity. But Buddy Willard turns out to be a hypocrite by having an affair with a sluttish waitress and all the time pretending to be a novice, innocent, and loyal to Esther. Not to be outdone, Esther takes the big decision not only to ditch Buddy Willard but also to pay him back in the same coin by having some affair herself, But then, there is the fear of ending up with a baby. So, with the permission of her genial psychiatrist, Dr. Nolan, she goes for a "fitting." While climbing the examination table, she feels like climbing to her freedom; and after the fitting is over, she is beside herself for being her own woman, for effectively stalling the injustice done to her by nature and becoming "the presiding genius of her own body."[12]

Now Esther is ready, both physically and mentally, to take on Buddy Willard: "Ever since I'd learned about the corruption of Buddy Willard my virginity weighed like a millstone around my neck." (240) She gears herself up for taking revenge on Buddy's faithlessness, as well as for being intimated into the experience of the other world. But her initial search for a suitable partner proves futile. Constantin, the simultaneous interpreter at the U.N.O., proves cold enough for the job, and conditioned as Esther has been all along, she fails to take the lead herself. Eric, another boy-friend, turns out to be abnormally puritanical who would keep his beloved unsullied and would rather go to a prostitute for sexual gratification. Esther does not accept the lesbian advances of her girl friend Joan, and so her hunt goes on. She finally finds out Irwin, a young professor of Mathematics at Harvard, who is an expert hand in such matters. As Esther at her age is "one in a million" virgin, she suffers a massive haemorrahage, but she bears everything, for blood is her answer that she has crossed the Rubicon. As she has now achieved her heart's desire, so she ditches Irwin immediately after making him pay the hospital bill and by taking all the precaution that he can find her nowhere.

But the path to freedom from inhibition and imposition of society has not been easy for Esther; at every step she has to encounter obstacles put in her way by social code and convention. She has been offered several old-models—her own mother, Mrs. Willard, Jay Cee, Philomela Guinea—the famous novelist and her benefactress, and a host of others: "they all wanted to adopt me, and, for the price of their care and influence, have me resemble them." (232) Esther refuses all these models as "dolls, zombies, and mannequins;"[13] as a true independent artist, she wants to seek her own individual salvation. But society demands conformation, conform and continue, rebel and be punished and perish. Her shock-treatment is one of the several ways of society to make one fall in line.

The first shock-therapy is a jolting experience for Esther:

> Then something bent down and took hold of me and shook me like the end of the world. Whee-ee-ee-ee-ee, it shrilled, through an air crackling with blue light, and with each flash a great jolt drubbed me till I thought my bones would break and the sap fly out of me like a split plant.
>
> I wondered what terrible thing it was that I had done. (151-52)

Not only shock-therapy but several suicide attempts are also the part of the necessary price Esther has to pay to her Muse. Plath has always equated death with art: "Dying/Is an art, like everything else/I do it exceptionally well." ("Lady Lazarus") So, her protagonist in *The Bell Jar* has to pass through the ultimate ordeal of attempted suicide, which, incidentally, does never succeed. It is through the fire and blood of shock and suicide that the spirit of Esther forges ahead like a Phoenix flame. By the end of the novel, the tight lid of the bell jar around her neck is shifted slightly and Esther is "Open to the circulating air." (227) Still her emotional resolve is entangled, because the "tranquillized fifties" of her country is yet not ripe for full expression of the female experience:

> I wasn't sure. I was not sure at all. How did I know that someday—at college, in Europe, somewhere, anywhere—the bell jar, with its stifling distortions, wouldn't descend again. (254)

The bell jar does indeed descend, not on the protagonist of the novel, but on the novelist herself—Plath gases herself to death barely few days after the publication of this novel.

Why this little bit of dichotomy between the created and the creator? The surmounting torments and tensions in the life of Plath can get artistic resolve in the novel only partially and temporarily. While the bell jar is "suspended" for the time being in the novel, it chokes the novelist to death because her ever vulnerable self lacks the strength of any ideological stance—feminism is still few months away from Plath. Yet, what she leaves behind in the form of *The Bell Jar* will ever remain a powerful example of the pre-feminist scenario.

NOTES

1. Jane Anderson (Joan Gilling of the novel) has filed a suit against the producer of the film based on *The Bell Jar*. Her contention is that the implicit lesbianism of the novel has been made explicit in the film version. For details see "Who will bell the Jar?" *The Times of India*, Sunday Review, 22 February 1987, p. 3.
2. Edward Butscher, *Sylvia Plath: Method and Madness* (New York: Seabury Press, 1976), p. 309.
3. Butscher labels Plath a bitch-goddess in the same book.
4. Lois Amis quotes Plath's mother in "Biographical Note," *The Bell Jar* (New York: Harper and Row, 1971), p. 215.
5. Sylvia Plath, *The Bell Jar* (1963; rpt., London: Faber and Faber, 1982), p. 126.
6. Barnett Guttenberg, "Plath's Cosmology and the House of Yeats," in Gary Lane, ed., *Sylvia Plath: New Views on the Poetry* (Baltimore and London: The Johns Hopkins Univ. Press, 1979), p. 149.
7. Nancy Hunter Steiner, *A Closer Look at Ariel : A Memory of Sylvia Plath* (New York: Harper's Magazine Press, 1973), p. 33.
8. George Stade, "Introduction," *A Closer Look at Ariel*, p. 18.
9. Sylvia Plath, "Johnny Panic and the Bible of Dreams," *Johnny Panic and the Bible of Dreams* (London: Faber and Faber, 1977), p. 18.
10. Joyce Carol Oates, "The Death Throes of Romanticism: The Poetry of Sylvia Plath," in Edward Butscher, ed., *Sylvia Plath: The Woman and the Work* (New York: Dodd, Mead, 1977), p. 219.
11. Murray M. Schwartz and Christopher Bollas, "The Absence at

the Centre: Sylvia Plath and Suicide," in Lane, ed., *Sylvia Plath*, p. 188.

12. Lynda K. Bundtzen, *Plath's Incarnations: Woman and the Creative Process* (Ann Arbor: The Univ. of Michigan Press, 1983), p. 256.
13. *Ibid.*, p. 127.

Iris Murdoch: The Feminist Perspective

A.K. SINHA

Iris Murdoch (b. 1919) is an English woman novelist of the twentieth century who has travelled the complex and difficult path of the "soul" along with her characters. She approaches the problems of the modern life with a typically English interest in ethical problems and knows how to "embody" complex philosophical and ethical questions in gripping story plots. With twenty-one novels, a handful of plays and poems, a number of influential articles, a book on Sartre, a book of her own moral philosophy and a book on Plato's theory of art to her credit, she is a writer of international reputation.

It is significant to note here that in the fifties have also emerged a new group of English novelists, popularly called Angry Young Men, comprising William Cooper, Kingsley Amis, John Wain, John Braine, Alan Sillitoe, Colin Mac Innes, Stan Barstow and Stanley Middleton protesting against a hollow welfare state and an intolerably cruel society. The bitter experiences during the Second World War and the agony at the explosion of the first nuclear bomb seem to have made these rebels believe that all the standards set for them by their elders were misleading and had to be rejected. The economic programmes, brought out by the Labour Government of the post-Second World War England proclaiming to help the working class particularly, were not being fulfilled in practice. The spread of education had promoted a belief in the full range of opportunities opening to all. But when these young men, coming from a low income group, left their colleges they found frustration awaiting them. General industrialization, unemployment, persistence of class distinctions and cultural snobberies made the post-Second World War society distracted and diseased.

So the angry young rebels find it to be their duty to point their fingers against these bewildering wrongs of their society. The generation gap, hypergamy, the primacy of the provincial background, and the general selection of the protagonist from the lower income group become the dominant features of the young English rebels. From these rebels comes into being the new idea of an anti-hero, opposing everything that can be cried over. This anti-hero appears as the small, good-hearted rebel, protesting against his society with almost clownish gestures.

Similar to the beliefs and attitudes of these angry rebels and yet different from them all, Iris Murdoch's richly resonant and sardonically angry tone emerges in a very striking manner. Murdoch begins her career in *Under the Net* (1954) where others of her generation look like ending theirs, with a work which is witty and hilarious. Her Jake Donaghue of this novel is akin to Kingsley Amis's Jim Dixon and John Wain's Charles Lumley, Jake is an angry middle-aged man who mocks at society and its respectability. He moves playfully around with law and order and does small things on the sly, swims in the Thames at night, steals a performing dog, sneaks in and out of locked apartments, even steals food.

It is in *The Bell* (1958) that Iris Murdoch presents Dora as the first of a series of innocent sympathetic worldlings married to insensitive ascetics. Bullied by her pompous unhappy art historian husband Paul, who is studying medieval documents at the Abbey, Dora feels imprisoned in a relationship of unequals. Paul is jealous and unpleasant and has no idea of her as a person. Besides, he is thirteen years older than her. He has merely installed Dora in his flat and has only added to his collection of beautiful objects:

> Once married and installed in the Knightsbridge flat, in the midst of Paul's unique collection of medieval ivo-

> ries, Dora set about the business of being happy, at first with success. But as time went on, she discovered that it was not as easy as she had imagined to grow into Paul's wife.[1]

Dora comes from a lower middle-class London family, with her father dying when she was nine years old, and her mother, with whom she had never got on very well, marrying again. Moreover, she had been an ugly and wretched schoolgirl, and was still very young though she vaguely thought of herself as past her prime.

Dora comes out as an anti-heroic woman protesting in her own way against the domination of Paul. The novel starts, as it ends, with Dora. Her encounter with her husband is presented with a subtle psychological insight. Paul stands with one hand on his hip and stares at her. She looks back at him, uneasy, yet admiring the solidity of him. She feels flimsy, and ephemeral by comparison, as if she were merely a thought in his mind. Paul overwhelms her self-surrender with a love that is paternal and predatory. As the novel progresses, Dora finds space to grow. She begins to acquire a sense of identity, to value herself. And in the open-ended final chapter of *The Bell*, she even turns back to painting, and plans to live independently. If she will return to Paul at all, it will be only as an equal.

Thus, in *The Bell*, the novelist can be said to have adopted the feminist perspective by having so meticulously painted the portrait of a lady. The initial description of the Imber community is humorous and very much from the point of view of a Dora who sees the Imber as a prison whose inmates would be set before her as judges. She sees them as dreariest who have contrived to produce a stale smell.

Even the Abbess in the novel, with whom Murdoch has admitted a little to identifying, calls the inmates of the Imber Court a kind of sick people, disturbed and hunted by God, unable to live either in or out of the world. Michael is singled out by the author to be an accidental man, the plot's fool and a man who accumulates disaster.

The Unicorn (1963) takes us to a prototypical "horrid" province of European Romanticism, a wilderness in West Ireland. The houses neighbour a sea which kills people, we find here rocks with carnivorous plants, and an unfeathered dog which picturesquely floods at seven-year intervals. The governess Marian who enters the landscape in the opening chapter is appalled by the terrible isolation of the place. In five days she is beginning to forget who she is and she fails to understand how the natives of the place stay sane and she even conjectures that they do not. Marian has hoped to escape from an unhappy love-affair in coming to this place, Gaze. She finds that there are no children for her to teach. Her pupil is the beautiful and imprisoned Hannah Crean-Smith, who represents the Unicorn of the title, and who appears in two opposed aspects, half nun, half unconscious vamp and seductress. She accepts her imprisonment by her absent husband Peter for her crimes of adultery. Marian finds herself getting carried away in a unique sort of relationship with Hannah:

> "Well you know that I love," said Marian. She was surprised to hear herself saying this. It was not the sort of thing she came out with usually.. Yet it seemed quite natural here, or as if it were compelled from her.
>
> "Yes, Thank you. I think, don't you, that one ought to cry out more for love, to ask for it. It's odd how afraid people are of the word. Yet we all need love. Even God needs love. I suppose that's why He created us."
>
> "He made a bad arrangement," said Marian smiling. Since uttering the word she felt that she did love Hannah more: or simply that she did love her, since she had given no name before to her affectionate feeling.[3]

Hannah has a stoical calm and a capacity to live in the moment. Her worshippers are also her galors. Peter is drowned. And when Denis and Marian go over to Hannah to tell her of this death by water, they find that she too is dead. This death of Hannah haunts Denis, who feels that they have all killed her.

Thus *The Unicorn* is primarily a story of two women. And as the novel ends, Marian does not know whether the world in which she had been living was a world of good or of evil, a world of significant suffering or a devil's shadow play, a mere nightmare of violence. Hannah has been for them an image of God; and if she was a false God they had certainly worked hard to make her so. Hannah looms largely as a doomed figure, a pale death-dealing enchantress.

The Black Prince (1973) of Iris Murdoch is a black book about marriage, a dark book about authorial rivalry and a reflective book about love. The novel's subtitle *A Celebration of Love* suggests the keynote. It is a story in three parts of Bradley Pearson's love affair with Julian Baffin. The first part ends at the point at which Bradley realizes that he has fallen in love with Julian. The second part deals with his declaration of this love and with the response of the small court of characters. The third part concerns elopement, consummation and almost immediate discovery of the lovers by Julian's father. The woman appears as a Life Force when Bradley confesses that his mother was proud of him and she filled him with exasperation and shame but he loved her. He simply disliked his father.

Yet another aspect of the woman emerges in the following confession made by Priscilla about Roger to Francis:

> The garden was always *his* garden. The house was *his* house. Even the kitchen was his kitchen. I've given my whole *life* to that man. . . . I haven't *got* anything else.[9]

Even Bradley experiences that trembling dedication to the totality of another only as he sits on the divan bed and waits for Julian.

Thus, although *The Black Prince* keeps up a running commentary about *Hamlet*, it assigns significant roles to the women. At the end of the novel, Bradley receives a letter from

Julian painfully ending their love affair; saying that she is going to stay with some friends of her father who live in a quiet remote village, a little place in the mountains.

In *A Word Child* (1975), Iris Murdoch presents Hilary Burde as the narrator who disclaims being a practising artist but creates a small enclosed world whose meanings he tries wholly to legislate. The novel is about the education of the narrator. At one point, Hilary is told by Christopher:

> Oh how tedious you are . . . you are nothing but a lout who has been taught a few tricks. You are the sort of lower class product who never grows out of his grammar school. Always the little prize boy who was top in the exam. Always envious, always anxious. You exist by excelling, by knowing just that little more than the others and understanding nothing.[4]

Hilary finds Ann coming to him first out of pity, wanting to show him that he could love a woman. At yet another significant turn of the plot, it strikes to Hilary as comic that he was being badgered by three childless women in their thirties, two wanting him to present them with a child, the other wanting him to sanction her marriage. And yet when Hilary tells Tommy that she *belongs* to him, her rejoinder is dramatically significant:

> 'I don't. Face the truth. I don't. What could that mean? Belong to you, like a possession you put away in a cupboard and look at once a week? No. It's good-bye, Hilary. Make it easy for both of us, please, at least spare me now.[5]

And it is only when the novel is about to end that Tommy ultimately agrees to marry Hilary.

The Sea, The Sea (1978) presents the story of Charles Arrowby, a famous theatre director and also an occasional actor and playwright who has retired to the sea to repent of something like a life of egoism. Charles writes something between a memoir and a diary and his self-deceptions speak through his confessional. If *The Black Prince* meditates *Hamlet,* this novel meditates *The Tempest* which in 1969 Murdoch has called perhaps her favourite of all plays. Charles's house, Shruff End, by the sea appears to be haunted. Rosina, a jealous, predatory, practical ex-lover is shown to have been haunting Charles in revenge for his having made overtures to another ex-lover, the gentle Lizzie. When Charles asks Rosina to clear off as she, according to him, is not a part of his life, the woman retorts by hissing:

> *I am* part of your life, you know. Yes, you *are* frightened, Charles. It's interesting, it's a revelation, it's so *easy* to frighten people, to bewilder them and persecute them and terrify them out of their wits and make their lives a misery.[6]

When Peregrine tells Charles that basically he seems to despise women, the protagonist hits back and says that he does not. In fact, Charles admits that he was in love with all Shakespeare's heroines before he was twelve. Charles here is however told by Peregrine that such heroines live only in the never-never land of art, all trickled out in Shakespeare's wit and wisdom. Charles enjoys power. He has carelessly smashed Rosina's marriage with Peregrine many years before, and then, once he had enjoyed Rosina's subjection to him, purged her of friends and apparently prevented her having children, he has just as carelessly discarded her.

Thus *The Sea, The Sea* is also the story of a male egoist, a lion becoming old and clawless, whom Rosina defiantly describes as an "awful crook" with his "own illusions of power that fascinated people." The woman here looks back in anger and makes the male realize the vanity of such human wishes.

In *Nuns and Soldiers* (1980), the novelist presents an anti-heroic Time who realizes the utter hopelessness of his situation, and thus seems to go a step beyond Charles Arrowby at the end of *The Sea, The Sea:*

> He thought, what's the matter with me? I feel terrible, useless, utterly sick of myself. Where am I going, what am I for? What has my life been, what will it be? I just live by lies, by deceiving myself. I can't paint, I can't earn money, I can't do anything. . . . He recalled Gertrude's crying face and he wanted to cry himself but he couldn't.[7]

In this novel, the two "friends," Anne and Gertrude, steal the show, as it were, and in this way *Nuns and Soldiers* has a strange relationship with *The Unicorn*, where Marian and Hannah enact a similar type of human drama. And yet the image of the prison can be found even here. Anne, who has moved away from the convent, recollects:

> Gertrude had said it must be like getting out of prison. Well, how hard, how ardently, she had tried to get *into* that prison, and it was like a prison, there were cells, bars, high walls, locked doors. God had put her under house arrest, and with a glad and willing heart she identified herself as a prisoner. . . . Ordinary relationship with the outside world soon wilted. . . . Love itself altered, was constrained, perhaps clarified.[8]

Thus one finds that through these six novels Iris Murdoch, like Jane Austen and George Eliot, defines woman as a subject in her own right. The portraits of the ladies in these novels seem to be more searching and more life-like than those of men. With a keen and fresh power of perception, Iris Murdoch presents a neat study of women in the twentieth-century society—a study which remains with her discreet and yet unobtrusive. Dora, the Abbess, Marian, Hannah, Julian, Priscilla, Tommy, Rosina, Anne, Gertrude and other women in these novels strive for and obtain a certain autonomy. They are not merely at the other end of their heroes's problems. They do not provide mere safety-valves for the release of the pent-up emotions of their respective protagonists, and are not content with merely playing the second fiddle. In fact, these women present their notes of protest with a certain intensity of tone, and are round characters, memorable for their psychological complexity. Sometimes motivated by weird impulses and desires that lie too deep in the unconscious to be named accurately, they are vital characters with marked individual tendencies. They emerge as strong-willed people commenting upon the messy, imperfect and unperfectable task of love and its failure. These women are actually proud without pretension, brave and defiant, and they subtly expose the shams of the contemporary society. In these six novels, therefore, Iris Murdoch hands all things over to the woman and denies and suppresses male authority. Thus these novels indeed appear to be dominated by a profoundly feminine view of life, and here truly emerges a feminist perspective.

NOTES

1. Iris Murdoch, *The Bell* (London: Chatto and Windus, 1958), p. 8.
2. Iris Murdoch, *The Unicorn* (London: Chatto and Windus, 1963), p. 63.
3. Iris Murdoch, *The Black Prince* (London: Chatto and Windus, 1973), p. 103.
4 Iris Murdoch, *A Word Child* (London: Chatto and Windus, 1975), p. 79.
5. *Ibid.*, pp. 353-54.
6. Iris Murdoch, *The Sea, The Sea* (London: Chatto and Windus, 1978), p. 103.
7. Iris Murdoch, *Nuns and Soldiers* (London: Chatto and Windus, 1980), pp. 172-73.
8. *Ibid.*, pp. 57-58.

Women No Longer Swing in the Ancient Orbits: Margaret Drabble's *The Millstone* and *The Realms of Gold*

SANGEETA JAIN

I

Men and women are two halves of the same species, so one expects them to fit together like two sides of a coin. Yet, throughout history, the sexes have regarded each other less as fellow human beings and more as aliens—to be loved, feared or confined. In the relationship between the sexes, women have been forced to occupy a secondary place, not imposed by their inherent deficient characteristic but rather by strong cultural forces and social tradition. This has resulted in the failure of women to occupy a place of human dignity as free and independent beings. They find themselves living in a world where men condemn them to "immanence" and their existence is justified only as objects of sex— "absolute sex, no less."[1] They are defined, as Simone de Beauvoir says

> with reference to man and not he with reference to her, she is the incidental, the inessential as opposed to the essential. He is the subject, he is the Absolute—she is the other.[2]

Theological statements emphasized the subordinate position of woman as willed by heaven. Woman was accused of the original sin and of being the root of all evil. She was considered impure and sullied, contaminating all and opening the gates of hell. This derogatory opinion was further reinforced when serious philosophical debate arose as to whether woman was a complete human being possessed of a soul, or merely a breeder for the superior race of men.

The history of patriarchy reveals varieties of cruelties and barbarities levelled at women. They were forced to live in a crippling state of utter humiliation and abjection—bought, sold, raped, beaten, tortured and finally murdered. They were always the oppressed class dominated through male self-interest, prevented from development as human beings by the system which prostituted them in and out of marriage. After marriage, the woman became a minor of sub-average intelligence in the eyes of the law. Her legal existence was suspended, or at least incorporated and consolidated into the hands of the husband. She could not dispose of the money earned, hold property, have a say in the upbringing of the children, sue her husband or hold him to an argument. Her husband could be an adulterer, or a sodomite, or stained with every crime, yet he was still her husband and she could not leave him, get a divorce or remarry. While the man could divorce, kill his wife and still be freed from punishment. For the male dictum was:

> My wife and I are one and I am he.[3]

The wife was no more than a chattel, a slave who had to suffer the aggravated assaults committed by the husband.

Mores were strict and women were weighed down by the operation of the double standard and neurotic sexual ideology, which punished with social ostracism any woman who breached the sexual taboo, but blandly ignored male offences. Women were typed to a mere biological existence and the path to their intellectual and economic upliftment was closed.

The moment of awakening came in the latter half of the nineteenth century, when women became aware of their imprisonment and there came a need to break away from the stultifying male ideology. The bomb of discontentment which had been simmering for quite sometime exploded with a loud blast and shook the foundation of the patriarchal citadel. Women waged a whole-sale war against the male-oriented society and the organized suffrage committees won a few battles. They won the local franchise and to some extent carved out equal opportunities; in education and employment. But concessions were slow in coming. Discrimination in hundred different ways continued. Women's confinement to the home and private life went unquestioned.

The aging and abating women's movement was revived and revitalized in the nineteen sixties. The intensity of women's activism for liberation grew at an extraordinary rate. Development of consciousness transformed the movement from elite lobby to a mass movement. Their politics was one of total involvement and a commitment to changing through direct participation all inequitable social realities. Feminists re-examined the concept of womanhood and challenged the existing patriarchal ideology. They condemned pre-marital chastity, marriage and romantic love. They strove for liberation from sex roles and the traditional ways of defining gender identity. Philip Snowden says:

> The feminist asks for freedom in the exercise of those gifts, and in the use of those qualities of soul and mind, which are apart from the consequences of the sex-act. She objects to the pressing down of woman's personality into one channel, the directing of woman's emotion, with its specially rich quality, to one end, the confinement of woman's genius to one achievement.[4]

And the feminist movement was:

> The recognition, full and complete, of the humanity of women.[5]

Steady growth of women's emancipation, political and cultural uncertainties discredited the traditional image of woman being an evil force, or an inferior being. The old ideals of woman as passive, dependent and chaste were gradually transformed. A more human and egalitarian image of woman, with rights and duties, legitimate sexual passion and an independent existence emerged.

II

Amidst the medley of shrill feminist cries and vehement protests stands Margaret Drabble. Her novels are explorations of female development and the nuances of male oppression in society. Although her characters are revealed and developed in relation to familiar feminist issues of education, sexuality, marriage and economic dependence, yet Drabble is not a feminist. The author shatters female stereotypes and emphasizes women's competence and independence. The protagonists are single, separated or divorced women, who posit themselves in a world of profession, which provides alternative definition of what it means to be female. They do not mould themselves on anyone else's concept but are persons on their own account, who determine and shape their own lives. Drabble's two novels, *The Millstone* (1965) and *The Realms of Gold* (1975) are tied to the feminist perspective and cover significant liberationist territory.

"Emancipated woman, this was me: gin bottle in hand opening my own door with my latch key,"[6] says Rosamund Stacey, the young protagonist of *The Millstone.* She is a young intelligent scholar who faces a practical crisis in her life—pregnancy, ironically from her first sexual experience. With confidence and courage, she faces the dilemma and struggles through adversity to self-knowledge and authenticity.

Rosamund is basically a competent and self-reliant person who supports herself by research grants and by teaching an assortment of students. She believes "dependence to be a fatal sin." (10) Her mother, a great feminist brought her up to be equal. Rosamund declares: "She made there be no questions, no difference, I was equal. I am equal." (32) Rosamund plays the game of a totally emancipated woman with her men friends. She tactfully dates two people at once letting neither man realize that she did not sleep with the other. But, "unassertive" and "unassuming" George wrecks this excellent system and becomes the incidental father of her child. Rosamund meets him at a party and is impressed by his knowledge of English poetry, his pleasant voice and unobtrusive gentle manner and lowers the mask of inhibition. George's departure from her life is as sudden and unexpected as is his arrival. Rosamund loves him yet she does not want to impose herself upon him. Pride and self-respect are integral to her being and she avoids seeking him out.

Life appears in all its inscrutable incomprehensibility and complexity the moment Rosamund confronts the reality of her pregnancy from her accidental encounter. She is very much her own woman and precludes the socially acceptable act for an upper class British girl, of aborting the baby. She is also not amenable to the idea of marriage in order to provide respectability for her unborn child. She is made of sterner stuff and her "extraordinary confidence" (91) gives her a fillip to face the pregnancy alone without seeking anyone's assistance. Moreover, she plays her pregnancy openly and refuses to pretend that she is Mrs. Stacey in the ho$pital: "but I'm not Mrs. Stacey, I'm Miss." (67) And in light of defiant joy, she realizes that on the foot of her hospital bed was "U" which stood for unmarried.

Rosamund's commitment to her pregnancy signifies an enrichment of experience, deeply felt rather than superficially acknowledged. As a result of giving birth to the baby, she comes to know love: "Love, I suppose one might call it and the first of my life." (118) With it comes the most beautiful development of her commitment—happiness. Motherhood is not regarded as a trap but the initiator of a special relationship between adults and children. Feminists declare:

> Children are often the only people with whom women have a close emotional bond, in whom they find the warmth they do not get elsewhere.[7]

Rosamund's pregnancy does not prove a hindrance to her work. She discredits female stereotypes related to pregnancy as she does not "go over from the camp of logic to the camp of intuition." (78) She follows an achievement pattern more prevalent with males and her career progresses unimpeded. Moreover, she accelerates her scholarly work which is acknowledged accordingly and she gets a job in a reputed university. Earning power allows her to remain independent and have the child.

Toward the end of the novel, in a rare encounter with George, Rosamund grasps the bare bones of her existence—her triumph and superiority over the father of her illegitimate child. She meets George almost after two years and invites him to look at her baby. Apart from a few pleasantries, George remains indifferent, reticent and uncommunicative. The "call of the blood" does not work miracles and Rosamund realizes that the time had come and gone, of asking George to play a part in her life. She had "endured and survived and spared him so much sorrow" (195) and now she could not go back on what she had done.

By committing herself to her pregnancy and choosing to keep her baby as an unwed mother, Rosamund frees herself from the strictures of marriage and defines herself in relation to non-patriarchal values. She transcends division and achieves authenticity based on human personhood, rather than on gender. From the patriarchal perspective one would expect the single woman to be a figure of derision and social ostracism, but as Annis Pratt says:

> In much of women's fiction she becomes a hero representing the possibilities of growth and survival.[8]

In *The Realms of Gold* (1975), Drabble presents a picture

of a hero successful in passion, intellectual achievement and spirit. Frances Wingate, a successful archaeologist, creates realms of gold from which women were banished and then becomes professionally and financially successful by going forth and discovering them in reality. As a strong, competent and powerful woman in her mid-thirties, Frances regards her boorish husband as an expendable stud and presides efficiently over a husbandless household. She thinks there is no need for a man and finds the nuclear family unthinkable. Her brother Hugh sees her "not a captive" of the male-dominated institution but a "queen, like Boadicea." (186) Her nephew Stephen gazes at her in wonder seeing her optimism and energy as though she were "another species." (86)

Frances is a woman used to getting her own way. She has many affairs but with Karel Schmidt it is serious. She loves this "nice, but weak" (52) historian for seven years. But, when she realizes that Karel is not planning to leave his violent wife, something rebels in her, "pride, conscience" (18) and she declares: "It simply isn't in me to spend the rest of my life ruining my career for a man who will never marry me." (66)

Frances's strong nature makes her leave Karel. She presents a vision of power, centred in her self and not controlled by patriarchy. Even her liaison with Karel is unconventional. Towards the end of the novel, after Karel's wife declares openly that she is a lesbian and leaves him, he moves into Frances's house and brings his children from her to raise.

As a professional woman, Frances reels from job to job, from country to country, from excavation sites to conference halls, organizing meals, preparing lectures, seminars, ringing stations and arranging elaborate travelling schedules.

Frances further articulates the malaise that characterizes the technological world: loneliness, despair and nothingness. The conditions of survival are "unnatural" and deadly and few characters have courage to confront them as Frances finally does. With her amazing power of survival she resolves to "defy nature." (6) Her approach to life is revolutionary, unlike her nephew Stephen who out of depression and fear kills himself and his baby while his wife Beata suffering from anorexia nervosa lies inert in the hospital. Moreover when old Con dies, Frances's father hands over the burial arrangement to his daughter, who is more competent than his son, and she sees herself "the matriarch arranging funerals." (266)

In a key subplot, Drabble counterpoints the dreadful marriage of Frances's cousin Janet Bird. The atmosphere of subjugation and female passivity in the humiliating norm of helpmate is the focus in Janet's case. Sacrificed at the altar of marriage, she endures a disconsolate and repressed life of "nothingness." While her egocentric husband breathes a sign of relief and carries on unharassed potting shots at her "as though she were a duck at a fair." (153)

Finally, a good part of the plot centres around the pathetic death by starvation of Frances's great-aunt Connie. Old Con rejects patriarchy which insists that women marry and raise children. She defies all social taboos and lives by herself, suffering "lost love, rejection, puerperal fever, guilt, interfering vicars, the death of a loved child, persecution of parents." (279) People called her a witch and perhaps she was. The history of witches reveals that in the sixteenth and seventeenth century, they were regarded as socially disruptive elements intolerable to patriarchal culture which burned them by millions. Mary Daly points out: "The witch craze focussed predominantly upon women who had rejected marriage (spinsters) and women who had survived it (widows)."[10]

Frances bows her head in respect to Old Con who had lived and died so solitary and had wanted to be buried in unconsecrated ground. Frances responds to the call of power in her old aunt and decides "to take over where Con had left off." (281)

In reading the novels of Drabble one is made aware of the heroic possibilities in women. Pressures from within and without weigh heavy upon them, yet the positive heroes achieve the desirable feminist synthesis. They free themselves from the tension of what a normal human being might desire and what women must become. They define themselves in relation to values other than male superiority and female dependency of patriarchy. Drabble's women discredit the ancient images of womanhood and embrace new orbits of definition, proclaiming overtly: "women no longer swing in the ancient orbits."[11]

NOTES

1. Simone de Beauvoir, *The Second Sex*, trans. H.M. Parshley (New York: Random House, 1968), p. xvi.
2. *Ibid.*
3. Quoted in Herbert Marder, *Feminism and Art: A Study of Virginia Woolf* (Chicago: Univ. of Chicago Press, 1968), p. 5.
4. Quoted in A.R. Wadia, *The Ethics of Feminism* (New Delhi: Asian Publication Services, 1977), p. 49.
5. *Ibid.*, p. 29.
6. Margaret Drabble, *The Millstone* (London: Weidenfeld and Nicolson, 1965), p. 10.
7. Selma Sevenhuijsen, de Vries Petra, "The Women's Movement and Motherhood," *A Creative Tension* (London: Pluto Press, 1984), p. 19.
8. Annis Pratt, *Archetypal Patterns in Women's Fiction* (Great Britain: The Harvester Press, 1982), p. 127.
9. Margaret Drabble, *The Realms of Gold* (London: Weidenfeld and Nicolson, 1975), p. 185.
10. Mary Daly, *Gyn/Ecology: The Metaethics of Radical Feminism* (Boston: Beacon Press, 1978), p. 184.
11. Nancy Poland, "Margaret Drabble: 'There Must Be a Lot of People Like Me'," *Midwest Quarterly*, xvi, 3 (April, 1975), p. 265.

Beyond Divided Boundaries: A Reading of Marilyn French's Feminist Ideology in *Her Mother's Daughter*

GANGA VISWANATH

Since its re-emergence as an important cultural and political force in the 1960s, feminism has presented one of the most important challenges to accepted academic approaches to literary studies. Feminist studies now form a branch of "interdisciplinary enquiry which takes gender as a fundamental organizing category of experience."[1] Such an enquiry is based on two related premises about gender. One is that the inequality of the sexes is neither a biological given nor a divine mandate, but a cultural construct. The second is that the male perspective, hitherto assumed to be "universal," gives only a partial picture of human experience.

In all societies, there exist two basic discourses, that of the "dominant group" and that of the "muted group."[2] Taking the sexual categories, this would mean the male and the female discourses. Both these discourses make certain statements about human experiences and express certain values. While these two kinds of discourses can be traced in all the different genres of literature, a study of fiction is important since women have expressed themselves for a longer period through this genre. "Women's fiction reflects an experience radically different from men's As Annis Pratt states, "the tension . . . between forces demanding [women's] submissions and [their] rebellious assertions of personhood, characterize far too much of [their] fiction to be incidental."[3] A feminist reading of such fiction reveals the patterns of pain and suffering of women which form a leitmotif in the narrative. It also points to the possibility of change in the social and cultural structures resulting from women's fight against these norms of subservience to a dominant gender. In Marilyn French's *Her Mother's Daughter*, suffering becomes a legacy passed on from mother to daughter till one daughter decides to break free from this inheritance. Frances, who belongs to the first generation, sacrifices her own preferences and joys for a better future for her children. Isabella (Belle), her eldest daughter, inherits a legacy of grief and thwarted dreams but this chain of suffering and submission is broken by Anastasia, Belle's daughter, who as Stacey Stevens, a famous photographer, enjoys independence, material comforts and a career she loves. She triumphs in a man's world and feels that her mother has failed in life while she has succeeded. In her maturer years, however, she realizes "that the occupations of [her] mother's days . . . were as important, more important than all the hydroelectric plants, the oil rigs, the articles, the photographs, the magazines that occupied the other world, the world she [Anastasia] was part of."[4] On reflection she also realizes that her mother was more heroic than all the men engaged in technological progress. People's lives should be judged by the "contribution they make to the huge intricate organism that is the world. . . . And there was no contest. To nourish children and raise them against odds is more valuable" than all the advancements in technology and war. (619) In its totality, the compromise that her mother and her father had together effected to nourish their family seemed a very valuable contribution to society. Anastasia had started life with the belief "that life was split into two parts, one for women, the other for men. If you were an extraordinary woman you could take the man's role." (620) She did succeed in a man's role but that did not bring happiness because the division between these two worlds still existed. These dividing boundaries should merge through compromise and, as men and women learn to live as equals, the necessity for compromise will also diminish.

Anastasia is the narrator and she views her life sandwiched between the lives of the two preceding generations of women in her family and the one immediately succeeding. The use of this technique and the constant movement from the present into the recent and remote past and then into the future, gives a unique dimension to the "time" in the novel and also helps the reader to understand Anastasia's own reactions to life as a woman. Through the employment of this technique of juxtaposition, Marilyn French gives a creative thrust to the problems of women that she deals with in her work, bringing them sharply into focus, but leaving them without comment much as a photographer captures reality but leaves interpretation to the viewer.

Anastasia has little knowledge of her grandmother Frances's life, hence Belle recreates it for her. The narration begins thus:

> My mother said her mother was a saint. . . . And then she'd go off toward one part of it . . . the incredibly cruel man, the submissive woman, the brutalized children; or the poverty or the ignorance although when it came to ignorance, the voice grew an edge, a bitterness that sometimes seemed almost ready to spill over onto her mother. (19)

Belle tells Anastasia that she often wondered how her father knew so much about so many things that her mother did not know. She remembers one particular day when her father threw a carefully prepared dish of creamed spinach on the floor. Though Belle was just a child, she could not eat all that day because "she kept seeing Momma on her hands and knees, with her back bent wiping up the mess." (38) Though she felt sorry for her mother, it seemed to her that her mother was being punished for her ignorance. The child Belle had intuitively hit upon the relation between knowledge and power for "power and knowledge directly imply one another."[3] Belle herself is denied that knowledge which her mother lacked because when her father Michael Brez died in 1913, his business was near bankruptcy and there was little money to educate Belle. It broke her mother's heart when she heard from his friends that her husband often used to say that he was determined not "to leave behind a rich widow who would turn over his hard-earned money to some new man." (61) To Belle it appeared as if her father, though dead, still had them in his power through the burden of poverty which he had left behind for them to bear.

Anastasia is now able to recreate the life of Frances through her study of three family photographs. The first, taken in 1901, shows Frances as a contented woman with a "round placid face." She also notes the arrogance and "something fierce" in the aspect of her grandmother. (47) Anastasia observes the resemblance she bears to her grandmother "except that the placidity got lost over the generations." (47) She traces the fierce sense of purpose she feels to her grandfather. In the next photograph taken in 1907, "that arrogant man had become pure tyrant" (47) and Frances has lines of anxiety on her forehead. "She looks enraged, fixed in anger." (48) When Anastasia examines the next photograph she reflects that there are probably worse things than anger since this picture, taken after her grandfather's death, shows her grandmother "old, worn and defeated." (48) "She is only in her forties but there is no life in her face. Whatever spirit she had is gone." (48) Marilyn French here makes explicit the link between sex-war and class-struggle. The socio-economic aspects of marriage and its effects on women are also indicated. "To be female is to inhabit, without hope of escape, the lowest class in a sexist structure. Men may work . . . to improve their own position on the social scale [as Michael Brez had done]. Women, denied any such recourse, flit about on the edges of the real world, dependent on men for maintaining even the most unsatisfactory existence within it."[4] Frances's children are taken away from her and put in an orphanage while she screams in helpless rage. She is allowed to keep one child with her and she chooses to keep Belle. Belle now takes on the role of "housekeeper" while her mother becomes the bread winner.

When Belle grows up, she works with her mother. Frances puts away money and gets back her children from the orphanage. Belle now understands why her mother always felt so tired and incapable of responding to life. She sees the exploitation of women who are made to work for long hours. When she reminisces about this phase of her life, she tells Anastasia that she "felt like one of a herd of cattle trudging down those stairs just one more of an infinitely replaceable species, seen by bosses as so many head, treated that way." (105)

During this period of her life, her friend Sue's love and support are the only rays of sunshine. Sue teaches her the manners of genteel life and makes her feel like a "lady." Belle gets her hair cut without her mother's permission. She asserts her independence by doing so but Frances does not understand and disapproves. Belle improves her prospects but meets new dangers. She experiences a different form of exploitation in the architect's office. "Everytime he [the architect] passed her, he put his hand on her shoulder or arm." (123) When she shows no interest, she is fired. Belle does not give up. She is "willing to suffer the consequences of a fight, but not the stifled bitterness of subordination."[7]

Belle's meeting with the young Ed Dabrowski opens up a new world of experiences for her. The ecstasy of passion soon dissolves into tears when she finds herself pregnant. Woman cannot forget her biological destiny. If she does, she is punished. She marries Ed, but the ceremony is clouded with shame and guilt. Ed sets up an automobile workshop but his business collapses during the days of the Depression. Belle again gets caught up in a world of sacrifice, self-denial and suffering. It is into this world that Anastasia is born. Writing about her birth, she says: "She [Belle] wept, and from her pain, I emerged. I Anastasia, her punishment, the midge daughter." (139) The pieties of a traditionally defined motherhood are shattered in this statement. Belle has to learn to accept and love her baby daughter. Ed is a good husband and supports his family. Belle remains unhappy, yearning for a better life. A good part of the novel is about Belle's struggle to raise her family. Ed's interest in another woman poses a new threat, for "she knew that when man withdraws his presence, his comfort and companionship, the woman almost ceases to exist; she needs the continual validation of a male in a society which decrees that she is nothing of her own."[8] During these difficult years, Belle's friendship with other women gives her a lot of comfort. She experiences "sisterhood" as a sustaining force in her life.[9]

Anastasia sympathizes with her mother but grows up determined not to inherit her legacy of suffering. She expresses her determination thus:

> I saw the bloody cord connecting us. I set my teeth to bite myself free. I would not take my place in the sacrificial ranks . . . I would not repeat their experience. Above all, I would construct a new personality for myself that did not, like hers, absorb all the light and air surrounding it and turn it into darkness . . . surrounded by the proofs of my enslavement. (322)

When Anastasia grows up, she sees that men are always feared and women are expected to cater to their needs. When she goes out with boys and does not allow them to pet her, she is told: "I'll get you yet young lady." (157) Anastasia comments: "I couldn't stand the way he said that, as if I were a *thing* and he could *get* me, the way you get a puppy and domesticate it." (152) Like her mother before her, she finds that is what men do, and women have to accept their biological destiny. Bradley Carpenter treats her like a princess and their period of courtship ends when she finds herself pregnant. He marries her, gives up his dreams of becoming a musician and settles down as a real estate agent. Anastasia is unable to make a compromise between illusion and reality. "Making a compromise is difficult" for her, she feels "corrupt," "weak" and dishonest when she does so. (675) Her marriage becomes "pure surface with nothing underneath." (264) Such a relationship is stifling but Anastasia realizes that "integrity [is] a luxury few women [can] afford." (264) She decides to give herself that luxury and asks Brad for a divorce. Brad's ego is hurt. He does not agree to it when she asks for it but later suggests it himself when he gets interested in another woman. Anastasia sees the selfishness of man. She also learns to fight and emerge the winner and gets an assignment with *World*, an internationally recognized magazine. The hobby which she developed when she kept house for Brad, which Brad had resented, now proves to be a source of income for her. As Stacey Stevens, the photographer, she makes a name for herself but her children do not share the happiness she feels when she gets her first assignment abroad. She despairs: "I couldn't tell them that I felt I'd suddenly been recognized as a person, as a human being and not just a woman, a mother, which is to say, nobody at all, a cipher." (357) The conflict that a woman experiences when she breaks away from stereotyped roles and chooses a self-assigned role is well portrayed. Often a woman acts according to the wishes of her family especially those of her children. For Anastasia, however, the assignment is not only the fulfilment of an ambition but an economic necessity. She goes against the wishes of her family and accepts it.

The attitude of men towards women of talent is well pictured by Anastasia when she expresses the difficulties experienced by her while working with a man called Russ Sonders: "I can't just dismiss him as a drunk and a bully. He is a *man*. And automatically, because he is a man, he has a kind of authority. . . . Why! Shouts the other part of my heart/head." (414) While doing her assignments, she gets several opportunities to study the attitude of society to women: A women's convention is referred to as a convention of Broads, a photo essay on poor Indian women shows them "whirling in the same condition." (96) As a war-correspondent, she proves her capacity to endure the travails of war as well as any man. She also marries Toni, her landlady's nephew, several years younger to her, who keeps house for her. This experiment in reversal of roles does not work out. When Toni gets a job in

Hollywood, he leaves his family including his own child Franny (named after Anastasia's grandmother Frances) *The World*, the magazine for which Anastasia worked, collapses and she finds herself burdened with the children:

> Women, caring about kids or ending up with them, somehow we cannot give them up. . . . What can I call it? Not love. More than love and not excluding hate. My heart is tied to them with [an] unbreakable code. The cord is scarred, pulled thin, hacked at, but it does not break . . . it is strong enough to rip apart the heart before it breaks. (590)

The authenticity of Anastasia's experience and the frankness of her expression combine to shock the reader into recognizing the mingling of love and hate even in the idealized relationship between a mother and her children.[10] Weighed down with her responsibilities, she visualizes the lives of women in her family. She states: "I saw our inconsolability—mine, her's [Belle's], her mother's before her, as the natural consequence of being alive for forty years as a woman." (605) She also sees this struggle pass on to her daughter, so that in one sense the daughter re-lives the life of her mother as the title of the novel indicates. Marilyn French thus challenges the alienation from and rejection of the mother that the daughters learn under patriarchy. She goes beyond matrophobia to a subconscious quest for the mother who upholds all that is truly meaningful and heroic in life.

Marilyn French's feminist ideology is nowhere explicitly stated but has been unobtrusively expressed through the characters. The consciousness of gender in all the characters in the novel focuses the reader's attention on a key force of oppression in the contemporary world and the consequent division of the world into a "man's world" and a "woman's world." She engages these issues and works through them to reveal that woman, like man, is a gift to the world. One must learn to dissolve the dividing boundaries to "embrace the full reality of human society."[11]

NOTES

1. Gayle Greene and Coppelia Kahns, eds., *Making a Difference: Feminist Literary Criticism* (London and New York: Methuen, 1985), pp. 2-3.
2. Joe Andrew, *Women in Russian Literature, 1780-1863* (London: Macmillan, 1988), p. 3.
3. Annis Pratt, *Archetypal Patterns in Women's Fiction* (Bloomington: Indiana University Press, 1981), p. 6.
4. Marilyn French, *Her Mother's Daughter* (New York: Summit Books, 1987), p. 619.
5. Michel Foucault, *Discipline and Punish: The Birth of the Prison*, trans. Alan Sheridan (New York: Pantheon, 1977), p. 27.
6. Rosalind Miles, *The Female Form: Women Writers and the Conquest of the Novel* (London: Routledge and Kegan Paul, 1987), p. 135.
7. William Drake, *The First Wave: Women Poets in America 1915-45* (New York: Macmillan, 1987), p. 170.
8. Rosalind Miles, p. 123.
9. Nina Auerbach, *Communities of Women: An Idea of Fiction* (Massachusetts: Harvard University Press, 1978), p. 13.
10. This idea has also been stated by Adrienne Rich in her book *Of Woman Born: Motherhood As Experience and Institution* (London: Virago, 1976).
11. Nina Auerbach, p. 191.

Female Experience and Redeeming Violence in Joyce Carol Oates's *them*

N.P. SINGH

Although Joyce Carol Oates won the National Book Award for fiction in 1970 for her novel *them* (1969), critical response to the novel has been sharply divided. Alfred Kazin has described it as "her best novel to date."[1] Dorothy Curley has opined that *them* is "a rather sadly old-fashioned novel about a poor family.[2] Walter Sullivan has pointed out, "*them* is more ambitious than *A Garden of Earthly Delights*—it has more characters, its scope is wider—and as a chronicle of life among the poor of a big city, it rings all true."[3] Writing in *Newsweek*, G.W. lamented, "This novel is a charnel house of Gothic paraphernalia; blood, fire, insanity, anarchy, lust, corruption, death by bullets, death by cancer, death by plane crash, death by stabbing, beatings, crime, riot, and even unhappiness."[4]

An effort has been made in this paper to look at the novel *them* as a chronicle of the life of the poor in a big city like Detroit which acts both as the loadstar and also as constraint for its protagonists. Powerlessness and social deprivation of the major characters in the novel leads to violence, violence both in thought and in action. It is true that the novel is steeped in violence and it is through violence that the major protagonists redeem themselves and affirm their humanity in a world that gives them very little choice to act and manoeuvre. Violence articulates women's predicament in a society where they are doubly victimized.

G.W. Waller has pointed out in his study, *Dreaming America*, that "the book is a tripartite account of two generations of the Wendall family, whose lives never make newspaper headlines but are nonetheless darkly determined by the limiting, hostile environment of Detroit."[3] The drama of the life of Loretta Botsford is unfolded against the backdrop of a big industrial city like Detroit where she lives downtown in a drab apartment. She is a young woman, sixteen years old, who stands before a mirror and scrutinizes herself in it. Joyce Carol Oates visualizes her feelings in these words, "Looking into the mirror was like looking into the future; everything was there, waiting."[4] Loretta's father has been out of work for ten years and her brother Brock has been with his peers on the street. While her father immerses himself in alcohol, Brock invariably carries a gun with him. Loretta works in a laundry and also bears the drudgery of home as her mother has been dead for many years. The drama of Loretta's life begins in August 1937 and she has a soaring dream, a dream of happiness and love.

It is Saturday, a day of rest and fun. Loretta goes out of the house and sees people moving briskly on the street. She meets her lover Bernie Malin, spends some time with him and then invites him to her house. She reassures him that her father will be dead drunk and her brother will not return till morning. She also affirms that nobody is likely to enter her room and she is the architect of her life. The lovers are together and it is after their blissful union that the nightmare of Loretta's life is depicted. She is awakened by the shot of a gun and discovers her lover to be dead. She apprehends that her brother must have perpetrated the crime. He has always been madly jealous of her lover and also tried unsuccessfully to exert the authority of the father in the family.

Loretta runs frantically out of the room. She finds it difficult to believe that her lover has been shot dead— "One shot had done it, like magic." (38) She runs out of the apartment and goes to her friend Rita. She tells her that she wants a gun. Rita consoles her and wants to know what has really troubled her. Loretta simply says, "I'm in trouble, I need a gun." (45) Rita, however, gives Loretta only a dress. It is while returning home that Loretta chances to meet Howard Wendall, a cop. He interrogates her sharply but she is not able to make a frank confession to him. She simply says, "I'm in awful bad trouble." (47) Howard Wendall reaches her apartment and discovers the dead body in Loretta's room. He becomes angry and admonishes her that she is in deep, deep trouble. His authoritarian impulse is aroused and, realizing her vulnerability, he seizes her and rapes her in the kitchen. Joyce Carol Oates has described Loretta's sad plight in memorable words, "And then, struggling with Howard, struggling to make it easier for him, she did think of Bernie for the first time: he was dead. She had loved him and he was dead and she would never see him again. Never would he come to her the way Howard was trying to come to her. He was dead, it was over, finished, that was the end of her youth." (50)

The opening scenes of the novel portray vividly the dream and the nightmare of Loretta. She marries Howard Wendall who helps her in disposing of the dead body and moves to another apartment in the city, the south side of Detroit. Her youth comes to an end at an early age and her life as a married woman begins. Her son Jules is born first. He is a restless and energetic child. Mama Wendall, the grandmother, lionizes the child and is awfully proud of his restlessness. Her husband is, however, suspended from his job and the family moves to the country. It is Mama Wendall, who is the boss of the country house, and Loretta is always in awe of her. The family grows and Jules has a sister, Maureen, who in turn is followed by Betty. Mama Wendall is happy in the country and affirms, "America is really the country, not the city." (65) Loretta, however, is not convinced. She finds the life in the country rather dull and vegetating. There is nothing in the country for the children except fresh air and it is no wonder that "Loretta wept for the lost city and its dirty air." (65)

Howard Wendall is drafted and sent to Europe during the Second World War and Loretta defies Mama Wendall and returns to Detroit with the children. She castigates her mother-in-law sharply: "Oh, you big old horse! You let me alone! I'm free to go where I want." (79) Loretta's life is a quest for autonomy and freedom. She knows that her freedom will remain a myth as long as she stays with Mama Wendall. She has, however, no choice in Detroit but to stay with her old friend Rita. She also becomes a street-walker. While soliciting a customer, she is caught by a police squad. Joyce Carol Oates visualizes her predicament in these words, "Loretta was led up to it to be introduced officially to the city of Detroit." (84) Mama Wendall's prophecy that she will become a whore indeed comes true. Loretta reduces herself to become a street-walker, a commodity for sale in a big city.

Jules, Maureen and Betty grow up in the city and discover both the lure and the trap of Detroit in their own way. Even when in the country, Jules had set the barn on fire. Mama Wendall had whipped the boy furiously and cried, "You'll wind up in the electric chair and I'll pull the switch." (78) Jules grows up to be a wild young man who drops out of school. He loiters on the street and commits petty thefts. Once he receives a sound thrashing at the hands of a cop. It hurts him deeply: "He wept silently in pain, ashamed, and made his way back out to the street." (124) While Jules manages to escape from home and school to the street, Maureen is a student who finds school a sanctuary from the chaos and disorder of home. She is particularly fond of the order and peace in the library which is like a real home for her. She also nurses a dream to be a good but stern mother, spanking the naughty ones and fondling the good ones. Even a kid as wild and unruly as Betty will be tamed and disciplined.

Howard Wendall returns from the war and becomes a factory worker. He dies in an accident and Jules and Maureen do not hide their dislike of their father because he had ceased to count in the family. Loretta finds Maureen grown into an attractive woman and she begins to worry. She has no control over Betty, the youngest one, but she does try to curb Maureen's movements. She screams at Maureen and at anyone who comes in her contact. Maureen has to do school's homework and is also burdened with the drudgery of the kitchen.

She works incessantly and dreams. Her dreams are her only solace in her home which she hates intensely. She dreams of being a teacher at the school and commanding children, even bullying them into submission. She wants to be perfect as a teacher, free from all human errors. Joyce Carol Oates recounts Maureen's dream in these words, "Even when she played, even in her imagination she was somehow afraid of making a mistake." (138)

Maureen is, however, fined in the library and she has to pay the fine. She tells Jules that she needs some money to pay the fine. She borrows money from Jules but she feels sick because she has not told her brother the fact that she has savings of her own. She is afraid to communicate with Loretta and she also does not want to depend on Jules's charity. Loretta has a new husband named Furlong. Maureen finds it difficult to address him as dad. Her stepfather teases her occasionally but Maureen dislikes him immensely. Loretta has become Mrs. Furlong but Maureen is gradually drifting from home: "But she was measuring everything against the time when she would leave home, like Jules." (178)

Maureen is once slapped by her stepfather. He slaps her because she defies him while he is quarrelling with Loretta. While her mother wants her to apologize to him, Maureen remains adamant and also resolves to attain economic emancipation and end her dependence on Jules. She is preoccupied with the question, "How do you get money?" Maureen chances to meet a man while returning from her school. He gives her a ride in his car and takes her to the river. Without feeling any love for the man, Maureen submits to him, thinking all the time of the money that he will give her. She also has a realization that, with the acquisition of money, she will get freedom from the restrictions at home.

Maureen takes to the street and becomes a street-walker at an early age. She hides her earnings inside her books very meticulously. She also begins to regard a man primarily as an intricate machine through which money can be squeezed if one follows methodically the motions of a street-walker. Her emotions are not at all involved in her adventures and there is no trace of any guilt feeling in her. What really matters for her is the money she hides inside her books. Nemesis, however, overtakes her when her stepfather discovers the money hidden inside her books. Joyce Carol Oates has described the stepfather's fury in memorable words:

> He came toward her and seized her by the neck and dragged her into the room. He was shouting something she couldn't catch. She heard the words but they were so close to her, battering her, that she could not make them out. With his free hand he began striking her. He held her up so that she couldn't fall and struck her again and again, while she tried to get away, to fall backwards away from his hand. She screamed. He began to strike her body. He let go her and she fell. She put her arms over her head and screamed against the floor, the linoleum floor, while he bent over to pound her flat on the back with his fists. (219)

The first section of the novel titled "Children of Silence" comes to an end with Maureen's merciless battering by her stepfather. She has never regarded him as her father but Furlong exercises the formidable authority of a father in a patriarchal society. Brock had shot dead the lover of Loretta and Furlong nearly kills Maureen. She is bed-ridden and is hospitalized for months. She is driven to the brink of insanity. While Loretta and Maureen figure prominently in the first section of the novel, Jules occupies the dominating position in the second section of the novel entitled "To Whose Country Have I Come?"

Jules worries about Maureen's illness but Loretta assures him that she will recover. Jules spends much of his time on the street, away from home. He chances to meet downtown Fay, a rich woman. As he meets her for the first time, he is nearly hit by a car. He is told by Fay, "That was pretty close." (233) This fleeting moment is, perhaps, an index of the contemporary

America and the violence that is swirling around. Jules is infatuated with Fay because she is not an ordinary woman. She is a woman with a diamond on her finger. He tells her that he will go to California and make his fortoune. Fay interrupts him, saying, "There's nothing out there." (237) Jules does not believe her and yearns to go out of Detroit. Joyce Carol Oates visualizes Jules's dream in these words: "He could smell Detroit about him, a kind of stretched-out hole, a hold with a horizon." (232)

Jules meets through Fay a guy named Bernard Geffen who employs him as his car driver. It is through Bernard that Jules discovers the suburb of Grosse Pointe. The houses in the suburb are beautiful, surrounded with lush lawns, and the people lead a life of luxury and affluence. The people living there seem mysterious and utterly fascinating to Jules who is only eighteen. When he earns dollars while serving Bernard Geffen, he is simply thrilled. He also starts planning his future. He stops thinking of his sister Maureen and becomes infatuated with Bernard's niece Nadine who too lives in the suburb. After Bernard's gruesome murder, Jules is irresistibly drawn to her. She has a strange apprehension while he makes love to her, "I can feel myself lying on my back somewhere, like this, in some strange room in Detroit, with my throat cut and the blood down under my back, getting me wet. I can almost see it. And you're squatting over me, looking at me." (284)

There is a strange irony in this terrible vision. We know that at the end of the second section of the novel, it is Nadine who shoots Jules and also tries to shoot herself. Alfred Kazin has described the novel *them* as a frightening book. The violence in the mind of Nadine is, perhaps, far more frightening than the violence she actually commits. There is also a touch of the picaresque in the novel as Jules steals a car and runs off with Nadine to far-off Texas. He falls ill, terribly ill, and Nadine deserts him. Jules slowly recovers in Texas, performs odd jobs and eventually returns to Detroit. He begins to work with his wealthy uncle Samson and also cherishes the American dream: "With his looks and his brains, he thought, why couldn't he make as much money as his uncle Samson had made? That is, on his way to become a millionaire." (297)

Nadine once again gets involved with Jules but she is not happy by any stretch of imagination. She admonishes him, "But you can't push me around like that. You can't tell me what to do." (286) When she chances to meet Jules in Detroit, she is a married woman. She lives comfortably in the suburb and Jules is again fatally driven to her. She confesses to him her acute dissatisfaction at being a woman:

> A woman is like a dream. Her life is a dream of waiting. I mean, she lives in a dream, waiting for a man. There's no way out of this, insulting as it is, no woman can escape it. Her life is a waiting for a man. That's all. There is a certain door in this dream, and she has to walk through it. She has no choice. (367)

The Nadine-Jules encounter has been described by Joyce Carol Oates in clinical details. "Really they were trapped together, struggling together. They were enemies. He imagined her body lacerated with deep red gashes, the frantic maniacal slashes of a dog, and the idea of her blood, the sight of her blood excited him." (394) It is clear that their relationship is not of equals. It is a relationship between the hunter and the prey. It is, however, an irony that ultimately Jules becomes the victim and Nadine turns out to be the hunter. She shoots Jules and also tries to shoot herself in a frenzy. She wants to extricate herself from a relationship that demeans her in her own eyes. She asks Jules vehemently, "You're thinking that I'm a pig? For all this? A pig, a slut?" (397)

While Jules has a traumatic experience with Nadine who seems to be ashamed of her sexuality, Maureen recovers gradually from her insanity. She is nursed back to health by Loretta and uncle Brock who has returned unexpectedly. She resumes her studies and finishes school education. She becomes a student of Joyce Carol Oates at the University of

Detroit. She introduces herself to her teacher and writes letters to her. Her second letter to her teacher is indeed a remarkable document and unfolds her growth and the pangs of a woman's growth against the backdrop of the contemporary America of the sixties. She hates her teacher because she has given her an "F" and failed her. Joyce Carol Oates has also told her that a work of art like *Madame Bovary* is far more important than life. A work of art contains order and beauty and is, therefore, superior to life which is full of disorder and chaos. Maureen challenges her teacher's formalism:

> Oh, we women know things you don't know, you teachers, you readers and writers of books, we are the ones who wait round libraries when it's time to leave, or sit drinking coffee alone in the kitchen; we make crazy plans for marriage but have no man, *we dream of stealing men,* (italics mine) we are the ones who look slowly around when we get off a bus and can't even find what we are looking for, can't quite remember how we got there, we are always wondering what will come next, what terrible thing will come next! (341)

Mary Allen has rightly pointed out in *The Necessary Blankness: Women in Major American Fiction of the Sixties*, "No one is better at showing the female consciousness aware of the possibilities of rape than Joyce Carol Oates. She is a master at depicting women's anxieties of many sorts, and she makes a striking contribution to our understanding of contemporary America as seen by women. Here is an author to read if one dares to know the particular fear there is in being a woman."[7] It is through the image of Maureen Wendall that the writer has made concrete the sad plight of a young woman in contemporary America. The third section of the novel entitled "Come My Soul, That Hath Long Languished" begins with Maureen in 1966 looking at her reflection in a mirror. She is sick of being Maureen Wendall and she wants to be a different person. She wants above all to have a husband and a house of her own. She wants a home where she can take her own decisions.

The sight of Maureen at the mirror reminds us of Loretta at the beginning of the novel. While Loretta was waiting for something momentous to happen, Maureen is not that optimistic. She has the trauma of battering at the hands of her stepfather behind her. She has also the painful experience of being a street-walker and a failure at the University of Detroit to chasten her. It is clear that Maureen has the capacity to shed her illusions and face the bleak reality around her far better than her mother who keeps on living in a world of make beliefs and great expectations. She is a woman of twenty six, living alone in the city and not the starry-eyed Loretta, a girl of sixteen, who stares into the mirror and dreams of the future.

them is a contemporary American novel that is written in the naturalistic mode and is saturated with the mundane details of living in the suburb and in the city. It reeks with violence, violence both in thought and in action. There is, however, another dimension in the novel. Loretta looks into the mirror as a sixteen year old girl but Maureen looks into the mirror as a twenty-six year old woman who feels old enough to be a woman of fifty. Mama Wendall denounces Loretta as a whore when she defies her and goes to Detroit and, at the end of the novel, Loretta also denounces Maureen as a whore when she comes to know that her daughter is going to marry a teacher who is already married and has children. There is a circularity of narration embedded in the naturalistic texture of the novel which poignantly draws our attention to the conflict of generations and the reversal of roles. Rebels of one generation become the tyrants of the next generation who are themselves challenged by the new rebels. Loretta challenged Mama Wendall and is herself challenged by Maureen towards the end of the novel. The endless flux of life is communicated by Joyce Carol Oates through the recurrence of certain cardinal situations and the reversal of roles.

The naturalistic mode of the writer is also coupled with the prophetic mode, especially in the last section of the novel. It is the summer in 1966 and the temperature goes up steeply.

A riot breaks out in the streets of Detroit and the stores are set on fire. Men, women and children from the city begin to loot the stores and take goods home. Even Loretta joins the mob and carries a portable television home. It is an irony, however, that the set does not function properly and eventually it is burnt when the rioters set fire to Loretta's apartment. She becomes homeless, and along with others, gets shelter in the house of a lady living in the suburb.

The police and the administration take stern measures to restore law and order. Jules is also infuriated by the frenzy of the mob and shoots a cop. The act of murder is the culmination of Jules's life, liberating him from his inert and directionless existence. It gives some meaning to his unproductive and sterile life. There is no reason to disagree with Josephine Hendlin who is of the opinion, "Violence in her novels is accepted, legitimized, and even idealized."[8] Jules gets into the company of student activists and Dr. Piercy, an Assistant Professor of Sociology at Wayne State University. While riots grip Detroit, the staid don unfolds calmly his distant dream:

> I know that our society must be leveled before a new, beautiful, peaceful society can be erected. This means the end of the world as we have known it, we middle-class whites, but it must be realized, it must be acknowledged, and we ourselves must attain it—or go down in history on the side of the Hitlers and Stalins, the oppressors of mankind, involved at this very moment in a bloody war to put down a revolution in Vietnam. (501-2)

There is, however, a big gulf between the radicalism of the University don and the men and women who loot and burn stores. The rioters are moved primarily by greed and do not have any revolutionary ardour. They are at best victims of the values of a consumerist culture. As we have seen, even Loretta becomes a victim of the culture of grab and seek and steals a portable television. She also sees on her benefactor's television a programme on Detroit riots. The don's speech is followed by that of her son Jules. He is of the view, "Everything in America is coming alive. It's breaking out and coming alive. It is only necessary to understand that fire burns and does its duty, perpetually, and the fires will never be put out" (502)

The fire without doubt stands for the riot, the looting and the arson that breaks out on the streets of Detroit. It is evident that Jules regards the riot as a manifestation of the people's desperate revolt against the status quo. He doesn't realize the fact that the rioters are prompted by naked greed and they do not have any vision of revolution and social reconstruction. They are the victims of the glaring contrast between the suburb and the city. They constitute the lumpen proletariate of the modern city. As long as they roam on the streets of Detroit, the fires would continue to burn and destroy. The writer has created Detroit as a symbol of a modern city in which an explosion can take place any moment.

Loretta, however, weeps bitterly at the stance taken by her son. She weeps inconsolably and keeps on wondering, "What had happened to Jules? Why had he said such crazy things? She was ashamed of him. She remembered him burning down a barn as a child. She remembered him pushing through a crowd to stare at a burning plane. Why, he is a murderer. She thought clearly, he is a murderer, and she had given birth to a murderer." (503)

The novel comes to an end with an encounter between Maureen and Jules. She has married her teacher and lives in a suburb. She is surprised to see Jules and he can also sense her uneasiness. He tells her that he has come to say her goodbye. He also wants her to keep in touch with mother. Even Betty, the wild one, always roaming the street, helps her occasionally. Jules wants Maureen to help mother and also to give her a ring. Maureen retorts sharply: "Don't talk to me like that! You know! You know everything I know. Jules, please, could you leave now? I don't feel well. I feel sort of sick. We don't have any money, he has to pay child support. . . . We don't have enough money for ourselves." (505) She expresses further her resolve never to see her mother and her sister. She will have absolutely no connection with them. Jules, however, questions her sharply, "But, honey, aren't you one of them yourself." (507)

Maureen gives no answer to Jules's pertinent question. She indeed belonged to *them*, the dispossessed and the poor living beastly in overcrowded apartments in the city. But now she is a different person, living in the suburb. She is also going to have a baby. She asks her brother if he has become a communist, a revolutionary. Jules replies that he does not know what a communist is. He is simply trying to get along and make money. He is on his way to California with the university don, his mentor. He will begin his life afresh in California and realize his dream.

Jules eventually gets ready to leave Maureen. He tells her that he loves her and after making his fortune in California he will try to marry Nadine, the woman who tried to kill him. He will one day return to Detroit and see her. His final words to Maureen are both a comfort and a warning:

> I love you for being such a sweet sister and suffering so much and getting out of it, using your head, but don't forget that this place here can burn down too. Men can come back in your life, Maureen, they can beat you up again and force your knees apart, why not? . . . Can't it happen? Won't it happen? Wouldn't you really want it to happen? (507)

Maureen tells her brother that it will never, never happen. She thinks that her home will ever remain intact and protect her from the chaos and disorder widely prevalent in the city.

A critic like Walter Sullivan wonders, "One does not know where the focus should fall in these novels or who the main characters are."[9] The focus of the writer in my view is on the family and women in different societal contexts. In spite of the naked terror of living in contemporary America where apartments can be burnt and women can be raped, *them* is a saga of the survival of the Wendall family. Jules has a hope of going to California and realizing the American dream and Maureen has a faith that her house in the suburb will never be destroyed. Loretta dreams of becoming a nurse because nurses have a respect in society. All the buffets of fortune fail to destroy her faith in future and grief hurts her but does not entirely corrode her soul. Frederick R. Karl is rightly of the view, "Joyce Carol Oates's fiction is in one form or another concerned with the female experience—best achieved in her novel *them*, which I see as a key text of the sixties."[10]

To conclude, both Loretta and Maureen always strive to realize freedom and autonomy through marriage, not outside marriage, They do not submit passively and always try to attain a life of dignity and self-respect. When Maureen is severely mauled by her stepfather, Loretta does not accept it meekly. She manages to get her husband convicted and sentenced to imprisonment. Joyce Carol Oates has given us memorable portraits of women in her novel *them*, and showed us both their vulnerability and their innate strength. Their fond dreams and illusions are indeed shattered but they have the courage and the resourcefulness to survive in a violence-saturated world. The writer has neither idealized women nor shown them as bitches. She has depicted them as they really are—caring, vulnerable and yet resourceful, resourceful enough to survive in an essentially paternalistic, male dominated world in which fires will continue to burn perpetually.

Alfred Kazin has described *them* as a frightening book. It is, however, a half-truth. The flood of violence in the novel is frightening as well as redemptive. To cite an example, the violence that Maureen's stepfather inflicts on her is indeed frightening but the violence that Nadine and Jules perpetrate is both frightening and redemptive. They redeem themselves through violence and assert their humanity and autonomy through their desperate acts. It would not be out of place to quote the writer on the cathartic nature of her art: "A writer's job, ideally, is to act as the conscience of his race. People frequently misunderstand serious art because it is often violent and unattractive. I wish the world were a prettier place but I wouldn't be honest as a writer if I ignored the actual conditions around me."[11] It is through the remorseless rendering of violence and disorder that Joyce Carol Oates endeavours to achieve the catharsis of our fears, apprehensions and phobias in the contemporary world. The violence in her novel *them* is only the means to an end. It is not an end by itself.

NOTES

1. Linda Wagner, *Critical Essays on Joyce Carol Oates* (Boston: G.K. Hall, 1971), p. 159.
2. *Ibid.*, p. xxv.
3. *Ibid.*, p. 83.
4. *Ibid.*, p. xxv.
5. G.W. Waller, *Dreaming America* (Baton Rouge, Louisiana State University Press, 1979), p. 127.
6. Joyce Carol Oates, *them* (New York: The Vanguard Press, 1969), p. 15.
7. Linda Wagner, p. xxvii.
8. *Harvard Guide to Contemporary American Writing* (Cambridge, Mass.: Harvard University Press, 1979), p. 253.
9. Linda Wagner, p. 81.
10. Frederick R. Karl, *American Fiction 1940-1980* (New York: Harper and Row, 1985), p. 420.
11. Linda Wagner, p. xvii.

Feminism as Pop Fantasy: A Reading through Sidney Sheldon's *If Tomorrow Comes*

SHRUTI DAS

I

Serious or mainstream literature is read by the academics and the serious-minded people. But popular literature is voraciously consumed by the mass. The popular-fiction writers shape the attitude of the mass. As the mid-twentieth century saw the rise of feminist consciousness, feminism became a commodity that sold. Male writers pretended to sympathize with the cause of feminism. In fact, men who propagate feminist discourse today rarely question whether or not their perspective on women's reality is true to the lived experience of women as a collective group. More often than not, they project the sexist-racist stereotype of the strong, superhuman woman which is the operative myth in the minds of many.

Sidney Sheldon is a prototype of the American thriller novelists. His novels are popular thrillers, translated into multiple languages and sold in million copies internationally. His readers call him a feminist because his books *The Other Side of Mid-night, Bloodline, The Rage of Angels, Master of the Game, If Tomorrow Comes*, and *Windmill of the Gods* feature famous and infamous heroines. These heroines have beauty, intelligence and ice-cold nerves; with these weapons they wage war against a world that has cheated them of conventional success and happiness. This image of woman fogs the major issues of feminism. Feminism proposes to expose and view a suppressed image of humanity and thereby define woman as a subject in her own right. Unfortunately, the popular-fiction writers indulge in "literary transvestism" in the name of feminism. Literary transvestism not only impersonates women-as-subjects but also women-as-perceivers.

II

This paper attempts to study the protagonist in Sidney Sheldon's *If Tomorrow Comes*[1] (1985) as an embodiment of feminism as conceived and manifested by him. The heroine Tracy Whitney is projected as a woman who fights for existence in a society that denies her justice and a normal life. Sheldon, like his tribe of popular-fiction writers, attempts to champion the cause of feminism and endows Tracy Whitney with superhuman character. Tracy's metamorphosis from a vulnerable, young woman suffering in a patriarchal system into an invincible hood is indeed fantastic. Tracy becomes more of a female-man than a female, trying to find her identity in a male-dominated world. Though Tracy expresses only one of the facets of feminism, that is, rebellion against oppression, Sheldon does not allow her complete freedom of thought and action. There is always a man in the picture to whom she turns for direction. It is men who propel her out of her complacence into rebellion, it is men who use her spirit and intelligence and finally, it is a man who subordinates her. Sheldon's manifest is a parody of the philosophy of feminism. One does not learn what Tracy as a woman has felt or experienced but only what Sheldon thinks Tracy should be—this is Sheldon's transvestism.

Women have always been considered as subordinates. Vern Bullough in his book *The Subordinate Sex* has said: "The very word woman . . . emphasized (a) passive anonymous position. It derives from the Anglo-Saxon *wifman*, literally "wife-man," and the implication seems to be that there is no such thing as woman separate from wifehood. As individuals, with few exceptions, women did not count. They were mothers, wives, daughters, sisters, proper and forgotten."[2] In establishing a rigid difference between "male" and "female," society appeared to have allocated to "female" all the qualities that males thought were undesirable. To conform to the stereotype of "womanly" or "feminine" meant to display those characteristics that distinguished women from men. It meant behaviour that was passive or weak, compliant, and indecisive. It meant being susceptible to suggestion from others, easily led or persuaded. It meant being non-aggressive and non-competitive, and dependent, in need of companionship and affection. In short, women were meant to be inadequate, self-doubting, and essentially incapable of a strong, independent and autonomous existence. Feminists maintain that the sex-role stereotype of woman was a prescription for failure, for victimization. Gradually, women became aware of the limits and dangers of femininity, both as an individual psychological state, and as a wider social phenomenon. Consciousness-raising of women became the first step to change. The faint echo of protest took the form of a strong voice and a concrete movement by the 1960s and 70s. Women were no longer willing to accept male oppression. They demanded political, economic, and sexual rights. For women, liberation meant self-determination within a definable environment. The real female combined in her the so-called feminine qualities of nurturance, compassion, tenderness, sensitivity, affirmativeness, co-operativeness with the so-called masculine qualities of aggressiveness, initiative, and competitiveness.

In *If Tomorrow Comes*, Sheldon introduces Tracy Whitney as a traditional feminine character who is solely concerned with being a daughter, a girl-friend and ultimately a wife. She wants to impress people, especially her fiance, Charles Stanhope's parents into accepting her: "She wanted Charles's parents to see her at her best. I have got to make them like me." (17) She is the stereotype of woman who is passive, dependent and indecisive. To emphasize this point, Sheldon writes:

> She was nervous. Her beautiful hair-do had succumbed

> to the dampness in the air. She had changed dress four times. Should she dress simply? Formally? She had one Yves Saint Laurent she had scrimped to buy at Wanamaker's. If I wear it, they will think I'm extravagant. On the other hand, if I dress in one of my sale things from Post Horm, they'll think their son is marrying beneath him. Oh hell. . . . (18)

Tracy undergoes hell due to her indecisiveness. Her worth as a person is in direct proportion to the way in which she dresses and projects herself. Her simple complacency is shattered one night when a telephone call informs her that her mother is dead. Her shock becomes manifold when she learns that her mother had been driven first to bankruptcy and then to suicide by Joe Romano, the Chief henchman of the underworld king of New Orleans, Anthony Orsatti. Tracy innocently sets out to avenge her mother's death. She naively confronts Romano in his own house. Instead of admitting to his guilt, Romano tries to molest her. She attempts to defend herself by shooting at him, then calls for an ambulance and flees. Romano, who is not seriously injured frames Tracy. He accuses her of armed robbery of a valuable Renoir painting. She is arrested at the airport. Attorney Perry Pope and Judge Lawrence also trick her into admitting something she is not guilty of. She is convicted. For the next fifteen years, she is "to be incarcerated in the Southern Louisiana Penitentiary for Women." (44) Charles too betrays her. She is all alone in the world: "Tracy realized . . . she had been tricked. They were going to destroy her. Just as they had destroyed her mother." (44) "They" were men who made or broke the law as was convenient to them. "They" were men who dominated over and used both Tracy and her mother as it suited their purpose. Distressed, Tracy searches for an alternative.

Radical feminists imagine an alternative reality, a "Herland," which is a woman's utopia. This kind of alternative reality and utopian feminist vision is the central theme of Charlotte Perkins Gilman's *Herland*.[3] The society in Gilman's

Herland is matrilineal. This isolated community is ruled by women and worships a woman who has solved the riddle of life and death. Women work constructively and collectively with other women. They do not bicker; they are well organized; they do not admire aggression in men; they can invent. The sexiest stereotype woman is discarded. The three man team of explorers to Herland is forced to observe: "We had expected pettiness, and found a social consciousness. . . . We had expected jealousy, and found a broad sisterly affection." (81) On the other hand, Sidney Sheldon's "Herland"—the Southern Louisiana Penitentiary for Women is the antithesis of this feminist ideal.

It is also very much unlike Gloria Naylor's celebrated Brewster Place. Naylor's fictional Brewster place, in her novel *The Women of Brewster Place*,[4] is a haven for women suffering from sexism and racism. Women of all colours and all walks of life lived in the shelter of Brewster place in perfect co-operation with one another. They were one in prosperity and in adversity. Their unity and intensity is well observed by Naylor when she describes a scene where the women are pulling down a wall that had been stained by the blood of one of their inmates:

> Women flung themselves against the wall, chipping away at it with knives, plastic forks, spiked shoe heels, and even bare hands; the water pouring under their chins, plastering their blouses and dresses against their breasts and into the cracks of their hips. . . . Suddenly, the rain exploded around their feet in a fresh downpour, and the cold waters beat on the top of their heads—almost in perfect unison with the beating of their hearts. (186-88)

"Unison" is the keynote of this feminist utopia. But the atmosphere of Southern Louisiana Penitentiary described by Sheldon tells another tale.

It is a distopia where abnormal activities are rampant. Lesbianism is an accepted norm; women rape women; the catch-word is "fresh-meat"; and the new prisoners are "fish":

> First offenders who were sexually normal never had a chance. They came in timid and frightened; the bull-dykes were there, waiting. The drama was enacted in planned stages. In a terrifying and hostile world the bull-dyke was friendly and sympathetic. She would invite her victim to the recreation hall, where they would watch television together, and when the bull-dyke held her hand the new prisoner would allow it, afraid of offending her only friend. The new prisoner quickly noticed that the other inmates left her along, and as her dependence on the bull-dyke grew, so did the intimacies, until finally, she was willing to do anything to hold on to her only friend.
>
> Those who refused to give in were raped. Ninety percent of the women who entered the prison were forced into homosexual activity—willingly or unwillingly—within the first thirty days. (79)

One of the inmates explains to Tracy:

> We don't just rape for sex. We rape for power, to show them right off who's boss. The new fish who come in here are targets for everybody who wants to gang-fuck 'em. The only protection they got is to become the wife of a bull-dyke. (79-80)

This is the mode of survival in the penitentiary for women. Instead of helping one another reform on living with "sisterly affection," they destroy what little femininity they possess.

Thrown into such a world, isolated from her normal surroundings, Tracy abandons her femininity and resorts to masculine aggressiveness as her means of survival. She plans and trains herself for the revenge she has pledged to take on the male-world outside. Tracy's odyssey begins after her release from prison. From a bewildered sufferer, she has metamorphosed into a brilliant criminal. She neither redefines her identity nor does she revive in herself a woman-consciousness. Rather, from a stereotype female, she is transformed into a stereotype male. The only feminine characteristic that Sheldon attributes to her is her willingness to succumb to male-domination time and again. Bloody revenge does not do the image of a woman good, so Tracy does not shed blood to destroy her oppressors. Instead, she cleverly manipulates situations and destroys them. Revenge has become an obsession with her. Sheldon writes:

> For so long now, her every working thought had been to avenge what had been done to her mother and herself. And now that it was almost finished, there was only an emptiness inside her. (145)

Revenge does not bring about a psychological growth in Tracy. It does not make her satisfied and complete. Her isolation makes her feel miserable. She wants a come-back in search of peace and happiness, into the same male-dominated society that had destroyed basic tenets of feminism by wishing to become non-aggressive and non-competitive again. Tracy's achievement is merely two dimensional. It is lesser than life because it lacks "insight" which is the third dimension. She satisfies only her ego and feels whole but empty. She wants to fill the moral void by trying to assume her former self. Tracy contacts her former employer at the Philadelphia Trust and Fidelity Bank and asks for her old job as a first step. She is refused. On one occasion, she even cries out pathetically: "I am not a criminal. I came here looking for a job." (160) She is denied a normal place in society. She is a convict or outlaw. Dejected, Tracy lets her life drift. She drops anchor when she associates herself with Conrad Morgan. Morgan leads Tracy into the underworld, where with her unusual intelligence she reigns supreme. Sheldon elevates her to the status of the popular, invincible superman albeit distorted. She is a daring and brilliant criminal. She acquires a lot of wealth and property with the help of Morgan. She becomes addicted to cheating and stealing. The C.I.A., the Interpol, the Scotland Yard and the global police are hoodwinked by her. Sometimes she uses disguises, sometimes mud masks to give the police a slip when she's caught red handed, she leaves convincingly wrong clues for the police to follow while she steals a valuable painting and the Lucullan diamond with great ingenuity. She is always the winner in all these breath-taking duels. Yet at times Tracy is troubled:

> It is time to begin my new life. . . . But what kind of life? I have gone from an innocent naive victim to a . . . what? A thief—that's what. . . . No. An avenger. That's what I have become. And an adventuress perhaps. (206)

"She had outwitted the police, two professional con-artists and a double-crossing jeweller." (206) Guilt, false-pride, uncertainty and indecisiveness are all jumbled up in her consciousness. She is drawn again into the web of crime by a man—Jeff Stevens. Her spirit, which could have been constructively channelized by her, is misused by men. Sheldon fantasizes the concept of female superiority. He makes a mockery of this concept by making Tracy Whitney a mentally superior being, a superior criminal. He fails to understand that at the heart of feminism is an egalitarian impulse, seeking to free woman from oppression by removing all the obstacles to their political, economic, and sexual self-determination. To erect a doctrine of female superiority to men only by virtue of their spirit is a step backward. Morally Tracy is underdeveloped. Instead of using her unique courage to constructively overcome her problems of existence, she uses it destructively in a battle of wits against the protectors of law. Sheldon's attribution of boundless spirit to Tracy is simply sensational. It is a pointer to the lack of understanding that springs from inadequate immersion, from inadequate empathy, involvement and commitment to the serious problems of women.

Close analysis of Tracy's life reveals Sheldon's view of

feminism. He simply inverts certain dominant values in the name of feminism. One has to agree with the French feminist Antoinette Fouque:

> Inversion does not facilitate the passage to another kind of structure. Reformism suits everyone! Bourgeois order, capitalism, phallocentrism are ready to integrate as many feminists as will be necessary. Since these women are becoming men, in the end it will only mean a few more men.[5]

Sheldon makes Tracy extraordinary, a fantastic female-man. Through this narrative, Sheldon has tried to show that this serious movement which clamours for a woman's better tomorrow is only "full of sound and fury signifying nothing." Female desire for self-identity is seen by males as irresponsible and whimsical which he is willing to humour for sometime while he subtly drives home that the ultimate reality lies in woman's perennial subordination to man. Sheldon's chauvinism is explicit as he tails off his narrative in *If Tomorrow Comes* by stating with emphasis, that is, in italics, that after all her rebellion, Tracy is excited about the fact that "Life will be thrilling enough just being Mrs. Jeff Stevens." (384)

NOTES

1. Sidney Sheldon, *If Tomorrow Comes* (New Delhi: Rupa, 1985).
2. Vern Bullough, *The Subordinate Sex: A History of Attitudes Toward Women* (New York: Penguin, 1973), p. 3.
3. Charlotte Perkins Gilman, *Herland* (New York: Pantheon, 1979).
4. Gloria Naylor, *The Women of Brewster Place* (London: Sphere Books, 1980).
5. Antoinette Fouque, "Warnings," in Elaine Marks and Isabella de Courtvron, *New French Feminisms* (Amherst: University of Mass. Press, 1980), pp. 117-18.

Establishing Visibility: Contemporary Fiction by Afro-American Women Writers

SUMITA PARMAR

I
am a black woman
tall as a cypress
strong beyond all definition still
defying space
and time
and circumstance
assailed
impervious
indestructible
look on me and be
renewed.

Mari Evans

The last two decades have seen the flowering of the talent of the Afro-American women writers as has no other period in history. In fact there always has been a tradition of women writers among the blacks going back to 1787, when the first slave narrative by a woman was published in the United States. Phillis Wheatly, Lucy Terry and Harriet E. Wilson are names who have continued this tradition. But despite their existence, acknowledged women writers have been few and far between. The intention of this paper is to account for the emergence of so many black women novelists in the last two decades and to focus on the major themes in the work of some of these authors.

I

The matrix of work by these women forms a kaleidoscope of many splendours, enriching and extending the international corpus of black literature. These are women who are no longer willing to be either relegated to the background, or be culturally and historically erased as their sisters in the past have been. Among the most acclaimed are Alice Walker, winner of the 1983 Pulitzer Prize and the American Book Award for her novel *The Color Purple*. (Walker has written three other novels besides books of prose and poetry.) Toni Morrison, author of four novels, of which *Song of Solomon* won the National Book Critics Circle Award in 1977, Paule Marshall who bagged the American Book Award for her novel *Praise Song for the Widow* and Gloria Naylor, the 1983 recipient of the American Book Award for a first novel for The *Women of Brewster Place*. Naylor has since then written two other novels. Literary awards are generally an arbitrary yardstick by which to measure a writer's worth, but certainly they are an indication of the kind of critical attention contemporary black women writers are drawing. Other writers who have won wide recognition are Nikki Giovanni, Maya Angelou, Toni Cade Bambara, Gwendolyn Brooks, Lucille Clifton, Mari Evans, Audre Lorde and Sonia Sanchez.

Explaining the emergence of these writers, Stephen Henderson says: "the contradictions between knowledge and action that surfaced in the Civil Rights and Black Power Movements forced sensitive and intelligent women to re-examine their own positions vis-a-vis the men and to conclude that they were the victims not only of social injustice, but of a sexual arrogance tantamount to dual colonialism—one from without and one from within the Black community."[1] Black women saw that both the media and literature projected their distorted portrayals. These portrayals were strengthened by the creation of characters in fiction with twisted racial characteristics. The black matriarch, the dominating and overpowering black woman, the castrating black female—these caricatures of black femininity were eternized. Disappointingly, black male writers too wrote from a well-defined male viewpoint; even they resorted to deformed stereotypes depicting black women as "queens and princesses or as earth mothers and idealized big mommas of superhuman wisdom and strength, unrecognizable as individuals."[2] Women characters in the hands of the male writer were often rendered without due perception and sensitivity. Mostly the women were confined to roles of wives and mothers—other aspects of their personality remaining ignored. Black women invariably lived for children, for parents, "bereft always of an autonomous self."[3]

Faced with such a situation, confronted with a fait-accompli that erased them from history and bound them in unfair and untrue images, when "even Black men as scholars and thinkers writing in this century could not free the images of black women in the national psyche, it remained for black women to accomplish the task themselves. The emergence, therefore, of black female expression in drama, poetry and fiction was long overdue."[4] Black women decided to rescue themselves and their sisters in the past from historical and cultural invisibility and set about creating a literature of their own.

When asked about why they write, these women are articulate and moving in their replies. "I wrote *Sula* and *The Bluest Eye* because they were books I had wanted to read. No one had written them yet, so I wrote them,"[5] says Toni Morrison. Audre Lorde states, "I write for myself. When I say myself, I mean not only the Audre who inhabits my body, but all those fiesty incorrigible black women who insist on standing up and saying, 'I am, and you cannot wipe me out.' I write for those women for whom a voice has not yet existed, or whose voices have been silenced."[6] A simple yet powerful statement comes from Maya Angelou: "I write because I am a black woman listening attentively to her talking people."[7] Gloria Naylor is direct and acid. Says she, "I wanted to become a writer because I felt that my presence as a black woman and my perspective as a woman in general had been under- represented in American literature."[8]

A crucial part of this activity, this creation of their own literature, was the discovery of many lost talents—the work of numerous women writers in the past whose efforts had gone unaccounted, to add and strengthen the tradition. A tradition that undeniably existed but was tenuous and full of gaps. Thus the re-discovery of Jessie Fauset, Georgia Douglas Johnson, Nella Larson and especially of Zora Neale Hurston has been very significant starting from the first slave narrative written by a woman in 1787, called "*Belinda or The Cruelty of Men Whose Faces Were like the Moon*," black women realized how it had always been the male slave narrative that was considered. The enlightened and articulate female slave was nowhere in the picture, nor was her writing. Even the publication of *Incidents in the Life of a Slave Girl* by Harriet Jacobs in Boston in 1861 was scarcely noticed. "We have been as invisible to the dominant culture as rain. We have been knowers but we have not been known,"[9] was the bitter but inevitable conclusion. This trend of invisibility continued right into the twentieth century when black women started writing about themselves.

II

After having answered the question why black women write, the ineluctable next question is what do they write about? At this point, a short divergence will help to both widen and straighten the perspective of women's work in general.

As far back as 1950, Elizabeth Hardwick was convinced that women writers could never compete with men on an equal basis because of the "absolute and immutable difference in experience."[10] Elaborating this point, she says:

> If women's writing seems somewhat limited . . . (it is

> because) women have much less experience of life than a man as everyone knows. But in the end are they suited to the kind of experience men have? *Ulysses* is not just a work of genius, it is Dublin pubs, gross depravity, obscenity, brawls. Stendhal as a soldier in Napoleon's army, Tolstoy on his Cossack campaigns, Dostoevsky before the firing squad, Proust's obviously first hand knowledge of vice . . . these horrors and the capacity to endure them are experience. Experience is more than going to law schools and having the nerve to say honestly what you think in a drawing room filled with men; it is the privilege as well to endure brutality, physical torture and unimaginable sordidness. . . . In the end it is in the matter of experience that women's disadvantage is catastrophic.[11]

But the definition of the word "experience" has come full circle. Contemporary historians of women assert the need for a woman-centered analysis of both experience and the past. They point out that "women's social reality and experience are different from men's. They draw attention to the female life cycle—especially to risky and recurrent childbirth, to the paucity of rites of passage, of women's special experience of medical practice. They stress the gap that separates most female lives from public events and remind us that the invention of reliable contraception has more decisively affected the lives of women than the majority of political revolutions."[12] In a strongly worded redefinition of history, Coppelia Kahn states:

> History has been a record of male experience, written by men from a male perspective. What has been denigrated historically significant has been deemed so according to a valuation of power and activity in a public world. . . . As long as the transmission and experience of war are its primary focus, as long as war and politics are seen as more significant to the history of mankind than child rearing, women remain marginalized or invisible. . . . It

> is therefore imperative for historians of women to reconstruct the female experience and to fill the blank pages and make the silences speak.[13]

For black women writers, the considerations are somewhat different. Although the yardstick of conventional femininity is as applicable to them, being black makes them different from all others. They do have to fill in the blank pages and make the silences speak, but they apply no one else's standards but their own. And well can they afford to do this. Their work has been subsumed to the side and ignored by the white critical establishment for too long. Their black male counterparts also have been hardly encouraging. Commenting on this, Alice Walker states acidly, "And look at the ignorance of black men about black women. Though black women have religiously read every black male writer who came down the pike . . . few black men have thought it of any interest at all to read black women."[14] Therefore what started out as being a disadvantage has proved to be a boon—an unexpected advantage. Black women writers take special delight in charting out the frontiers of their own subjects and write about just what pleases them and what they want to. They realize that there is a vast unchartered territory, a terra incognita which awaits them for exclusive exploration. And they are reassured to find an enthusiastic section of readers willing to read their work.

The fiction of these writers is generally linked by similar themes and motifs. There is usually a black heroine who is involved in a quest to find a meaningful identity and to survive with dignity and integrity in a social environment that is both dominantly male and white. Often she is a mother with children and thus is rooted to a place. She has strong links with other women in her community, a dependable sisterhood, on which she relies in times of crisis. Turning the focus inwards, these writers probe the male-female relationship among their own people. A recurrent theme is that of the psycho-sexual abuse of black women and how they cope with racism and sexism in everyday life. They talk of the experiences of being in double jeopardy," the special violence and violation to the combination of being black and female."[15] They present the Afro-American reality as they see it, trying to convey what hundreds of years of abuse and humiliation has done to the black people. Referring to the shackles that her people have been bound by, Alice Childress says:

> We are the only social group within the United States ever forbidden by law to read and write. The law also forbade any white to teach us to read. We and the native Americans were the only citizens or aliens legally forbidden to enter libraries, concert halls, theatres and public schools. In order to change such laws we spent many lives and much money and time. Any who allied themselves with us had to pay similar penalties.[16]

Just as Zora Neale Hurston wrote against the stereotypes of the day and tried to provide "new categories of perception and new ways to consider the stuff of our lives,"[17] so in their interviews, autobiographical statements and in their fictional themes these writers demolish the old images that black women have been caged with and provide contrasting models of strength. Maya Angelou refers with pride to her grandmother who with wise management and foresight not only ran a successful store which catered to the needs of the blacks of Stamps, Arkansas and helped them in times of crisis with credit, but which also supported the white establishment tottering under the great Depression. Writes Maya:

> Welfare was absolutely forbidden. My pride had been starched by a family who assumed unlimited authority in its own affairs. . . . My grandmother had begun her business in the early 1900s . . . by selling meat pies to saw men in a lumber mill then racing across town in time to feed workers in a cotton gin four miles away.[18]

At another place, she quotes the words of her mother:

> People will take advantage of you if you let them. Especially Negro women. But you remember this now. Your mother raised you. You're fullgrown. Let them catch it like they find it. If you haven't been trained at home to their liking, tell them to get stepping. Stepping, but not on you.[19]

Commenting on Angelou's statements, Mari Evans writes, "If there is one enduring misrepresentation in American literature, it is that of the black southern matriarch. When blacks appeared first in James Fenimore Cooper's novel *The Spy*, the black woman was silent, post-forty, corpulent and in the kitchen. By modern times, the images of non-Mulatto southern black women are still not progressed. When seen at all, they were powerless pawns related only to contexts of white aspirations. But Angelou's depiction of her paternal grandmother is a singular repudiation of that refraction."[20]

Another rare but positive image that originates from the slave narratives is that of the black woman full of sass and quick-witted, using her intelligence to outwit her white masters and attempting to gain freedom for herself and her children. Toni Morrison's *Beloved* describes such an episode in the life of Sethe. A point of interest is that often these women sacrificed chances to escape alone and waited for opportunities when they could take their children along. No such concern is apparent in the narratives of the men. A mother's love tends to be taken for granted, not just among the blacks but universally. For the black woman, however, the socio-economic circumstances have been exceptionally harsh and consequently demonstrations of maternal devotion have extracted higher prices. Frequently abandoned by her man, almost always without resources, often illiterate and uneducated, she has still been the glue to keep the family unit together, painstakingly attempting to give her children an education so they might lead a better life. This aspect has been highlighted by black women writers and the theme of love and devotion that the Afro-American woman gives to her family is depicted in Walker's *The Third Life of Grange Copeland*, Morrison's *Beloved*, Naylor's *The Women of Brewster Place*, besides various other works of fiction. Thus these writers have provided images of faithful and loyal wives, devoted and supportive mothers and reliable friends, and given their readers new images to think about.

III

As their work is linked by a commonality of themes and their intentions bound by a common vision, similarly the aesthetics used by these artists are also akin. All of them use black speech as a major device. The rhythm and structure of English as spoken by blacks is so typical and characteristic that it becomes an effective tool to establish authenticity of character and tone and create a vibrant interaction between the reader and the text. In fact, black literature stems from a storytelling tradition of oral literature. Says Gayl Jones:

> When you tell a story, you automatically talk about traditions but they are never separate from the people, the human implications. For you're talking about language, you're talking about politics and morality, and economics and culture . . . you're talking about all your connections as a human being.[21]

Attempting to define this elusive characteristic of blacks, Toni Morrison says:

> There are things that I try to incorporate in my fiction that are directly and deliberately related to what I regard as the major characteristic of black art—whatever it is. One of which is the ability to be both print and oral literature: to combine those two aspects so that the stories can be read in silence, of course, but one should be able to hear them as well.[22]

Not only do these writers draw from the spoken language, but they also use expressions of black music like jazz, events in history and religious and cultural symbolism. Often in the fictional canvas, an ancestral figure looms large, a comforting and reassuring presence *(Song of Solomon, Sula)*. The community plays an integral role as part of the structure of many of these novels *(Women of Brewster Place, Sula, Song of Solomon, The Third Life of Grange Copeland)*. Mari Evans effectively sums up in the following words:

> To address specifics: I insist that black poetry, black literature if you will, be evaluated stylistically for its imagery, its metaphor, description, onomatopoeia, its polyrhythms, its rhetoric. What is fascinating, however is that despite the application of all these easy criteria, no allegation of "Universality" can be imposed for the simple reason that black becomes a catalyst, and whether one sees it as a colour, a substance, an ancestral bloodstream or as a lifestyle, historically when black is introduced, things change.[23]

IV

What has been significantly changed for the black woman and by her is her sudden visibility. This visibility and the inclusion in literature of new dimensions of experience and feelings can be counted as one of the most meaningful achievements and contributions of Afro-American women writers. The affirmative note in their work is emphasized by the fact that they all insist that black people must assume responsibility for their behaviour. Grange Copeland's words in *The Third Life of Grange Copeland* are representative of what these writers think. Says Grange, "never blaming himself done him weak. . . . By George, I know the danger of putting all the blame on somebody else. . . . And I'm bound to believe that

that's the way the white folks can corrupt you even when you done held up before. Cause when they got you thinking that they are to blame for *everything,* they have you thinking they're some kind of gods."[24]

In spite of racism, these writers say, black people still have the responsibility to attempt to nurture their dignity and self-esteem. The spotlight here is on the women for whom the task of self-nurturance, the quest for selfhood is even more challenging. They document the anguish, pain and often the inferiority that black women suffer from when their own men slight them for straight-haired, fair-skinned women. They describe the tragedy that occurs when the yardstick to measure beauty and femininity is impossible and white *(The Bluest Eye, Maude Martha).* But by the conclusion of the novels, the heroines learn to appreciate their own singular beauty. They become "subjects not objects for another's ambition, designing roads to destinies of their own choosing. They develop and mature frequently a painful and lonely process, but they realize that they have to confront not only their strengths but also their weaknesses. They learn that to love another they must first learn to love themselves."[25] And finally they all echo at one level or another the affirmation in the ringing words of Celie in Alice Walker's *The Color Purple,* "I'm poor, I'm black, I may be ugly and can't cook . . . but I'm here."[26]

NOTES

1. Mari Evans, ed., *Black Woman Writers* (London: Pluto Press, 1984), p. xxiii.
2. *Ibid.*, p. xiv.
3. *Ibid.*, p. 11.
4. *Ibid.*, p. 25.
5. Claudia Tate, "Black Women Authors: An Emerging Voice," *Topic,* No. 153, p. 60.
6. *Loc. cit.*
7. Mari Evans, p. 4

8. David Bradley, "Nine Novelists," *American Review* (1/1989), p. 42.
9. Joanne M. Braxton, Harriet Jacob "*Incidents in the Life of a Slave Girl*: The Re-Definitions of the Slave Narrative Genre." *The Massachusetts Review*, p. 379.
10. Elaine Showalter, *A Literature of Their Own* (Princeton: Princeton University Press, 1977), p. 217.
11. Gayle Green and Coppelia Kahn, *Making a Difference: Feminist Literary Criticism* (London: Methuen, London: 1985), p. 14.
12. *Ibid.*, p. 12.
13. *Loc. cit.*
14. David Bradley, "Novelist Alice Walker: Telling the Black Woman's Story," *The New York Times Magazine* (8 Jan. 1984), p.33.
15. Mari Evans, p. 14.
16. *Ibid.*, p. 113.
17. *Ibid.*, p. 45.
18. Maya Angelou, *Singin and Swingin and Gettin Merry Like Christmas* (New York: Random House, 1976), p. 53.
19. Maya Angelou, *Gather Together in My Name* (New York: Random House, 1974), p. 128.
20. Mari Evans, p. 28.
21. *Ibid.*, p. 238.
22. *Ibid.*, p. 342.
23. *Ibid.*, p. 167.
24. Bradley, p. 29.
25. Tate, p. 60.
26. Alice Walker, *The Color Purple* (New York: Pocket Books, 1982), p. 214.

Endurance and Survival in Gloria Naylor's *The Women of Brewster Place*

AMINA AMIN

"Writing by women about women," says Le Ann Schreiber, "is no longer seen as a distaff literature."[1] She rightly maintains that women writers have become increasingly conscious of the fact that in their own feminine experiences, they have a huge "unchartered territory" to explore and project through their work. The impact of black women writers has been specially dramatic in this respect, for they have brought to American Literature, dimensions of feelings and analysis that were previously missing. Black women writers are said to be writing primarily for themselves. Writing becomes a means of understanding their experiences and discovering the deeply hidden meaning of these experiences. Most of these writers have been pre-occupied with the problem of the multiple oppression, i.e. racism-sexism-capitalism, which black women in America have undergone for years together. Maya Angelou's words come to mind here:

> The Black female . . . is caught in the tripartite crossfire of masculine prejudice, white illogical hate and Black lack of power.[2]

Gloria Naylor examines this "tripartite crossfire" in *The Women of Brewster Place*. Her fictional characters engage in a fierce struggle for survival in an environment of "poverty and prejudice, violence and violation and an almost crushing adversity." Though black women writers write for themselves, they have succeeded in creating a readership which shares their concerns. These writers have contributed substantially to Afro-American Literature in the depiction and revelation of character. The image of black women has rarely been a positive one. This is because they have been portrayed both by white and black male writers as slaves or servants, as marginal beings on the socio-economic scale. Mainly, it is the plantation tradition that has been the source of black female characters in much of the literature produced before the arrival of black women writers on the literary scene. These writers have succeeded in substituting a positive view of black women as individuals who are intelligent, and who have an indomitable will and a firm determination to survive in a harsh world, without losing their humanity towards their fellow beings.

The Women of Brewster Place deals with seven women residents of an unidentified northern city somewhere in urban America called Brewster Place, which has become a slum for blacks. Although each woman has her own individual problems, all of them collectively share the problems of the black urban female. As Naylor herself says, "Each woman has her dream and each story is the tale of dream deferred just a bit, which is the problem of the black female experience in America."[3] William Bradley Hooper describes these women aptly: "these women are of different ages, come from different backgrounds, react differently to their blackness and to men, and have different notions of personal accomplishment, but all are burdened by being both black and female."[4]

The novel is composed of seven narrative units that work as independent short stories, each concentrating on a single woman's life. The dominant character in one chapter takes a subordinate place in others. The work is bound together as a novel because of the related episodes which though they do not move chronologically, span the whole narrative.

The first section of the book focuses on the experiences of Mattie Michael who has spent her childhood and adolescence in Tennessee, under the strict vigilance of a father who loves her fondly. Mattie's life in her parents's home is typical of the life of any black girl living on a plantation. There is love, care, warmth and joy in her home, but there is also a constant fear and apprehension on the part of the parents about the safety of their girl. Most of all, as Mattie's experiences show, there is fear on the score of a young girl's sexual vulnerability. And it is this vulnerability that brings Mattie's ruin. On an innocent outing with Butch Fuller to the Morgans's sugarcane field to pick a few nice fat canes left around, Mattie falls a prey to Fuller's advances and becomes pregnant. Mattie's ordeal begins the day her pregnancy is discovered by her self-righteous father. At first, Samuel Michael broods over it in a "torturing silence" but soon breaks into a violent rage, battering and bruising both Mattie and her mother; Mattie, because she has ruined the family name and Fannie, because she has dared to condone Mattie's sin. Needless to say Butch Fuller disappears completely from Mattie's life. Even without condemning the double standards that operate in a male-dominated society, Naylor expresses her anger both at Fuller's cowardly behaviour and Samuel's sexist-bias, which assumes that in an illicit relationship between a man and a woman, it is the woman alone who is guilty and therefore she alone has to be punished.

On the other hand, Fanny Michael is elated over the prospect of her daughter having a baby. When Mattie expresses the guilt and shame she undergoes because of her sin, Fanny blurts out:

> Ain't nothing to be shamed of. Havin' a baby is the most natural thing there is. The Good Book call children a gift from the Lord. And there ain't no place in that Bible of His that says babies is sinful. The sin is the fornicatin,' and that's over and done with.[5]

All the same Mattie decides to leave her home and, like many other dark children of the South, travels toward "the seductive call of wartime jobs and freedom in urban areas," carrying the child that would tie her to the past and future as "inextricably as it was now tied to her heartbeat." The economy with which Naylor narrates Mattie's experiences so far is brilliant. In prose that is terse and chiselled but which rises to the level of poetry, Naylor quickly brings us to the point when Mattie meets Etta Mae Johnson whose story forms the second part of the novel.

We are not told when and where Mattie's son Basil is born. Mattie undergoes all the hardships that a single woman, with a meagre education and an equally meagre income, would undergo, bringing up a child. However, what is remarkable about Mattie is the tenacity with which she faces her ordeal in a harsh and impersonal world. How callous is the world in which Mattie finds herself becomes clear when she leaves the boarding-house to look for another accommodation, little realizing that her choices are few. She knows quickly that there is no sense in wasting her energy finding a place in the white neighbourhood that displayed vacancy signs and she even learns to shun certain neatly manicured black neighbourhood. With her characteristic economy, Naylor projects the hypocrisy of the society when Mattie finds the following three sentences staring in her face as she moves from place to place in her search for accommodation:

> "Where's your husband?"
> "I ain't got one."
> "This is a respectable place!" (30)

Exasperated, Mattie is almost tempted to say that her husband has been killed in the war, when she is asked for the umpteenth time: "Where's your husband?" by Eva Turner. But that would be a denial of her son and Mattie feels nothing shameful about what he is. But Eva does not give her that opportunity. Instead she chuckles good-humouredly: "I had five husbands—outlived them all. So, I can tell you, you ain't missing much."

Mattie's meeting Miss Eva, as she is popularly called in the neighbourhood, marks a turning point in her life. She plays a crucial role in reviving Mattie's sagging confidence in herself and her faith in the goodness of human beings. As Naylor says, Mattie soon finds herself "accepting the kindness of the woman with a hunger of which she had been unaware." And,

> In the unabashed fashion of the old, Miss Eva unfolded her own life and secret exploits to Mattie, and without realizing she was being questioned, Mattie found herself talking about things that she had buried within her. The young black woman and the old yellow woman sat in the kitchen for hours, bleeding their lives so that what lay behind one and ahead of the other became indistinguishable. (34)

Needless to say, in this scene Naylor is emphasizing the commonality of the black female experience. This is one of the many instances in the novel, of a woman unfolding to another woman, regaining her lost confidence and acquiring the strength and fortitude to survive in a brutal world. From the way Eva Turner cares for Mattie and Basil, it looks as if Mattie has found another mother. In depicting the close Eva-Mattie relationship, Naylor follows the convention of many Afro-American women writers who emphasize the necessity of "female bonding" among black women.

In her article entitled: "Nobody/ But Nobody/ Can make it out here alone: Mother-Daughter Relationship in the Novels of Contemporary Afro-American Women Writers,"[6] Uma Alladi suggests that historical reasons necessitated the Afro-American woman to emphasize the role of the mother in the absence of the father, who either went to seek jobs in the North or deserted their families. As a result, mothers and daughters formed a relationship which was emotionally very close. In times of crises, such a close emotional relationship helped women to endure and survive. The relationship between Mattie and her mother Fannie and that between Mattie and Eva Turner are relationships of this kind. Further, the relationship between Mattie and Eva Turner is only an extension of a woman to woman relationship or of female bonding. One can see this pattern throughout the novel. The relationship between Mattie and Etta Mae Johnson whose story forms the second section of the novel and that between Kiswana Browne and her mother in the third section; that of Mattie and Ciel Turner in the fourth section, and that between Kiswana and Cora Lee in the fifth section are all examples of this female bonding. Even the relationship between the lesbians Theresa and Lorraine, at one level at least, is an example of such a kind.

All these women, Naylor feels, face the problem of womanhood in a society where women are undervalued and abused. They experience a sense of alienation which is ameliorated by "the networking or nurturing" by women, which one can see throughout the novel—sometimes it is very violent and a life is saved (as in the case of Mattie Michael and Ciel Turner) and sometimes it is less dramatic and there is a kind of cultural awakening from one woman reaching out to another (as in the case of Kiswana Browne and Cora Lee).

Mattie relates to the other women in the novel primarily as a mother. In fact, as Dorothy Wickenden says: "*The Women of Brewster Place* is a novel about motherhood, a concept embraced by Naylor's women, each of whom is a surrogate child or mother to the next."[7] This is not to suggest that Naylor's concept of motherhood conforms to the image of the "black matriarch" which is so much a part of the Afro-American literary tradition. Black women writers in general have freed their heroines from the roles their male counterparts had assigned them as "big Mommas" of superhuman strength and wisdom. Naylor deviates from the stereotype by making Mattie a multi-faceted character. Through her, Naylor projects the struggle of a black single woman, the mother of an illegitimate child—to survive in an environment of poverty, neglect and racial discrimination. Fate deprives Mattie of the only support she had i.e. her son, who also deserts her. What is remarkable about Mattie is that she is deserted by all the three men in her life—first by Butch Fuller, her lover, then by her father and finally by her son Basil. They desert her at moments when Mattie needs them most. However, Mattie does not allow these experiences to break her. Instead she comes out of each of these ordeals a little more strengthened, with dignity, and as sense of self-awareness which enables her to chart her own destiny. She spends her life usefully by bringing succour and relief to other women who, like her, are victims of a harsh and hostile world.

It is through her relationship with Lucielia Louise Turner, whose story forms the fourth section of the book, that Mattie's real mettle becomes evident. Ciel is the granddaughter of Eva Turner who in the past has stood by Mattie. Ciel is living a life of humiliation and degradation with Eugene who wants to desert her as soon as he comes to know of her pregnancy. It is as if it is Ciel's fault alone that she has got pregnant, as if it is Eugene alone who will have to endure the hassles of bringing up another child. Ciel even undergoes an abortion in order to please and keep Eugene, but to no avail. Ciel's only solace is Serena, her daughter, whom also a cruel fate takes away in an electric shock. Ciel reaches the limits of her endurance, shuns food and drink, and is on the verge of slipping from life. No amount of consolation from the other women of the block works to revive her. However, it is Mattie who succeeds in administering the healing touch. Naylor paints a graphic picture of Mattie's efforts at bringing the dying Ciel back to psychic health. Mattie is determined that Ciel will not die. So she enfolds Ciel's tissue thin body in her huge ebony arms and rocks her back and forth as a mother would rock a baby, till a moan breaks forth from the mute Ciel and tears flow down her face freely. It is in this scene that Deirdre Donahue's remark about Naylor's language sounds most true: "Naylor's potency wells up from her language. With prose as rich as poetry, a passage will suddenly take off and sing like a spiritual . . ."[4] Naylor's description of Mattie's rocking and bathing Ciel acquires religious overtones and lifts the whole scene from the level of the realistic to the mythic:

> Mattie rocked her out of that bed, out of that room, into a blue vastness just underneath the sun and above time. She rocked her over Aegean seas so clear they shone like crystal, so clear the fresh blood of sacrificed babies torn from their mother's arms and given to Neptune could be seen like pink froth on the water. She rocked her on and on, past Dachau, where soul-gutted Jewish mothers swept their children's entrails off laboratory floors. They flew past the spilled brains of Singalese infants whose mothers had dashed them on the wooden sides of slave ships. And she rocked on. (103)

Mattie bathes Ciel's emaciated body in a kind of a ritual that approximates a baptism. One is reminded here of Annie Gottlieb's remark: "*The Women of Brewster Place* isn't realistic fiction—it is mythic. Nothing supernatural happens in it, yet its vivid, earthy characters (especially Mattie) seem constantly on the verge of breaking into magical powers.[9] To say that *The Women of Brewster Place* isn't realistic fiction is to deny it the immediacy and conviction which go a long way in making the novel great. The fact is, Naylor combines the realistic and the mythic with superb skill. The flashback technique which Naylor uses throughout the novel with great command helps her to combine these two levels artistically.

Mattie is sure Ciel's tears will end, that she will sleep thereafter and morning will come. What kind of a morning came for Ciel we come to know only towards the end of the novel, when unexpectedly Ciel makes her appearance at the Block Party the women of Brewster Place are having, to raise the money they need to fight their white landlord. Ciel now lives in San Francisco and works for an insurance company. She is about to start another family. With the help of Mattie, who continues to call her "child," Ciel has come out of her ordeal with self-sustaining dignity and has become a self-reliant woman in control of her destiny.

Naylor shows that practically all the women of Brewster

Place are victims of sexual abuse and exploitation. Mattie is seduced by Butch Fuller and then deserted, Etta Mae Johnson meets the same fate at the hands of the various men she meets, including Rev. Woods. Ciel receives a brutal treatment at the hands of Eugene; Cora Lee is burdened with half a dozen kids who are not sure who their father is; Ben's lame daughter is offered by her own mother to satisfy Mr. Clyde's lust, in exchange for the extra land he has rented them. Finally, Lorraine, who has been living a life of alienation and ostracism with Theresa, also becomes a victim of the savage sexual violation by C.C. Baker and his buddies. Through Lorraine's gang-rape and her subsequent death, Naylor shows how vulnerable a woman is. Talking about Lorraine's rape, Naylor says:

> The thing is, Lorraine wasn't raped because she is a lesbian, they raped her because she was a woman. And regardless of race, regardless of social status, regardless of sexual preference, the commonality is the female experience. When you reduce that down in this society even to something as abysmal as rape there is no difference between women.[10]

One can sense Naylor's outrage and contempt for the rapists when she says:

> Lorraine found herself, on her knees, surrounded by the most dangerous species in existence—human males with an erection to validate in a world that was only six feet wide. (170)

The brutality and savagery, which the boys of the alley perpetrate on Lorraine, unleashes a fury which drives her to butcher Ben who is the only person visible in the morning sun, as Lorraine crawls to death along the alley. Naylor's irony is obvious. For it was Ben who had confronted Lorraine when she was humiliated by Sophie, one of the women in the block.

Shattering though this experience is for the women of Brewster Place, it doesn't succeed in breaking them down completely. On the contrary, the blood stain that Cora spots on the brick that her daughter Sonya has been scraping with a Popsicle stick, drives her to yank the brick out of the wall as she cries out with determination:

> Blood—there's still blood on this wall. . . . It ain't right; it just ain't right. It shouldn't still be here. . . . Blood ain't got no right still being here. (185)

Impulsively the other women join her and collectively tear down the wall. In the act of tearing down the wall, the women experience a sense of regeneration and a feeling of solidarity and hope. Even the reluctant Theresa, who has decided to move out of the block after Lorraine's death, is won over to join in this symbolic act, which in turn gains her her acceptance in the community of the women of Brewster Place.

While Naylor devotes the major part of the novel depicting the experiences of the seven women in terms of their "femaleness," she also examines their predicament in terms of the effect of racism. And racism, in the novel is symbolized by the wall that makes the street a dead end. As Naylor herself has said, the wall was put up to keep apart the people who are down and out. Yet these "Afric" children cling to the street with a desperate acceptance that whatever was here was better than the starving southern climates they had fled from. For,

> Brewster Place knew that unlike its other children, the few who would leave forever were to be the exception rather than the rule, since they came because they had no choice and would remain for the same reason. (4)

Even a plucky girl like Etta had no choice but to come to Brewster Place. Rock Vale, Tennessee, had no place for a black woman who was not only unwilling to play by the rules but whose spirit challenged the very right of the game to exist.

But Rutherford Country wasn't ready for Etta's blooming independence and so she left the place one rainy summer night. Naylor puts it succinctly:

> Etta soon found out that America wasn't ready for her yet—not in 1937. And so along with the countless other disillusioned, restless children of Ham with so much to give and nowhere to give it, she took her talents to the street. (60)

Both Etta and Mattie end upon Brewster Place although they have taken totally different roads. If at one level the breaking of the wall, brick by brick, becomes symbolic of the solidarity of the women of the block, at another level it is symbolic also of the breaking of the racial barrier which the wall symbolizes. Naylor seems to be suggesting that it is only through a collective effort that such barriers can be broken. And it is to the credit of Kiswana Browne, the young idealistic woman from a rich family, who lives in a sixth floor studio apartment in Brewster Place and who is fond of her African roots, that the women of the block unite to fight their white landlord. Naylor gives a graphic picture of Kiswana's efforts to bring the women of Brewster Place together in a meeting which threatens to break down on issues less important than the exploitation of the landlord. But because of the backing of such people as Mattie and Etta and their fierce determination to make the block party a financial success, the women of Brewster Place make it. Naylor employs a celebratory tone as she describes the party and the subsequent breaking down of the wall even as the rain continues to pour heavily over Brewster Place. Once again here, as in the scene where Mattie rocks and bathes Ciel, Naylor describes an ordinary event as if it were a religious ritual. The high point of the scene is Cora trying to pass a brick to Kiswana and the latter imploring Cora,

> There's no blood on those bricks! . . . You know there's no blood—it's raining. It's just raining! (187)

And Cora asking in return,

> Does it matter? Does it really matter? (187)

Which means blood or no blood, the wall has to be torn down. The continuous rainfall does not dampen the spirit of the women of the block. After a week, Brewster Place is bathed in a deluge of sunlight and the women are getting ready for another party. Gloria Naylor fits into, what Claudia Tate calls, the general tradition in Afro-American Literature[11] of celebrating black survival by overcoming racial obstacles. It is not as if the women of Brewster Place have succeeded in breaking the wall of racism but Naylor pins her hope on the united effort that the women are determined to make. What is significant is that the women want to forget their prejudices and their bickering and unite to fight their common enemy.

NOTES

1. Quoted by Claudia Tate, "Black Women Authors: An Emerging Voice," Reprinted from *Topic*, No. 153, p. 59.
2. Quoted by Mari Evans, *Black Women Writers: A Critical Evaluation* (New York: Anchor, 1984), p. 12.
3. Quoted by William Goldstein, "A Talk with Gloria Naylor," *Trade News*, Publishers Weekly (Sept. 9, 1983), p. 35.
4. William Bradley Hooper in a Review of *The Women of Brewster Place*, *Contemporary Literary Criticism*, Vol. 28, p. 304.
5. Gloria Naylor, *The Women of Brewster Place* (London and Sydney: Sphere, 1984), p. 20.
6. *Indian Journal of American Studies*, 16, I (Winter, 1986), p. 101.
7. Dorothy Wickenden, *Contemporary Literary Criticism*, Vol. 28, p. 305.
8. Deirdre Donahue, *Contemporary Literary Criticism*, Vol. 28,

p. 305.

9. Annie Gottlieb, *Contemporary Literary Criticism*, Vol. 28, p. 305.
10. William Goldstein, p. 36.
11. Claudia Tate, "Black Women Writers at Work," *Continuum* (1983), p. xxiv.

Alice Walker's *Meridian* as a Feminist *Bildungsroman*

CHRISTINE GOMEZ

Bildungsroman, a term borrowed from German literary criticism, literally means "Formation novel." It trances "the youthful development of a central character,"[1] as he or she "passes from childhood through varied experiences . . . into maturity and the recognition of his identity and role in the world."[2] Identifying some common characteristics in such novels of education, Buckley[3] says that it involves the journey of a sensitive youth from a provincial restricted life in a small town to a cosmopolitan city, where his true education begins. After a series of initiating experiences and moral encounters, the protagonist rearranges and formulates his values and pursues a career in earnest.

Analyzing the reason for the earlier paucity of the *Bildungsroman* representing a woman, Joe Andrew says that this was because women were perceived in literature as "partial creations, stereotypes, projections, static rather than dynamic images."[4] Even when they were the protagonists, perceived as persons and not as images, their development towards a better life was within patriarchal limits, towards marriage, for example. But in recent years, as Rosalind Miles points out, women writers have successfully developed "a female *Bildungsroman* as a long-overdue and necessary counterweight to the long tradition of Portraits of the Artist as a young Male."[5] Underlying this new trend is the conviction that the development of a young girl's consciousness into adult womanhood is as universal and relevant to the entire human race, as that of a boy into adult manhood.

This paper presents Alice Walker's *Meridian* as a *Bildungsroman*, a form particularly suited to deal with the themes of self-discovery, self-definition and self-affirmation. This novel presents Meridian, a sensitive and reflective young black woman, and traces her past life in a series of flashbacks, anecdotes and retrospective narration. Her earliest memories, relationship with parents, maternal history, ancestral legacy of traits, initiation into sex, entrapment in motherhood out of ignorance and therefore in marriage and the disintegration of the marriage are presented. Stereotypical images of womanhood and motherhood are examined and found wanting. Determined to break out of these stereotypes, Meridian chooses to discard enforced motherhood and marriage and achieves self-actualization through education. Her participation in the Civil Rights Movement of the 1960s, belief in non-violent protest, emotional entanglement with Truman Held and Lynne Rabinowitz, her extrication of herself from the triangle, while continuing to love and help both Truman and Lynne, who get married, her sense of social responsibility and commitment to the black community are traced. The novel becomes a feminist *Bildungsroman*, working out the formation of a self-defined woman with a positive self-image and social commitment.

Commenting on the structure of *Meridian*, Alice Walker says, "I wanted to do something like a crazy guilt. . . . A crazy guilt only looks crazy. It is not patched; it is planned. . . . A crazy guilt story is one that can jump back and forth in time, work on many different levels and one that can include myth."[7] The arrangement of chapters is apparently haphazard, as in a crazy guilt, darting back and forth in time. Just as some pieces in a guilt are very small, some chapters are short. Such is chapter V, "Gold," which is only one page long. Since the guilt represents the black woman's talent to make something useful and beautiful out of rejected bits of cloth, it may be taken as an objective correlative of the black woman's life and experience. Perhaps this is why Walker has adopted the guilt structure for her novel of a black woman's quest for identity and her role in life. Meridian succeeds in making something useful and beautiful out of the apparently disjointed bits of her life and experiences. Thus there is perfect harmony between the content and form in this *Bildungsroman* of a black American woman.

Susan Willis[6] sees the novel as being made up of anecdotes. This is true particularly of Part I consisting of anecdotes from the past and Part III composed of episodes in the novel's present. Anecdotes are the narrative equivalents of the individual bits which make up the guilt. The myth- making faculty of Walker is seen in the legendary figures whom she introduces in the anecdotes to illuminate various aspects of the black woman's experience. Such are the Wild Child, Louvinie, the slave whose tongue had been cut and buried, out of which spot grew the magnificent magnolia tree Sojourner in Saxon College. While the Philomela-like cutting of the tongue symbolized the silencing of black women whose creativity is thwarted, the flourishing of the tree represented alternative fulfilment. The cutting down of the tree by the enraged black students represents the paradoxical nature of Black anger, which in its helplessness turns against itself, its sprouting at the end signals the regeneration of the black community. Fast Mary is another such legendary figure, a former Saxon student, who killed her baby and then killed herself, depicting what might have happened to Meridian and her child, if she had not broken out of accepted stereotypes.

The opening chapter of the novel contains significant clues regarding the content and form of the novel. Important themes in the novel are introduced here and structurally, the chapter reveals Walker's narrative technique. The novel begins in the mid-1970s in the small town of Chicokeam where Meridian has pitched her camp among the poor black people. Truman Held has come once again in search of her as he had done often during the past ten years. He finds her leading a band of poor black children, insisting on their right to enter a decorated circus wagon immediately and not on the day set apart for the blacks. She protests against the continuing racial discrimination even after the legal abolition of segregation. This first glimpse of Meridian reveals her social commitment to the black community, her belief in non-violent resistance and her link with children. The circus wagon contained a white woman's mummified corpse. Four slogans described her: "Obedient Daughter," "Devoted wife" "Adoring Mother," "Gone Wrong." (19) The first three phrases depict stereotypical images of women in relation to others, usually men. Women are usually defined not in themselves, but as female relatives of a man. Woman is thus seen as a function or role and not as a person.[9] She is a two-dimensional figure, with just a single quality considered appropriate by patriarchy to her function as daughter, wife and mother. The fact that these slogans are applied to a corpse suggests that a woman who tries to live up to these stereotypes will end up mummified. Meridian rejects these images, disobeys her mother, forgets the husband who deserts her and gives away her son for adoption. It is significant that when Meridian reaches a dead-end at the age of seventeen, Alice Walker describes her in terms of these stereotypes: "She was only seventeen. A drop-out from high school, a deserted wife, a mother, a daughter-in-law." (75-76) Only after she breaks out of these stereotypes, she finds her true self and recreates a definite positive identity for herself and discovers her individual role in the black community. The rejection of traditional definitions and images of woman is a major theme in the novel.

Though the novel starts in the 1970s, it goes back and traces Meridian's past life over twenty-five years and more. This is not done in chronological sequence. A complex retrospective technique is used. Chapter I, for example, presents a flashback within a flashback within a flashback. Starting with the novel's present in Chicokema, when Meridian meets Truman Held, the narrative goes back to an incident ten years before that, when Meridian had been a member of a Black Revolutionary group which demanded violence from its members. Unable to meet their demand and declare that she would kill for the movement, Meridian had remembered a day when she was thirteen, in church with her mother. Though deeply moved by the church music and her father's singing, she could not meet her mother's demand that she should publicly accept Jesus as her personal Saviour and Lord. On that day in church, she had remembered her parents's usual conversation on Red Indians, whose dispossession had been a matter of grief to her father. After thus tracing Meridian's journey in place and time, from Chicokema in the novel's present, to a New York apartment ten years earlier, to the church when she was thirteen, to her childhood and home a few years earlier, the author brings the reader back to the church, and then to the apartment in New York and then to Meridian's cell-like room in Chicokema. In the course of this journey in time and space, Meridian's present committed involvement with the black community, her past link with Black Revolutionary group, her rejection of violence, her estrangement from her mother, her rejection of formalized religion and her sympathy with the pre-Christian tradition of the Red Indians are all revealed. The journey backwards and forwards in Meridian's mind is like the peeling of the layers of the onion, after which the layers are rearranged in the same order. After peeling the layers of experience, both the past and the present are altered, illuminating each other. Later in Chapter IX, Alice Walker herself compares Meridian's thoughts to onion layers. (75)

The importance of maternal history in the understanding of a woman by herself and others is recognized by women writers. Alice Walker expresses this idea in a prose work of hers: "Guided by my heritage of a love of beauty and a respect for strength—in search of my mother's garden, I found my own."[10] In working out the evolution of Meridian, Walker brings out the impact of her maternal history, tracing it back to three or four generations. Walker presents a fairly detailed portrait of Meridian's mother and examines Meridian's relationship with her mother. It is against this background that Meridian's own motherhood must be viewed. Her rejection of physical motherhood over a particular child and her gradual assumption of a spiritual and emotional maternal attitude towards the black community and black children are seen as the results of deliberate choice.

Walker traces Meridian's maternal history in Chapter XV through five generations of heroic women, who sacrificed themselves for the sake of their children. Meridian felt inadequate and thought that she would never be able to live up to this legacy of her maternal ancestors. At this point the authorial voice comments, "It never occurred to her that her mother's and grandmother's extreme purity of life was compelled by necessity." (124) Her gradual realization of the possibility of choice and her deliberate exercise of choice are part of Meridian's formation.

As a result of this maternal history, the myth of black motherhood had become part of Meridian's consciousness. The black mother is seen to be a self-sacrificing and hard-working woman who has totally annihilated her individuality. As Barbara Christian points out, in this novel Walker has scrutinized "the monumental myth of black motherhood"[11] and shown how it imposes a stereotype on black women and denies them the freedom of choice.

While Meridian's mother had conformed to the stereotype, with bitterness and resentment, Meridian breaks out of it. In tracing the past of Meridian's mother, there is a deliberate demystifying of the mystique of motherhood. Motherhood is seen as a loss of freedom and personal identity. Having children is compared to "being buried alive, walled away from her own life, brick by brick." (51) Her way of taking revenge was to keep herself aloof from her children, deliberately withholding love and understanding from them. "In the ironing of her children's clothes, she expended all the energy that she might have put into openly loving them. Her children were spotless wherever they went. In their stiff, almost inflexible garments, they were enclosed in the starch of her anger." (79) Meridian's subconscious had picked up vibrations of her mother's resentment. Meridian had therefore built up a guilt complex. (51) This feeling of "primeval guilt" (96) continued and reached a crisis during a high fever and delirium at Saxon

College. At that time Miss Winter, her teacher at Saxon, understood the problem and whispered to Meridian, in the place of her mother, "I forgive you." (125) At that moment the burden of guilt regarding her mother, which had been weighing down Meridian, fell away and she started recovering after being almost on the brink of death.

Meridian's own motherhood is also presented in a deliberately anti-romantic manner. For Meridian, her pregnancy came as a shock and she was forced to marry "the latest lover," Eddie. (61) She felt sapped of all energy and even the ability to think. "She was so exhausted that it was futile to attempt to think straight, or even to think at all." (69) The resentment built up within her led to the thought of murdering her child and "to suppress it, she conceived, quite consciously, methods of killing herself. (69) The thought of suicide released her tension and calmed her and she was told that "she was an exemplary young mother." (69) She spent her time reading popular magazines, which projected stereotypical images of womanhood. "According to these magazines, woman was a mindless body, a sex creature, something to hang false hair and nails on." (71) By the age of seventeen, she had reached a dead-end, as a result of drifting through life lethargically, conforming to stereotypes.

Just when Meridian had reached the nadir of a stereotypical existence came the moment of awakening. The Black Activist movement came to her town. The house, in which the Black Voter Registration Drive was launched, was bombed. That explosion was a critical turning point and jolted her out of a lethargic and passive existence. "And so it was one day in the middle of April in 1960 Meridian Hill became aware of the past and present of the larger world." (73) After the awakening, Meridian joined the Civil Rights demonstrations in her town. It was then that she began to know and care for Truman Held.

The major breakthrough in Meridian's life was the offer of a college education to her. Meridian's mother strongly disapproved of her plan to go up for higher studies, after giving away her child for adoption. (90) But rather than resentfully bring up an unwanted child, withholding love from him, like her own mother, Meridian preferred to give him in adoption to those who wanted him and could love him. This would set her free to educate herself and become a better person, unmindful of those who would call her selfish. Of course there was a third alternative. "She might have murdered him instead. Then killed herself. They would all have understood this in time." (90) Walker's irony is here very bitter. Society's willingness to "understand" a mother killing her child and then killing herself, but its condemnation of her giving him in adoption and educating herself, brings out the low value placed on children and mothers by traditional society.

Though at the conscious level Meridian was convinced that her decision had been right, her subconscious, weighed down by centuries of maternal stereotypes impressed upon it, accused her of guilt. (91) The thought of enslaved black women who were miserable at the sale of their children, made her feel guilty and unworthy of her maternal heritage: "The daughters of these enslaved women had thought their greatest blessing from 'Freedom' was that it meant they could keep their own children. And what had Meridian Hill done with her precious child? She had given him away." (91)

After giving up her child for adoption, Meridian is seen to gradually assume a maternal role towards all black children. This is seen when she tried to rehabilitate the Wild Child at Saxon College, led the black children in protest in Chicokema and carried the foul-smelling bloated corpse of a black child to the town council hall to protest against the hazard of flooded ditches in the black slum area. As Barbara Christian points out, Meridian's quest takes her "beyond the society's narrow meaning of the word *mother* as a physical state and expands its meaning to those who create, nurture and save life, in social and psychological, as well as physical terms."[12] Relinquishing physical motherhood in the particular seems to be a necessary prerequisite for assuming universal motherhood.

This does not mean that Walker condemns motherhood totally. What she protests against is society's reduction of a mother to a function and its denial of personhood to a woman, once she becomes a mother.

Meridian's link with her paternal grandmother and father is also significant. Both of them had felt an affinity with the Red Indians. They had experienced ecstasy in the forty feet pit at the centre of an Indian burial mound in their land. Once in her childhood Meridian had entered the pit seeking to understand her grandmother's ecstasy and her father's compassion for the Indians. At first, she felt isolated from all living things, then there was a stinging sensation which spread through her whole body and then there was a lightness in the head and then a sensation of flying and a feeling of oneness with all forms of life. (58) This mystic experience was an important stage in her formation and growth. It was a celebration of life in all its forms and made her a life-affirmer always.

Meridian's sexual initiation had come early, between the age of twelve and fifteen in Daxter's funeral parlour. There Daxter and his assistant had exploited her ignorance and curiosity. Her mother had not instructed her to sex. There is a distance and detachment in these descriptions, conveying Meridian's indifference and lack of involvement. In her early sexual encounters, she experienced herself as an object, used by a man for his sexual gratification. Her lack of interest in sex after marriage, of which her husband complained, stemmed from these early experiences: "Their pawing over her and her refusal to do anything more than tease them had seemingly separated her from her young husband forever." (67) Partly due to her lack of interest and refusal to indulge in sex during her late pregnancy, her husband took up a mistress and slowly the marriage disintegrated.

After the breaking up of the marriage, Meridian's next sexual encounter was with Truman Held. She had begun to care for him during their work together in the Civil Rights movement. But when he began dating the white exchange students, she felt embarrassed, let down, "ashamed as if she were less." (106) In spite of his infatuation with Lynne Rabinowitz, Truman met Meridian in her apartment once and made love to her. After that single sexual encounter, he went back to Lynne, unaware that he had impregnated Meridian. On her way to the abortion, Meridian saw Truman and Lynne together and "It enraged her that she could be made to endure such pain, and that he was oblivious to it." (114) The unfairness of it all, that woman had to bear the brunt of the consequences of sex, while man went away scot-free to another woman, is brought out here. In her fury, she told the doctor who suggested tying her tubes, "Burn them out by the roots, for all I care." (115) It is a deliberate decision to kill not only this foetus, but to sterilize herself for life.

Reviewing her past life, Meridian realized that earlier with Eddie "she had lacked courage, lacked initiative or a mind of her own." (110) Though now she is aware of her attempts "to claim her own life," there is also the painful realization that Truman would have liked the former Meridian better "as she had been, as Eddie's wife—an attractive woman—but asleep." (110) Later, after the exchange students left, Truman approached her again saying, "I think I'm in love with you, African woman." (115) She repulsed him with "It's over," but unabashed Truman whispered, "You're *beautiful. Have* my beautiful black babies." (116) This bit of male chauvinism of seeing her as a baby machine, together with her abortion of his baby, of which he was totally unaware and her subsequent sterilization, enraged Meridian. She hit him thrice, drawing blood, her only act of violence in the whole novel. It was only years later that she was able to really forgive Truman, while consoling Truman and Lynne, when they lost their child Camara. "It was then that her feeling for Truman returned, but it was not sexual. It was love totally free of possessiveness or contempt. It was love that purged all thought of blame from her all too accurate memory. It was forgiveness." (172-73) Meridian thus passed from sexual love and admiration for Truman, to anger, resentment and shame, to forgiving love which became capable of accepting him as he was and of setting him free to be what he wanted to be. (216) At the end of the novel, Meridian reaches a sublimation of sexual love, in a genuine *agape* love towards all.

In working out the development and growth of Meridian, education and Saxon College play an important role. It was here that she encountered the Wild Child, the Sojourner and the story of Fast Mary. These anecdotes of mythic dimension drew her to an understanding of what it means to be a black woman in a racist and sexist society. It was here during a chapel service that she articulated for the first time her rejection of western religion. Her participation in the Atlanta Movement and short-lived membership in a black revolutionary group enabled her to attain political maturity, eschewing violence and choosing a deliberate commitment to the black community as her life's mission. It was during her sojourn at Saxon College that she was able to view her relationship with her mother objectively, in the perspective of black motherhood. While at Saxon, Meridian was haunted by persistently recurring dreams: "She dreamed she was a character in a novel and that her existence presented an insoluble problem, one that would be solved only by her death at the end." (117) Walker brings out the obsessive power of the dream by repeating this passage thrice in three consecutive paragraphs. This is followed by a perceptive comment on the stereotypical image of woman presented in novels. "Even when she gave up reading novels that encouraged such a solution—and nearly all of them did—the dream did not cease." (117)

Death and suicide seem to be the only solution to the problem faced by women. This is the destiny allotted to women in the literature produced according to the specifications and expectations of patriarchy. Literature is here seen as a predominantly male construct imposing inflexible straitjackets on women. Walker brings her heroine to the brink of death after which she recovers. Miss Winter's whispered words "I forgive you" (125) break the vice-grip of a primeval guilt over Meridian's consciousness. The image of death and resurrection is evoked in this episode, subliminally. Later too, when

Truman witnesses Meridian willing herself towards good health, "his first thought was of Lazarus, but then he tried to recall someone less passive, who had raised himself without help." (219) The reference to Christ's resurrection is obvious. Perhaps the name of Miss Winter is symbolic, since she ushers in new life or "spring" in Meridian. Thus Meridian's life at Saxon marks a significant stage in her intellectual development, political and social commitment, emotional maturity and spiritual wholeness.

Part I of the novel, entitled after Meridian traces the protagonist's life through a series of flashbacks, shuttling back and forth in time. Though Part II is called "Truman Held," the focus is still on Meridian. Here Meridian and the events are viewed through the eyes of Truman and Lynne. For example, Chapter 14 in Part I presented Meridian's lovemaking with Truman and its aftermath of abortion through Meridian's eyes. Chapter 18 in Part II gives Truman's point of view and why he ditched her: "He had wanted a woman perfect in all the eyes of the world, not a savage who bore her offspring and hid it." (142) Lynne's observation, of Meridian's abstracted air of existing at another level, is seen in Chapter 18: "Meridian, no matter what she was saying to you and what you were saying to her, seemed to be thinking of something else, another conversation perhaps, an earlier one that continued on a parallel track. Or a future one that was running an identical course. This was always true." (141) Lynne's observation regarding Meridian's existence in the past, present and future simultaneously, must be related to the novel's structure, where temporal barriers are knocked down and the reader jets back and forth, through the past and present and in Part III glimpses at a visionary future also.

Part II presents a picture of the marriage of Truman and Lynne and its gradual disintegration under racial pressure and Truman's own inherent weakness. Meridian's ability to understand and empathize with others is brought out. A significant feature of Part II is the presentation of the growth of rapport, understanding and friendship between Meridian and Lynne.

The presentation of friendship and a close bond between women is a new trend in women's writing. Virginia Woolf records the rarity of a satisfying woman-to-woman relationship in literature. "'Chloe liked Olivia,' I read. And then it struck me how immense a change was there. Chloe liked Olivia perhaps for the first time in literature. Cleopatra did not like Octavia."[13] While men view women as antagonists competing for male favour, women writers are able to conceive the possibility of rapport, genuine understanding and friendship between two women, even when they are the wife and mistress of the same man. Instead of hatred, anger, or rivalry, there is mutual sympathy at having been betrayed and exploited by the same man. In Chapters 20 to 25, Lynne confides in Meridian, sharing with her the traumatic experiences in marriage. Though both realize the weakness of Truman, they feel no hatred or contempt towards him. This motif of the bond between the wife and the other woman is worked out again by Walker in *The Color Purple* (1982) also. But here there is no trace of a lesbian relationship as in *The Color Purple.*

Part III entitled "The Ending", deals mainly with the novel's Time Present. Meridian lives up to her resolution, "I'll go back to the people, live among them," (31) taken when she left the revolutionary group. The common people, among whom she lives, love her and supply her with a room and food in grateful appreciation of her efforts on their behalf. Truman joins her in a campaign for registering names for voting. In these encounters with the ordinary people like the Treasure Sisters, and the devoted black family where the woman is dying, Meridian's genuine concern for her people is brought out. In this return to the people, in bringing back the truth of personal discovery to them, "she is a hero in the classical sense, unlike the anti-heroes of much contemporary literature, who are alienated from self and society.[14] Meridian arrives at a clear realization of her role in the black community, in this part. She sees her role as not belonging to the future, as a poet or a prophet, or to the present, as a revolutionary, but as a folk-singer of past memories. (201) She will keep alive the living and life-giving tradition of the people. Having thus arrived at the protagonist's clear-cut self-definition of her identity and her role in the community, the *Bildungsroman* draws to a close with a glimpse of the future.

The hope for the future is suggested symbolically. The Sojourner which had been savagely cut down by the Saxon College students after the Wild Child's burial, starts sprouting again, more than ten years later, a symbol of regeneration, of the affirmation of life, despite forces of destructive violence being at work. Meridian's head, which had grown bald, due to loss of hair in sickness, is covered with newly grown hair like "soft wool." (219) This is a Samson image, where the re-growth of hair symbolizes renewal of life and strength. When Truman tells her that he does not like to think of her as being always alone, Meridian replies, "But that is my value. Besides, all the people who are as alone as I am will one day gather at the river. We will watch the evening sun go down. And in the darkness may be we will know the truth." (220) Holding the visionary picture, Meridian walks away into the horizon.

The growth of a young black girl into an adult with a clear vision of her identity and her role in life is thus presented in *Meridian* through the structure of *Bildungsroman*. This is not just a female *Bildungsroman*, but a feminist *Bildungsroman*, which embodies the ideals of feminism. It presents a woman not as a passive creature, but as an active agent; not as ruled by emotion, but as capable of rational choice; not as totally selfless or extremely selfish, but as discovering her own positive identity and individual role in life; not as one whose primary aim in life is only marriage and motherhood, as seen in the traditional image of woman under patriarchy, but as one who commits herself to serving her community, through non-violent protest against all injustice. Meridian is shown to recreate herself positively, after discarding the stereotypes imposed upon her. *Meridian* thus becomes a feminist *Bildungsroman*, working out the formation of a self-defined woman with a positive self-image and social commitment.

NOTES

1. Karl Beckson and Arthur Ganz, *A Reader's Guide to Literary Terms: A Dictionary* (London: Thames and Hudson, 1960), pp. 24-25.
2. M.H. Abrams, *A Glossary of Literary Terms*, Third Ed. (New York: Holt, Rinehart and Winston, 1970), pp. 112-13.
3. Jerome Hamilton Buckley, *Season of Youth: The Bildungsroman from Dickens to Golding* (Cambridge, Mass.: Harvard University Press, 1974), pp. 17-18.
4. Joe Andrew, *Women in Russian Literature, 1780-1863* (London: Macmillan, 1988), p. 7.
5. Rosalind Miles, *The Female Form: Women Writers and the Conquest of the Novel* (London: Routledge and Kegan Paul, 1987), p. 102.
6. Alice Walker, *Meridian* (New York: Simon and Schuster, 1976).
7. Alice Walker, *Black American Woman Writers at Work*, ed. Claudia Tate (New York: Continuum, 1983), p. 176.
8. Susan Willis, *Specifying: Black Women Writing the American Experience* (Wisconsin: University of Wisconsin Press, 1987), p. 114.
9. Cf. Simone de Beauvoir, *The Second Sex*, trans. H.M. Parshely (New York: Alfred A. Knopf, 1970), p. xviii. "Man defines woman, not in herself, but as relative to him; she is not regarded as an autonomous being."
10. Alice Walker, "In Search of Our Mother's Gardens," *In Search of Our Mother's Gardens: Womanist Prose* (New York: Harcourt, Brace, Jovanovich, 1983), p. 243.
11. Barbara Christian, *Black Feminist Criticism: Perspectives on Black Women Writers* (New York: Pergamom Press, 1985), p. 89.
12. *Ibid.*, p. 242.
13. Virginia Woolf, *A Room of One's Own* (New York: Harcourt, Brace and World, 1929), p. 86.
14. Barbara Christian, p. 243.

First Person Singular: The Raised Feminine Consciousness in Atwood's *The Edible Woman*

T.N. DHAR

Novels, like any other work of art, are characterized by what Mikhail Bakhtin calls "dialogic heteroglossia." The phrase implies that they are a function of a matrix of forces, "a set of conditions—social, historical, meteorological, physiological."[1] These condition their meaning, and everything that they mean is "understood, as a part of a greater whole—there is a constant interaction between meanings, all of which have the potential of conditioning others."[2] This accounts for different voices or perspectives in them. As a work of fiction written by Margaret Atwood in the 1960s, *The Edible Woman* embodies several voices arising out of her belonging to a distinct geographical terrain, her association and involvement with a specific cultural situation, and because of being a woman. These voices are simultaneous and condition each other. In this essay, I shall confine myself to the exploration of one distinct voice of the novel which is made available to us largely through Marian, its central figure.

The novel is structured like a journey in which through her association with several male and female acquaintances and friends, Marian sees and assesses different ways of understanding what it means to be a woman, and this gives the book the quality of the novel of ideas. The various alternatives before Marian are comprehensively dramatized in a series of scenes which are well-integrated to constitute the main action of the novel. Marian is present in almost all of them: either as an observer or as an active or passive participant. Her beliefs and modes of thought are out to a strenuous test till, after being battered in body and psyche, she finally passes into a state of "raised" consciousness. She comes to think of herself in the "first person singular," and acquires a confident voice of her own. Reading her account offers illuminating insights into several issues: such as, what does it mean to be a woman, what is her situation, and what constitutes femininity? It is true that because of the particular weather of the novel, the answers to these questions are culture-specific, but it is also a fact that we learn things which are relevant to women of all climes.

The first part of the novel uses the confessional mode: Marian tells us about herself in her own voice. The logic of events is largely determined by the contrast that Atwood builds into the narrative to project different attitudes to womanhood, out of which Marian eventually chooses one as her ultimate destiny. The significant thing about her choice is that it is made after she had gone over the options very carefully, and the impulse to choose comes from the stirrings of an identity crisis in her.

Marian is contrasted mainly with Ainsley with whom she shares an apartment. While Marian is sedate, subdued, accommodative and pliable, Ainsley is modish, short-tempered, excitable and forward-looking. Precisely because of this, they live together in a state of "symbiotic adjustment." However, their main difference is over the issues of marriage and motherhood. Marian is led to think about them because of the first of her identity-crises, which she experiences in her place of work.

The place where Marian works has a highly stratified, three-tiered, hierarchic structure. The top is manned exclusively by men and is not accessible to her; the bottom is managed mostly by old housewives and she does not wish to be there. The prospect of getting grooved into the fixed middle-point of the office structure for the whole of her life, with a pension at the end of her tenure, makes her feel that in front of her was a "self . . . waiting, pre-formed, a self who had worked during innumerable years for Seymour Surveys and was now receiving her reward."[3] This disturbing awareness is the direct offshoot of a technologically advanced society which by its very advancement forces individuals into prefabricated roles, and is therefore of a general nature. Marian's crisis, however, acquires a feminine coloration when she looks for alternatives to her present situation. These are concretized in Marian's association with Ainsley, her office colleagues Emmy, Lucie, and Millie, her friends Clara and her husband Joe, and Peter.

Emmy, Lucie and Millie, popularly known as "office virgins," avoid sexual relations with men for varied reasons, but all of them agree that the best course available to a woman is to get married; in fact, they regard marriage as her ultimate destiny. But what does marriage involve? This is brought home to Marian in the elaborate scene of the married life of Clara and Joe: they had married for love which bordered on worshipping each other, and were considered an ideal couple. But watching Clara now, in her third pregnancy, Marian finds that she looked like a helpless mass of protruding flesh. Her children messed everything around them, drawing Ainsley's remark: "I don't see how anyone can love their children till they start to be human beings." (33) Marian also perceives that in spite of all the attention and love he has given to Clara, Joe's attitude to women is patronizing: "he tends anyway to think of all unmarried girls as easily victimized and needing protection. He had several times volunteered fatherly advice to me." (35) Marian also sees the inadequacies in Clara: "Clara simply had no practicality, she wasn't able to control the more mundane aspects of life, like money or getting to lectures on time . . . her own body seemed somehow beyond her, going in its own way without reference to any direction of hers." (35-36) Ainsley thinks that Clara hardly exists as a person, because she cannot get herself organized and cope up with life: "She lets herself be treated like a *thing*." (38) Marian seems to share Ainsley's perception of Clara; for when Peter proposes to her, she visualizes her marriage to be different from that of Clara.

Ainsley offers a more radical alternative to Marian's situation. She does not want to get married, but to get pregnant, to have a baby. She feels: "Every woman should have at least one baby. . . . It's even more important than sex. It fulfills your deepest femininity." (40-41) She also thinks that a woman should care for "wholeness," which is not possible without experiencing motherhood. Ainsley makes it clear that she wants children by choice, not as chance products of emotional entanglements or as by-products of happy hours spent in bed. That is why she elaborately plans to have one by a strong, handsome man. Marian's intuitive response is that it is not correct, but she is bothered by Ainsley's reasoning: "I knew Ainsley was wrong, but she sounded so rational. I thought I'd better go to bed before she had convinced me against my better judgement." (43) Later, Ainsley marries to have a father for the child she is carrying, because she modifies her views on the best way of bringing up children.

Marian has a steady friendship with Peter; they see each other often and she sticks to him in spite of several ups and downs in their relationship. Peter thinks her a sensible girl, who has independence and commonsense, but is not of "the other kind," a "girl who wouldn't try to take over his life." (61) Marian sometimes has a disturbing feeling that Peter tends to be aggressive and tries to manipulate her: once he had driven her to make love on the bedroom floor, at another time on a scratchy blanket in a field, and much later in a bathtub. The incident in the tub disturbs her a great deal, almost precipitating another identity-crisis. Reflecting on herself in the tub, she thinks: "he had intended it as an expression of *my* personality; did he really think of me as a lavatory fixture. What kind of a girl did he think I was?" (62) In one of the parties, she is annoyed with his excessive drinking and his unsavoury attitude: "He was treating me a stage-prop; silent but solid, a two-dimensional outline." But these moments of unease and outrage, which could have forced her to reconsider her relationship with Peter, pass off. When he touches her softly, just after she had expressed her anger with him, she melts like the heroine of sentimental novels: "I suddenly felt limp as a damp kleenex. I leaned my forehead against his and closed my eyes." (82) When he proposes to her, she feels that she could see herself "small and oval, mirrored in his eyes." (83)

It is significant that Peter not merely proposes to her, he even explains to her the reasons for marrying her. First, he thought that he was of the right age to marry; second, he did not want to pass off as queer by continuing to be a bachelor; third, and more importantly, she fitted perfectly into his image of what a woman should be like: "Marian, I know I can always depend on you. Most women are pretty scatterbrained but you're such a sensible girl. You may not have known this but I've always thought that's the first thing to look for when it comes to choosing a wife." (89) Peter is, in effect, fitting Marian into a conventionalized, even stereotyped, image of a woman who, minus her chastity, recalls the mid-Victorian Ruskinian image of a passive and dependant woman. Marian, on her part, looks upon him as a "rescuer from chaos, a provider of stability"; (89) she thinks that marrying him would be a release from the anonymous existence at Seymour Surveys. She goes to the extent of allowing him to decide the date of marriage for her.

After accepting the marriage proposal, Marian has a brief encounter with Duncan, one of the odd people she had interviewed in connection with her work, but it does not deflect her from her resolution. In fact, her brief moment of escape with him is described in very unpleasant terms. Kissing him, Marian felt that both of them were like automatons: "The whole incident had been ridiculously like the jerky attractions and repulsions of those plastic dogs with magnets on the bottoms I remembered getting as prizes at birthday parties." (101) She puts a final seal on her choice by offering an elaborate rational explanation: "I'd always assumed through high school and college that I was going to marry someone eventually and have children, everyone does. . . . I've never been silly about marriage the way Ainsley is. . . . She's against it on principle, and life isn't run by principles but by adjustments. As Peter says, you can't continue to run around indefinitely; people who aren't married get funny in middle age, embittered or addled or something. . . . But although I'm sure it was in the back of my mind I hadn't consciously expected it to happen so soon or quite the way it did." (102) In these words we see that Marian is virtually repeating the rhetoric of Peter; she has ceased to be her true being.

The second part of the novel, in which Atwood employs the third-person narrative mode, offers a deep, penetrative probe into Marian's psyche, because she gradually begins to realize that by agreeing to marry Peter, she had ceased to be herself. That is why going through a series of fast-moving situations, we see her losing control over her mind and body, but her progressive deterioration is accompanied by vital insights into the truth of her relationship with Peter, and subsequently about Duncan. This deflates the soundness and authenticity of her rationally-exercised choice; she realizes that she had let herself be sold as some kind of a desirable commodity.

The initial dent in Marian is caused by her doubt about the real identity of Peter and consequently her understanding of him. She identifies him with an anonymous caller who introduced himself to ladies as a seller of underwear, but whose real identity was not known to anybody. She thinks: "this was his true self, the core of his personality, the central Peter who had been occupying her mind more and more lately. Perhaps this was what lay hidden under the surfaces, that secret identity which in spite of her many guesses and attempts and half-successes she was aware she had still not uncovered: he was really the Underwear Man." (118)

For a clearer perspective on her relationship with Peter, she deliberately starts cultivating Duncan. She began to see that with both of them she was being "what they called 'used,' but she didn't at all mind being used, as long as she knew what for: she liked these things to take place on as conscious a level as possible." (183) She also understands that with Peter she had to exert herself, while Duncan was not demanding. Besides, with Duncan she could live in the present without being encumbered by past or future, with Peter she had been "waiting for an event in the future that had been determined by an event in the past." (184)

The mounting awareness of her uncertain relationship with Peter is accompanied by a change in Marian's metabolism. She finds it difficult to eat things which she enjoyed earlier; in fact, the list of the things she could possibly eat goes on diminishing day after day. She experiences psychic changes as well. One day she sees Duncan cracking pumpkin seeds in a movie house, but a few minutes later her sense of assurance crumples; she is not sure of what she had seen, and feels that she was "the victim of a complicated hallucination." (125) Meeting Clara in the hospital fills her with dread; leaving her, "she had the sense of having escaped, as if from a culvert or cave." (132) Shopping in a store, she feels that she moved like a "somnambulist." The gradual loosening of control over her self makes her increasingly conscious of her unreality. She thinks that she is not normal and that she ought to see a psychiatrist. She asks her friends to comment on her state of mind. But Peter thinks that she is "marvellously normal," and Clara tells her that she is probably suffering from "bridal shivers." The climactic point of the awareness of her unreality is symbolized by her experience in her bathtub just before she leaves to attend her engagement party: "All at once she was afraid that she was dissolving, coming apart layer by layer like a piece of cardboard in a gutter puddle." (218)

In the party she is uneasy because she is plagued by the feeling that she is a fake. When Peter tells her that she looked marvellous (because she had been made up by Ainsley), she tries to see herself in the mirror, but she "couldn't grasp the total effect: her attention caught on the various details, the things she wasn't used to—the fingernails, the heavy earrings, the hair, the various parts of the face that Ainsley had added or altered. She was only able to see one thing at a time. What was it that lay beneath the surface these pieces were floating on, holding them all together? She held both of her naked arms out towards the mirror. They were the only portion of her flesh that was without a cloth or nylon or leather or varnish covering, but in the glass even they looked fake, like soft pinkish-white rubber or plastic, boneless, flexible." (229) When Peter asks her to pose for a photograph, she feels that she has turned into a stone.

However, the party also provides her an insight into her situation as Joe talks about the effect of university education on women which he considers baneful. At the university, he says, "she gets the idea she has a mind, her Professors pay attention to what she has to say, they treat her like a thinking human being; when she gets married, her core gets invaded. . . . Her core. The centre of her personality, the thing she's built up; her image of herself. . . . Her feminine role and her core are really in opposition, her feminine role demands passivity from her." (235) Joe's elaboration on the effect of marriage on women comes like an epiphanic wave to Marian. She understands what Peter expected of her, and has the vision of a large "globular pastry, decorated with whipped cream and maraschino cherries." (235) She quits the party, and after trying to find some way of overcoming her anxiety in the company of Duncan, she goes back to her place and makes a cake in the shape of a woman. When Peter comes to see her, she surprises him with the new truth about herself. Offering him the cake, she tells him: "You've been trying to destroy me. . . . You've been trying to assimilate me. But I've made you a substitute, something you'll like much better. That is what you wanted all along." (271)

Having realized that her decision to marry Peter was a denial of her womanhood, that it was only a base conformity to a predetermined image of woman, Marian is restored to her normal physical and mental health. Liberated of the false notion of having an existence in which she is some kind of appetizing food, she begins to enjoy taking food. The final chapter of the book is once again in her voice because now she has begun to talk of herself in the first person singular, a new and confident voice of a distinct being.

NOTES

1. Michael Holquist, "Glossary," in M. M. Bakhtin, *The Dialogic Imagination: Four Essays*, ed., Michael Holoquist, trans. Caryl Emerson (Austin: University of Texas Press, 1981), p. 428.
2. *Ibid.*, p. 426.
3. Margaret Atwood, *The Edible Woman* (Toronto: MacClelland and Stewart, 1973), p. 21.

Contributors

Amina Amin, Gujarat University, Ahmedabad

Shruti Das, K.B. College, Barang, Cuttack

T.N. Dhar, University of Kashmir, Srinagar

Christine Gomez, Bharathidasan University, Trichy

C.T. Indra, University of Madras

Jaidev, Indian Institute of Advanced Study, Shimla

Sangeeta Jain, Meerut University

Pashupati Jha, C.M. College, Darbhanga

Chaman Nahal, University of Delhi

Sarla Palkar, M.S. University, Baroda

Sudha P. Pandya, M.S. University, Baroda

Sumita Parmar, University of Allahabad

R.S. Pathak, Harisingh Gour Vishwavidyalaya, Sagar

P. Ramamoorthi, M.K. University, Madurai

Anita Singh, Vasanta College for Women, Varanasi

Mina Surjit Singh, Panjab University, Chandigarh

N.P. Singh, University of Delhi

Pankaj K. Singh, H.P. University, Shimla

Sushila Singh, Banaras Hindu University

T.N. Singh, Banaras Hindu University

A.K. Sinha, Patna University

Ramesh K. Srivastava, G.N.D.University, Amritsar

Charu Verma, H.P. University, Shimla

Ganga Viswanath, Bharathidasan University, Trichy

Index